Writing Home

Writing Home

AMERICAN WOMEN ABROAD

1830–1920

Mary Suzanne Schriber

UNIVERSITY PRESS OF VIRGINIA

Charlottesville and London

Acknowledgment for the use of copyrighted material appears on page 244, note 52.

THE UNIVERSITY PRESS OF VIRGINIA
© 1997 by the Rector and Visitors of the University of Virginia
All rights reserved
Printed in the United States of America

First published 1997

∞ The paper used in this publication meets the minimum requirements of the American National Standard for Information Sciences—Permanence of Paper for Printed Library Materials, ANSI Z39.48-1984.

Library of Congress Cataloging-in-Publication Data
Schriber, Mary Suzanne, 1938–
    Writing home : American women abroad, 1830–1920 / Mary Suzanne Schriber.
        p.   cm.
    Includes bibliographical references and index.
    ISBN 0-8139-1730-1 (cloth : alk. paper)   ISBN 0-8139-1779-4 (paper)
    1. Travelers' writings, American—History and criticism.
    2. American prose literature—Women authors—History and criticism.
    3. American prose literature—19th century—History and criticism.
    4. American prose literature—20th century—History and criticism.
    5. Americans—Travel—Foreign countries—Historiography.
    6. Women travelers—United States—Historiography.   7. Women and literature—United States—History.   I. Title.
    PS366.T73S37   1997
    810.9'355—dc21   96-53086
                                                                CIP

For Tony, my traveling companion

Contents

Acknowledgments

My thanks to the National Endowment for the Humanities for a stipend in the summer of 1988 that encouraged me to launch this project; to James I. Miller, Chair of the Department of English, Northern Illinois University, for a one-course equivalent research assignment in 1988 that enabled me to pursue this work; and to Northern Illinois University for a research sabbatical and a Presidential Teaching Professorship, each affording me a semester's leave in which to bring this work to completion. I thank the staff of the Interlibrary Loan Service of Founders Memorial Library, Northern Illinois University, under the direction of Tobie Miller, for invaluable assistance in locating texts of travel; and Susan Harshman and Elizabeth Mehren of Manuscript Services, under the direction of Karen Blaser, College of Liberal Arts and Sciences, for their expeditious manuscript preparation. I am grateful to the Watkins/Loomis Agency for permission to quote from the letters of Edith Wharton to Bernard Berenson at the Harvard Center for Italian Renaissance Studies, Villa I Tatti, Florence, Italy; and to Fiorella Gioffredi Superbi, Curator of Collections and Archives at the Villa I Tatti, for her gracious assistance. I owe thanks, as well, to anonymous referees whose critiques brought crucial matters to my attention. James M. Mellard, friend and colleague, has again generously shared his professional savvy with me. I continue to be grateful to Lynne M. Waldeland, friend and colleague, for persuading me, years ago, to write. Each time I reach for just the right word or wrestle with a recalcitrant sentence, I am reminded of her linguistic precision and enthusiasm as she "dared," as she might say, to press me to follow suit. Finally, I thank Anthony Edward Scaperlanda, who has frequently done both my half and his of our domestic round in order to give me time to work on "that damned book," as it came to be known between us. He has helped me to stay on task and encouraged me through disappointments and revisions. Best of all, he has shared and multiplied my joy in the work as he and I write "home" together. This book is dedicated to him.

Abbreviations

BP	Ella W. Thompson, *Beaten Paths, or a Woman's Vacation* (1874)
BT	[Helen Hunt Jackson], *Bits of Travel* (1872)
FF	Edith Wharton, *Fighting France: From Dunkerque to Belfort* (1915)
HA	Caroline Kirkland, *Holidays Abroad; or, Europe from the West* (1849)
HH	Kate Field, *Hap-Hazard* (1873)
HR	Mary Hannah Krout, *Hawaii and a Revolution: The Personal Experiences of a Correspondent in the Sandwich Islands during the Crisis of 1893 and Subsequently* (1898)
IB	Edith Wharton, *Italian Backgrounds* (1905)
LA	[Catharine Maria Sedgwick], *Letters from Abroad to Kindred at Home* (1841)
LOW	Sarah Haight, *Letters from the Old World. By a lady of New York* (1839)
LR	Lucy Bronson Dudley, *Letters to Ruth* (1896)
LW	Agnes McAllister, *A Lone Woman in Africa; or Six Years on the Kroo Coast* (1896)
MCC	Constance Fenimore Woolson, *Mentone, Cairo, and Corfu* (1895)
MF	Edith Wharton, *A Motor-Flight Through France* (1908)
NBB	[Elizabeth Cochrane Seaman], *Nellie Bly's Book: Around the World in Seventy-Two Days* (1890)
NE	Sophia Hawthorne, *Notes in England and Italy* (1870)
NV	Abby Jane Morrell, *Narrative of a Voyage to the Ethiopic and South Atlantic Ocean, Indian Ocean, Chinese Sea, North and South Pacific Ocean, in the Years 1829, 1830, 1831* (1833)
PI	Mary Elizabeth Wieting, *Prominent Incidents in the Life of Dr. John M. Wieting, Including His Travels with his Wife around the World* (1889)
RWL	Lucy Seaman Bainbridge, *Round-the-World Letters* (1882)

SG   Margaret Fuller, *These Sad But Glorious Days: Dispatches from Europe* (1846–1850)

SM   Harriet Beecher Stowe, *Sunny Memories of Foreign Lands* (1854)

SS   [Martha J. Coston], *A Signal Success: The Work and Travels of Mrs. Martha J. Coston: An Autobiography* (1886)

SSS   Madeleine Vinton Dahlgren, *South Sea Sketches: A Narrative* (1881)

TA   Lilian Leland, *Traveling Alone: A Woman's Journey around the World* (1890)

TEE   Harriet Trowbridge Allen, *Travels in Europe and the East: During the Years 1858–59 and 1863–64* (1879)

WFI   Elizabeth A. (Mrs. E. A.) Forbes, *A Woman's first impressions of Europe. Being wayside sketches made during a short tour in the year 1863* (1865)

Writing Home

Introduction

The woman who is known only through a man is known
wrong, and excepting one or two like Mme. de Sévigné,
no woman has pictured herself. The American woman
of the nineteenth century will live only as the man saw
her; probably she will be less known than the woman
of the eighteenth; none of the female descendants of
Abigail Adams can ever be nearly so familiar as her letters
have made her; and all this is pure loss to history.

—Henry Adams, *The Education of Henry Adams*

Like many historians before and after him, Henry Adams was beset by
insight and blindness on the subject of women. The epigraph that heads
this introduction shows Adams on the lookout for Woman in history and
convinced that her absence is "pure loss." He sees, insightfully, that a
woman "known only through a man is known wrong." Yet he is blind to
what is before his own eyes. Asserting that the American woman of the
nineteenth century "will live only as the man saw her," Adams overlooks a
fact both remarkable and evident: those "female descendants of Abigail
Adams" to whom he refers were everywhere inserting themselves into history and bequeathing to it a written record of themselves as they did so.
Had Adams looked as intently at the women of his own time as at the
medieval Virgin of Chartres, he would have discovered ready to hand a
repository of information by and about nineteenth-century American
women: their accounts of travels abroad. His oversight is all the more surprising because women's accounts of travel were routinely published in pe-

riodicals such as *Harper's New Monthly Magazine* and the *Atlantic Monthly*, staples of his class. Moreover, had Adams chosen to extend his interest in the dynamo to include one of its cousins, the publishing industry in Victorian America, he would have found that in addition to travel articles in magazines and newspapers, American women, drawing on diaries, journals, and correspondence, published numerous books of foreign travel. Henry Adams would have come upon the body of material that is the subject of this study—the book-length accounts of American women who, having traveled abroad before 1920, proceeded to write about it for public consumption.

Before the 1820s, women's travels outside of the United States were infrequent and "accidental," undertaken to accompany fathers and husbands going abroad, primarily for political or commercial reasons. With the advent in the 1820s of steam-powered ships, followed by the luxurious "steam palaces" that governed the Atlantic by the 1860s, American women began to journey to foreign lands in significant numbers, for their own reasons and independent of men. Having traveled, they then joined the historic fraternity of travel writers, transforming their adventures abroad into books of travel whose numbers increased in tandem with the numbers of women travelers. Between 1830 and 1900, books of travel written by women number at least 195, approximately 27 before and 168 after the Civil War.[1]

Writing Home studies these books and others published before 1920 and the conditions that made them possible. It examines the practice of white, middle- and upper-middle-class American women, the majority from the Northeast,[2] in the genre of travel writing between 1833, when Abby Morrell brought to press the first book of travels abroad published in the United States by an American woman, *Narrative of a Voyage to the Ethiopic and South Atlantic Ocean, Indian Ocean, Chinese Sea, North and South Pacific Ocean, in the Years 1829, 1830, 1831,*[3] and 1920, when Edith Wharton published her last book of travels, *In Morocco,* and an epoch in foreign travel drew to a close. I scrutinize the work of familiar women writers such as Margaret Fuller, Harriet Beecher Stowe, and Constance Fenimore Woolson; of now-obscure women travelers such as Sarah Haight (1808–1881), wife of a wealthy New York merchant and socialite known for her lavish entertainments, and Lucy Seaman Bainbridge (1842–1928), a philanthropic, social, and religious activist who worked in numerous causes, from caring for the wounded in the Civil War to lecturing across the United States for the Presbyterian Board of Foreign Missions; and of outright adventurers such as Caroline Paine (1820?–1880?), traveler in 1850 and 1851 to Turkey, Egypt, and up the Nile, and Fanny Bullock Workman (1859–1925), conqueror of Himalayan peaks. This book encompasses the formal transformation of women's travel writing from letters written by homemakers for private consumption, and later cobbled into travel books for allegedly reluctant publication, to letters written by global homemakers, often foreign correspondents, for public consumption in newspapers and magazines, and later collected into books. I analyze texts of travel written by professional amateurs who understood writing as an arm of religious, civic, and domestic discourse, as well as texts of "artists" who, in the last quarter and through the turn of the nineteenth century, valued writing as "high art," a discourse separate from others, divorced from popular writing in a market dominated by male writers and publishers.

Writing Home is concerned with the travel tales of women who first transformed themselves into travelers and then transformed their travels into autobiographical, political, and cultural occasions. Setting out the conditions in which women traveled and wrote and the reception at home of their travels and their travel writing, *Writing Home* analyzes the purposes of women's practice in the travel genre and, to use Jane Tompkins's term, its "cultural work," its "attempts to redefine the social order." [4] *Writing Home* proposes a way to assess the meaning and the historical significance of an important body of work and a heretofore unwritten chapter in the history of women's writing in the United States: the history of women's writing of foreign travel. Because women who came to travel writing inherited a literary tradition in which to work, texts of travel written primarily by men, a history of women's travel writing necessarily takes men's into account.

When travel writing by either gender is granted sustained analytical attention, it becomes clear that although the act of writing may require inspiration, the muse is decidedly this-worldly, emanating from economics, technology, politics, ideology, and the various institutions of literature that shape the writing practice of particular people in particular places at particular times. The travel work of women and men shares a common border because their writing was enabled by the technological and economic conditions of nineteenth-century America. Particularly in the Gilded Age and the Progressive Era, the comforts and the speed provided by new modes of transportation, from steamships to railroads, made travel more feasible, as well as less threatening to life and limb. Economic prosperity and burgeoning capitalism encouraged the development of applications of technology that made travel increasingly accessible. The evolution of print technologies, and ongoing public interest in foreign lands from the beginnings of the republic through the turn of the century and beyond, created a market for travel writing that heightened the incentive to write and to publish. The historical situation of the United States also promoted travel and travel writing: foreign peoples, their histories, governments, and cultures provided the "other" against which Americans sought to define themselves, their mission, and their place in the world. This confluence of forces led to an escalation of the numbers of American travelers, men and women, as the nineteenth century progressed, and of the numbers of books of travel they wrote. A total of some 1,765 books of travel were published in the United States between 1830 and 1900, 325 of them before and 1,440 of them after the Civil War.[5]

The travel accounts of men and women share certain subjects, themes, conventions, and rhetorical strategies. They are potpourris of historical information and common understandings about foreign lands, paraphrased and sometimes quoted from predecessor travelers and historians, novelists and poets. They are full of talk about travel talk, including charges of mendacity against other accounts and claims of veracity and merit for one's own. They offer ritual laments about the difficulties of writing about travels; ritual disclaimers of literary merit; and ritual protests about making public a body of materials intended as private letters and diaries. They provide predictable itineraries, descriptions of modes of transportation, conventional responses to sacralized sites and monuments, complaints about guides and beggars, expatiations on religion and politics, picturesque descriptions of landscapes, and accounts of the manners and habits of other peoples. Accounts of travel by men and women are routinely informed by antitourism, nostalgia for the past, and disgust with contemporaneous life in foreign lands. They express a sense of belatedness, of the traveler's eleventh-hour arrival at the table of travel and travel writing. They often couch their observations in millennial understandings of history, coupled with a belief in the manifest destiny of the American republic. Travel accounts are compendia of the discourses and discursive practices that circulated in the United States between 1830 and 1920, ranging from republicanism to abolition to technological developments and the "woman question." These common subjects, themes, and rhetorical strategies are the glue that binds travel writing into a body of generic material.

Indeed, the "sameness" of topics, itineraries, and writing strategies in male- and female-authored accounts of travel seems to beg the question of difference. Perhaps for this reason, together with what has been the androcentrism of literary scholarship until the last quarter of the twentieth century, the commonalities of generic practice, tacitly assumed to exist in the writing of both sexes, have been largely, although not exclusively, identified and studied in the travel writing of men. The works of Van Wyck Brooks, Percy Adams, Foster Rhea Dulles, Cushing Strout, Christopher Mulvey, Charles Batten, Neil Harris, Paul R. Baker, Allison Lockwood, and Paul Fussell, cited in the course of my study, provide frameworks in which to construct the meaning of travel accounts, particularly those written by men. More recently, studies such as Mary Louise Pratt's *Imperial Eyes: Travel Writing and Transculturation* (1992), James Buzard's *The Beaten Track: European Tourism, Literature, and the Ways to Culture, 1800–1918* (1993), William W. Stowe's *Going Abroad: European Travel in Nineteenth-Century American Culture* (1994), and Terry Caesar's *Forgiving the Boundaries: Home as Abroad in American Travel Writing* (1995) treat the travel writing of women as important.[6] What difference, therefore, justifies *Writing Home*, an analysis of women's writing in the genre as a body of work in its own right? The difference is sustained analytical attention to gender, to the reverberations in virtually every department of Victorian life of being female or male. By consistently focusing on the operations of gender and its rhetorical effects, I identify previously unnoticed, ignored, but nevertheless important dimensions of the writing practice of women travelers and its place and work in Victorian America.

Virtually everything in the world of the Victorian American was charged with gender ideology in both senses of "charged": energized by gender and held responsible to its laws. Virtually everything, that is, was informed by difference. The technological and economic developments discussed in chapter 1, from steamships and their accouterments to touring companies, luggage, travel costumes, travel guides, and conduct books, were driven by and adapted to the requirements of gender, male and female, as constructed in Victorian America. Like the material conditions of travel, the ideological conditions that informed travel were different for women and men. Questions of identity and of America's millennial promise, for example, bore differentially on women and men because Woman was the culture's icon of national destiny. American women were conceptualized as superior to the women of other countries, an idea that shaped the construction of the people and places of other lands by American women in ways that differ from male constructions. Even geography was gendered in nineteenth-century America. Women were allocated specified spaces that were stretched to the breaking point by the global ambitions that took women into the streets of the world as well as the streets of New York City.

Women's global ambitions were encouraged by the simultaneity of women's numerically significant initiatives in travel and travel writing and three waves of intensely gendered historical activity: the first wave of the women's movement, contesting and redefining women's place and prerogatives; women's coalitions in clubs and various political and social reform movements; and women's inroads into professions, including the profession that made space for an outpouring of travel writing, journalism. Other institutions of writing, too, such as genteel periodicals and book publishers, marched to the gender ideology that defined women's lives from the Cult of True Womanhood in the antebellum years to the New Woman of the turn into the twentieth century and beyond. The differing relationship of men and women to the institutions of writing and to the culture's concept of "writer" during each of these periods affected the purposes for which women wrote travels, the cultural work of their writing, and the angle from which women were attached to the genre and its conventions.

Gender is always in play in women's accounts of travel (and in men's) as it was always in play in American culture and society, and gender, as this book will show, is a matter for performance. First transforming themselves into "womanly" travelers as defined by conduct books, women perform in womanly fashion on the stage of the world. They then transform the persona of traveler into the personas of travel writers. Whether simply to please readers, or to effect a political purpose such as statehood for Hawaii or woman suffrage, or to market their texts by playing on "woman" in titles and subtitles, distinguishing their work from men's, women travelers strike a pose and construct a self for public consumption. Sometimes they introduce their gender into the text directly, as a subject to be discussed and debated; sometimes they hide it in fissures in the text, at intersections where specific works and generic conventions meet. Whoever they were and wherever they traveled, women performed their gender, drawing their long skirts (to echo Adrienne Rich's poem "Heroines") through their texts as they drew them through the world.

Whenever women wrote of travels, they effected transformations crucial to this study: the transformation of what had been largely a male generic practice into a vehicle for versions of the world according to women; and the transformation and revision (but sometimes simply the reinscription) of accepted understandings of home and the social order. At the same time, the gendering of the world in women's accounts makes visible the previously unrecognized gendering of the world in men's accounts of travel. Men's constructions of the world, taken to be normative, now become visible as male versions of the world and merely one set of possibilities. Moreover, accounts of travel function for women as vehicles for gender-specific cultural work. In *Writing Home*, gender is the key that opens the door to the distinctive purposes and meaning of women's travel writing, as it opened the doors of harems, off limits to men, to women travelers. Subjected to analytical pressure with gender in mind, the "sameness" of men's and women's texts of travel proves to be only apparent, and the difference that gender makes, the difference that distinguishes the writing practice of women from that of men, is disclosed.

Women took hold of the conventions of the genre as developed by men, historically the world's travelers and travel writers by privilege of their gender, and turned them to their own purposes. At a time when women were assiduously moving into public spaces both geographic and literary, travel writing was another space in the public domain for the voices of women. As travel carried women into the byways and cities of the world, so their transformations of travel into prose carried their voices and opinions into the public square, furthering the transformation of women from receptacles into creators of politics and culture, and women's writing from accounts of travel into agents of cultural work. Virtually all of these texts play themselves off against the culture's reigning ideas of and conversations about women, some to revise the concept of Woman, some to confirm the status quo ante, and all of them to shape, influence, and complicate the culture's talk about the "woman question."

In their ideological and formal variety, women's texts of travel advance on several fronts our understanding of the complexity of women's place and intellectual positions in the institutions and politics of the United States before World War I. Taking public positions on virtually every subject of their day, from art to Roman Catholicism, from railroads to sewing machines, and from harems to forms of government, these texts show that, nineteenth-century rhetoric to the contrary, all subjects were women's subjects. Women's travel writing extends the meaning of "the beaten track" to include the domestic round from which women were released when traveling and the round of propriety that would keep women close to their own front doors. Preparing the ground for Charles Dudley Warner's observation in 1889 that "a brace of spirited girls may now go clear round the world together in entire safety, and without exciting any sentiment more dangerous than admiration,"[7] this writing challenges and plays with the "rule of decency" that governed the lives of Victorian women. It insists, instead, on the propriety and, indeed, the exhilaration of traveling solo and independently, and uses the public's fascination with female vulnerability as a rhetorical device to engage if not to titillate an audience. Even though some of this writing is, of course, deadly earnest, some of it is playfully irreverent, putting the lie to the stereotype of the Victorian woman as dry and dour. Finally, women's accounts of travel continue, amplify, and enlarge what Nina Baym identifies as an activity of women from the foundations of the republic: participation in the institutions of literature and its multiple genres, and the demolition of "whatever imaginative and intellectual boundaries their culture may have been trying to maintain between domestic and public worlds."[8] Women's travel writing often offers personas who, in the act of freeing themselves physically from geographical constraints, free themselves from less tangible ideological boundaries hemming them in.

Before the Civil War, writing home from abroad often meant a literal writing of letters to family and friends at home. After the Civil War, allusions to travel letters are ordinarily merely conventional. But from the beginning to the end of the nineteenth century and into the twentieth, writing home from abroad meant writing—and rewriting—"home." Writing home from abroad entails seeing "home" in a new light and writing *about* home from a new vantage point. It sometimes means securing "home" as conventionally understood and valued by a white, Anglo-Saxon, Protestant middle class: as the space occupied by a biological family in which women hold a special place. The contrasts made visible by travel abroad magnify the perceived privileges of American women in their circumscribed but, as they come to see more clearly when they travel, nevertheless fortunate domestic role. Sometimes writing home from abroad means expanding the definition of home to include communal and municipal spaces, then national boundaries and, finally, the world. And although travel writing by both genders is ostensibly about other lands but paradoxically about home, travel writing by women carries a special relationship to "home" because by cultural assignment, women are "about" home in a particular way. Whether women's travel writing secures or transforms the definition of "home," it writes and rewrites the place and role of women, its rhetorical center.

Yet as women write home from abroad, they presume to remake the world in the image of the United States, which is to say in the image of white, Protestant, middle-class values. Women's texts of travel are often arms of nationalism, classism, racism, the practice of "othering," and patriarchal definitions of Woman reinforced even as they are sometimes contested. Seeing themselves as normative Woman by the plan of God, and seeing the United States as the latest stage in God's unfolding plan for humankind, they "other" the people and nations of the world, and particularly their own doubles, other women. In this way they define themselves as Americans and women, piously or smugly reveling in their nationality and status, or didactically exhorting their compatriots to do so. In short, women's travel writing is as much about American exceptionalism and the romance of America as about home and abroad.

The challenge of representing the variety of cultural work in women's accounts of travel, the variety of cultural workers who did it, and the role of travel writing and its conventions in both of these areas has shaped the organization of *Writing Home*. Travel writing is a generic hybrid, an annex to history, autobiography, the essay, and other literary forms. Because texts of travel are often adjacent to more than one genre, many of them invite analysis in the light of more than one set of conventions. I have selected texts and associated them with genres adjacent to travel writing with four aims in mind: to show the cross-section of practitioners of the genre (most of them white women of the privileged classes); to identify and underscore the characteristics, variety, and continuity of women's travel writing practices across time; to assess the impact of gender, nationality, race, and class on women's texts of travel; and to draw the difference between male- and female-authored books, accounting for the gender-specific work of women's texts and the construction of different worlds both at home and abroad, one according to men and one according to women.

To accomplish these aims, I focus in each chapter on specific writers and texts from the historical periods into which the ninety years from 1830 to 1920 divide: the antebellum period, the transitional period of the Gilded Age between 1865 and 1880, and the Progressive Era between 1880 and the end of World War I. To do the work of each chapter, I have selected female travelers from the ranks of occasional and professional, unfamiliar and familiar writers. I lay the groundwork for the examination of specific writers, texts, and travel writing practices in the two omnibus chapters with which the book begins. Chapter 1, "Mapping the Territory," recounts the historical circumstances in which white, middle- and upper-middle- and upper-class women of the United States proceeded to travel and in which virtually everything connected with their travel was gendered. Chapter 2, "Literary Inroads," establishes the historical context in which women's travel writing occurred, the generic conventions available to writers, and the visibility of gender difference in the travel writing practice of women and men. The next three chapters examine women's writing of travel as occasions for three kinds of cultural work. Chapter 3, "Autobiographical Occasions," examines the three major modes of women's practice in writing travel-as-autobiography: self-exploration, self-destruction, and self-presentation, each of them a different response to the culture's constructions of Woman and each of them a form of cultural work. Chapter 4, "Political Occasions," examines women's practice in writing travel-as-politics, an undertaking enabled by institutions of journalism and dividing into national politics and gender politics. Chapter 5, "Cultural Occasions," associates

women's accounts of travel with institutions of literature other than journalism between 1830 and 1920: woman's fiction, local color and realism,
and popular and high art conceptions of the writer and writing. I conclude
with a single work, a war work, by Edith Wharton: *Fighting France: From
Dunkerque to Belfort*. An account of Wharton's trips to the front lines in
World War I, *Fighting France* stands as the beneficiary, the repository, and
the culmination of women's practice in travel writing from its first publication in book form in the 1830s until 1920. The beginning of World War I
ushered out the world explored, exploited, and enjoyed by genteel, Brah-
min, and other travelers of the nineteenth century, and the end of World
War I ushered in a new era in American travel, culture, and accounts of
other lands. *Fighting France* stands at the historical juncture between these
two worlds.

Writing Home provides a way of thinking about women's practice in the
travel genre. Contributing to an ongoing conversation about the literature
of travel, it offers a perspective on a large, significant, but neglected body
of material written by women of the United States. It allows us to over-
hear the voices of women in their variousness, carried in a genre that is a
remarkable listening post by virtue of its eclectic, casual, and polyvocal
form. *Writing Home* makes visible a species of *écriture féminine*, defined by Marguerite Duras and Xavière Gauthier as "wild, scrawny grass
[women] . . . which manages to grow in the chinks of old stones [the travel
genre] and—why not—finally loosens cement slabs, however heavy they
may be, with the power of what has been contained for a long time."[9] To
an attentive reader, a women's "world" is visible in "the chinks," the sites
of difference, where the gender of the "world" according to men becomes
visible as well. Venturing into this world, *Writing Home* recovers an important chapter in the history of women's writing in the United States.

Chapter One

Mapping the Territory
The Who, When, Where, and Why
of Women's Travel

The woman has been set free. . . . One had but to pass a week in Florida, or on any of a hundred huge ocean steamers, or walk through the Place Vendome, or join a part of Cook's tourists to Jerusalem, to see that the woman had been set free.

—Henry Adams, *The Education of Henry Adams*

Instructing the American woman in intelligent housewifery in 1832, the redoubtable Lydia Maria Child singled out "the rage for travelling, and for public amusements" as "one of the worst kinds of extravagance," an extravagance that is "rapidly increasing in this country" to the detriment of "our purses and our *habits*." "People of moderate fortune," she wrote, "have just as good a right to travel as the wealthy, but is it not unwise? Do they not injure themselves and their families?"[1] Child's question echoes across the nineteenth century as traveling American women, departing the shores of the United States in ever more significant numbers, became a phenomenon. From the decade before Victoria came to the throne of England in 1837, and in escalating numbers thereafter, thousands of middle- and upper-class, white American women from all walks of life—missionaries, nurses, teachers, reformers, journalists, archaeologists, novelists, musicians, artists, and society matrons—left the home shores for foreign parts. In an unprecedented female exodus, they fanned out around the globe on the waves of ideological, economic, political, and technological developments.

Like their male counterparts, they made their way to Europe and to the rest of the world on steam-powered ships. As early as 1835 some fifty women were among the three hundred Americans who visited Rome during Holy Week. At mid-century, some thirty thousand Americans traveled abroad yearly.[2] After the Civil War, when Americans both known and obscure crossed the Atlantic by the thousands on a lengthy, once-in-a-lifetime trip to Europe, many women figured among them. By 1890, according to a writer in the *North American Review*, there were "more than eleven thousand virgins who semi-yearly migrate from America to the shores of England and France."[3] This figure accounts for Henry James's remark, in his preface to *The Portrait of a Lady* (1881), that "coming to Europe is even for the 'frail vessels,' in this wonderful age, a mild adventure."[4] More bracing adventures filled the itineraries of Victorian American women traveling in China, Palestine, India, Egypt, the East Indies, Greece, Arabia, Algeria, and other parts of Africa, Central and South America, Cuba, the Yucatan, and Jamaica.[5] Women's travels to destinations far from home make up a chapter in the changing destiny of American women across the nineteenth century until World War I. Travel was transforming women from private into public actors on the world stage. This chapter takes up the impact of technological, economic, historical, and ideological contexts on this massive movement of women. It examines why women traveled, how their travel was gendered, and how their travel was perceived.

I

The purposes for which women traveled abroad, like their numbers, distinguished Victorian women travelers from female travelers of earlier periods. Before the nineteenth century, women were ordinarily, to borrow modern novelist Anne Tyler's title, "accidental tourists."[6] Men both poor and rich had set out since at least the sixteenth century on the "Grand Tour" to complete their education, whereas the few women who traveled at all before the nineteenth century embarked primarily for purposes neither touristic nor of their own making.[7] They undertook travel for religious purposes, like Chaucer's Wyf of Bathe, or for practical purposes, or out of necessity: to get from one place to another, to domesticate new territories in the wake of male exploration, to fill out an entourage organized by men, or to accompany husbands or fathers who were ambassadors or officers in military forces.[8] Women who came to America early in American history were, of course, "accidental tourists" as well,. accompanying men to the New World or joining them there to found families and communities. Once arrived, colonial women made excursions into American territory: Sarah Kemble Knight, for example, traveled from Boston to New York City in 1704 and 1705; and Elizabeth House Trist traveled with her slave, Polly, from Pittsburgh to Natchez on the Ohio and Mississippi Rivers in 1784.[9] As captivity narratives record, white women taken hostage by Native Americans made forced excurions into the wilderness. But travel across the oceans, from America to Europe and other continents, was rare. When it did occur, it was ordinarily undertaken in the capacity of daughter or wife, as when Abigail Adams traveled with her parents in England and France from 1784 to 1787, and when Martha Bayard, wife of a diplomat attached to John Jay's mission to conclude a treaty with England, lived in England from 1794 to 1797.

With the advent in the 1820s of steam-powered ships, crowned by the "naval mansions" that governed the oceans by the 1860s, United States women increasingly left their own continental borders to see the world. Whereas in ordinary nineteenth-century usage the term "abroad" was used to designate simple departures from the home to the marketplace or to a neighbor's house, it increasingly took on the romantic connotations of distance and adventure. Many nineteenth-century women continued in the footsteps of their predecessors and were "accidental" travelers, joining men in their overseas ventures. With children in tow, Sophia Hawthorne, for example, accompanied Nathaniel to England and Italy in the 1850s. Others were both "accidental" and self-motivated travelers. Abby Morrell lived in 1828 the type of adventures ascribed by Sarah Orne Jewett in 1896 to a character named Mrs. Fosdick, who set sail at eight years of age for the East Indies with her family, including her mother and a newborn baby.[10] Abby Morrell, according to her own claim, left a child at home and took to the high seas to be with her husband on his commercial exploits in the Philippines and Polynesia. She did so, however, at her own behest, not that of her husband.

The travels of many other women were in no way accidental. On the contrary, women claimed to conceive and execute travel plans independently. Declaring purposes significantly different from those of their eighteenth-century sisters, they traveled in what they saw as their own interests quite apart from those of a man. Emma Willard, pioneer in women's education and founder of the Troy Female Seminary, went to France and England in 1830 for the sake of Troy Seminary and women's education. Harriet Beecher Stowe, taking her husband along, went to Europe in 1853 by invitation of the British in the wake of the publication of *Uncle Tom's Cabin*. Julia Ward Howe, known for "The Battle Hymn of the Republic" but, among other achievements, a biographer of Margaret Fuller and author of a book called *Sex and Education* (1874), made her first transatlantic voyage in 1853 on her wedding journey and returned to Europe on four occasions between 1853 and 1877 to speak on women's rights. Mary Lovina Cort went to Siam and remained there from 1874 to 1885 to convert the heathen to Christianity. In the last quarter of the century, Kate Field, Elizabeth Cochrane (Nellie Bly), Elizabeth Bisland, and Elizabeth Banks, journalists all, traveled on assignment for newspapers and magazines; and women such as the wealthy Kate Buckingham of Chicago traveled to collect art.

In the mold of such exceptional European women as Lady Mary Wortley Montague, the Countess Dora D'Istria, and, later, Isabella Bird Bishop and Marianne North, some American women were adventurers seeking challenges in territories infrequently if ever visited by women. Caroline Paine, for example, whose name has been lost to biographers and remains only on the title page of her book of travels, ventured to Turkey, Egypt, and up the Nile through Palestine in 1850 and 1851; May French Sheldon (1848–1936), born into a wealthy and cultured family, educated largely in Italy, translator and writer of stories and poems, and four-time traveler around the world, sought adventures in Africa in the 1890s; Annie Smith Peck (1850–1935), intrepid climber and a professor (one of the first American women to hold the title) at Purdue University, scaled the Matterhorn in 1895 and in 1909 became the first woman to ascend the summit of "the apex of America," Mount Huascaran, in the Peruvian Andes.[11] Fanny Bullock Workman (1859–1925), wealthy and energetic, observant and opinion-ated and an ardent "kodakist," visited the Karakoram, a mountain range of northern Jammu and Kashmir, on eight occasions with her husband, Joseph, and staked a claim to its peaks in 1913. Some sought more mild adventures, as did a Miss L. L. Rees who, beset with boredom after the close of the Centennial Exposition in Philadelphia in 1876 and "seeking something to occupy our minds," set out with three companions for what she calls "Utopia,—the most magnificent of cities,—the Paradise of the earth," Paris, and the Exposition of 1878.[12] Others, like the novelists Catharine Maria Sedgwick in 1839 and Caroline Kirkland in 1848, were earnest travelers, seeking culture and an aesthetic education in Europe. Still others were of the type chronicled in the fiction of Henry James and Edith Wharton: "drifting hordes . . . scattered to the four corners of the globe," as they are labeled in Wharton's *The Custom of the Country* (1913), restless and pleasure-seeking Americans shopping for dresses at Worth's in Paris, for marriageable nobility in England and elsewhere, and for sun and soci-ety at various watering holes.[13]

Whatever reasons were proclaimed for going abroad in the nineteenth century, travelers set out in part because their culture sanctioned and en-couraged it. Travel was a ritual, a "cultural performance" to which impor-tance, respectability, and meaning attached. Itineraries and routes were not original. Rather, they were prescribed in guidebooks such as Murray and Baedeker and Knox, making the traveler's choices clear and providing itin-eraries and routes to sacralized sites.[14] As early as the 1830s, "how-to" travel books were readily available in the United States and, by the last quarter of the century, constituted an industry sufficient to support a book on a topic so narrow (and an affliction so pervasive) as seasickness.[15] In addition to guidebooks and how-to books, Americans drew on compendia of infor-mation that ushered them into foreign lands and mediated their under-standings of the world. British literature and preconceptions of England and Scotland framed the tourist's progress through "our old home." Ma-dame de Staël's *Corinne* (1807), Goethe's *Die italianische Reise* (1816), and eventually John Ruskin's work on architecture and painting prepared the traveler for Italy. There was, as well, a library of information about the Middle East, the Bible being the principle but certainly not the only source of information for earnest Christians. Information about the Far East, too, was easily accessible.[16]

This wealth of printed material was the *ordines*, the order of worship, that governed what William W. Stowe calls the "liturgy of travel." Guidebooks provided, Stowe writes, "an order of worship at the shrines of the beautiful, the historic, and the foreign, telling the potential tourist what kind of behavior is appropriate to each site and indicating what kind of fulfillment to expect from it. They serve as the directories of services, aids to meditation, and handbooks of devotion."[17] Virtually every American was prepared for a *frisson* from the grandeur of the Alps; for the sensation of the picturesque from ruins, ivy, and lichens; for the moral elevation of sermons delivered by noted preachers. Virtually every American traveler kept a journal, wrote letters home, and purchased a range of souvenirs, from gewgaws to copies of the Old Masters to items like the flowered-glass tea-caddy and a beautiful pair of mugs from the Island of Tobago that Sarah Orne Jewett plants in the home of the fictional Mrs. Blackett.[18] Travelers routinely made pilgrimages to culturally sacred places such as Stratford-on-Avon to pay respects to Shakespeare; to Abbotsford, Sir Walter Scott's home in Scotland; and to the Louvre and the Coliseum.

Letters of credit (replaced by travelers' checks by the end of the nineteenth century) and letters of introduction to literary, theatrical, and political lions such as William Wordsworth, Joanna Baillie, and the Marquis de Lafayette eased the way of the American abroad. Those who ventured to the Middle East visited the Pyramids, biblical sites, and Seraglio Point. Their letters of introduction took them to the stations of missionaries or to American consuls and American schools. The *ordines* of the liturgy of travel was so strict that, should a traveler dare not to visit the prescribed sites or experience the prescribed sensations, she confessed her sense of sinfulness to the readers of her travel account. Caroline Kirkland's playful remark in her *Holidays Abroad* suggests the degree to which travelers felt driven to perform the liturgy of travel according to the rules. "We have walked through the British Museum, with how little satisfaction!" Kirkland exclaims, and adds: "If one had courage to omit such things, and come home with an honest confession that one had not seen them, how much fruitless labor would be spared."[19]

Like other religious exercises, the ritual and liturgy of travel required sacrifice and penance. All travelers tolerated inconveniences and many of them withstood considerable discomfort for travel's promised privileges. Whether crossing the Atlantic or the Pacific, and whether in what Harriet Beecher Stowe called "sea coops" or, later in the century, in "steam palaces," travelers not only suffered from dreaded and often excruciating seasickness, but from the worries occasioned by the fatal accidents to which ships were subject, such as fires, icebergs, and collisions with other ships. Once arrived in Europe, they often found hotels as cold and damp as the weather, and they persistently expressed annoyance with beggars, hawkers, thieves, filth, guides, and conniving salespeople. Edith Wharton's recollection of the vicissitudes of travel, undertaken voluntarily, as late as the 1880s is reminiscent of the grueling, hazardous, and often involuntary travels of American women on the Oregon Trail between 1841 and 1868. Like the diaries of these westering women, Wharton reminds us of the persistence of physical discomfort and danger across the century. Travel from Florence to Urbino and the Adriatic, Wharton recalls, "was a toilsome expedition, in a heavy carriage drawn by tired horses, a journey full of the enchantments of discovery but also of fatigue and discomfort, since the well-organized travel of coaching days was over, and the inns off the direct railway routes had been almost abandoned." As late as 1912, traveling now by motor-car to the monastery of La Verna, Wharton found herself "hanging over dizzy precipices in the Apennines" where "the car had to be *let down by ropes* to a point about ¾ of a mile below the monastery, Cook [her driver] steering down the vertical descent, & twenty men hanging on to a funa [rope] that, thank the Lord, *didn't break*." [20]

Travelers to the Middle and Far East were subject to even greater difficulties. They were vulnerable to disease, erratic shipping schedules, red tape, and quarantines. They found hotels to be "invariably wretched" and, in Jerusalem, nonexistent before 1850.[21] Often they encountered severe hardships. Elizabeth B. Dwight, a missionary dispatched with her husband to Constantinople in the 1830s, found herself in the midst of a raging plague and of "dreadful fires, which have driven hundreds of people to beggar and thrown multitudes of others into scenes of distress."[22] The adventures *chosen* by some women were as difficult and life-threatening as those withstood by missionaries answering a divine call. In the 1850s,

Caroline Paine tolerated lizards in her rooms, sandstorms in the desert, and life in a tent for forty days, carrying with her from America into foreign fields the spirit of the pioneer woman. Fanny Bullock Workman and her husband, the same who conquered the peaks of the Karakoram, had earlier traveled in Spain and Algeria by bicycle (or "rover")—but at their peril. As they passed "farmhouses and native habitations" in Algeria, she reports, "the dogs would rush out at us, sometimes singly, sometimes in twos and threes, barking furiously, snapping and showing their teeth in a most threatening manner. . . . What would have happened to us had we not been provided with steel-cored whips, it is not difficult to predict." [23] Such experiences account for the derivation of the word *traveler* from *travail*, taken in turn from the Latin word *tripalium*, an instrument of torture. [24]

Why is it that despite such trying conditions, women nevertheless tolerated the "travail" of travel? [25] Like their fathers, brothers, and husbands, they did so for sometimes ordinary, sometimes pragmatic, sometimes venal, and sometimes idealistic reasons. By "ordinary" reasons I mean, simply, the curiosity, the exhilaration, the pleasure, and the escape from routine associated with travel, whether domestic or foreign. On the domestic front, Anna Dickinson, for example, a controversial lecturer whose speaking engagements took her across the United States, took time out to ascend Mount Washington with its "crystal clear air" and its "mists and vapors lovely enough in themselves," only to have "royal views" break upon her vision "as to assure [her] of imperial splendor at the mountaintop." [26] On the foreign front, virtually every traveler to Switzerland and the Alps claimed a pleasure in nature similar to Dickinson's. Travelers also set out on pragmatic rather than pleasure expeditions, often for reasons of health, traveling to domestic and foreign spas to take the water cure,[27] as did Catharine Beecher in the United States in the middle of the nineteenth century and Edith Wharton in Europe in the first quarter of the twentieth.

Yet hierarchies of social class and the desire for various forms of distinction, always complicit with the accumulation of cultural capital, inform travel activity.[28] Both before and after the Civil War, foreign travel placed on its devotées the mantle of cultural and intellectual superiority that Americans were pleased to assume. Following the Civil War, when the American acquisitive instinct found its ideal mate in a booming and industrializing economy, Americans traveled to buy culture, to acquire bits of it,[29] even importing it for installation in private homes—witness Mark Twain shipping to Nook Farm a massive carving-encrusted Bavarian bedstead and an Italian marble fireplace. Travel bespeaks, particularly after the Civil War, the economic superiority and success of newly rich Americans. Travel becomes an instrument of social leverage in a ferociously competitive economy in which, paradoxically, the class mobility associated with a rhetorically classless, middle-class society makes Americans sharply conscious of class and anxious to scale the ladder of class status by way of what Thorstein Veblen calls "the performance of leisure."[30] Moreover, in the last quarter of the century, old money and the newly rich were able through travel to escape temporarily the massive influx of immigrants to the shores of the United States. Citizens poured out of the nation on the upper decks of eastward-bound steamships as immigrants poured into the nation in the steerage of the same steamships, westward-bound. The vulgarity and disorder associated with immigrants in the minds of many established Americans, the traveling classes, stood to cast Europe and its high culture as yet more desirable and genteel.[31]

Ideal motives, as well, were embedded in the ritual and liturgy of travel. Like the economic and class considerations that made travel accessible and desirable, these ideal motives were part of the complex web of Victorianism. Women's travel opportunities expanded in a cultural and historical milieu that encompassed concerns with the self, identity, history, and the American mission. These concerns enabled Americans effectively to justify travel as a duty, as an imperative that bordered on the religious. Particularly before the Civil War, but continuing across the nineteenth century, Americans rationalized travel on three counts. First, equating travel with self-improvement, Americans undertook travel to better themselves culturally and intellectually, even as their contemporaries who traveled into what was then the "west," Ohio and Michigan, and eventually to Oregon and beyond, undertook to better themselves materially. As American cultural studies make clear, the romance of European culture drove the sons (and eventually the daughters) of all of the "best" people abroad despite the temptations to which European *im*morality, sophistication, and aristocracy were presumed to subject them.[32]

Second, the Victorian preoccupation with national identity authorized travel. From as early as 1782, when J. Hector St. John de Crèvecoeur posed

the question, "What . . . is the American, this new man?"[33] the observation
of other lands and peoples served the construction of American identity by
reference to "the other," making possible the meaning of "American" and
making travel an exercise in national definition. As Ralph Waldo Emerson
said in 1847, "We go to Europe to be Americanized, to import what we
can."[34] The association of travel with identity persisted beyond the turn of
the century.

A third rationale for travel is connected with the second. Particularly
before the Civil War, a sense of political and moral superiority, rooted in a
belief in America's millennial promise instantiated in the trajectory of history, drove Americans to the monuments and remnants of the past, of
history made palpable in Europe and the East.[35] As Elizabeth Peabody put
it in 1851, "The events of history are God's conversation with man upon
his nature, duties, and destiny."[36] Travel fits into this scheme as an excursion into history, into the linear progression from which the role of the
United States in God's grand design for the human race becomes visible.
History offers the vantage point certain to improve the American's grasp
of national identity, difference, and the mission that Catharine Beecher
articulates: "[T]his is the nation, which the Disposer of events designs
shall go forth as the cynosure of nations, to guide them to the light and
blessedness of that day [when "all nations shall rejoice and be made
blessed"]."[37] American travelers abroad were pushing eastward, making
excursions into the past in search of history already lived, even as many
Americans were pushing westward, creating history in the act of making
excursions into the future, enacting the American mission and God's millennial promise, and defining national identity and purpose in their difference from Native Americans. Writing in 1849, Caroline Kirkland registers
the degree to which the traveler's physical presence abroad was believed to
make palpable the otherwise abstract design of God and to revivify the
past—a past rendered particularly intangible for Americans who conceived
of themselves as lacking a past. Upon visiting Kenilworth and the dressing-
room of Queen Elizabeth, Kirkland observes, "I do not love Queen Elizabeth's memory much but could not help feeling that the certainty of standing where she had stood, was something, if only as giving a sort of tangible
reality to the past, which is apt to be to us rather an abstraction" (HA, 41).

Geographical excursions into history took on particular importance in a Victorian America suffering from fear of fragmentation. The nation sought assurance that—despite the economic upheavals of the 1830s and 1840s, the Civil War, the challenges to republican virtue of industrialism and catapulting wealth, the fight for woman suffrage, the influx of immigrants, the development of urban slums, and the recalcitrance of Native Americans in the Gilded Age and the Progressive Era—America was nevertheless God's chosen nation, poised and indeed charged by God to lead the human race into the millennium.[38] Thus the motives behind women's travel are complex. In the course of the century, numbers of women increasingly traveled in foreign lands with purposes and designs of their own, transforming themselves from "accidental tourists" into self-motivated travelers. Yet it is also the case that the variegated landscape of Victorian America, marked by questions of identity, wealth, status, millennialism, and manifest destiny, aided and abetted both their numbers and their plans.

II

The Victorian landscape included a preoccupation with gender, which, bearing on economics, nationalism, and ideology, defined Victorianism and its impact on travel in significant ways. The alliance of technology with gender is a telling example. One of the most remarkable technological advances of the period, the "steam palace" inaugurated in the 1840s and commanding the Atlantic by the 1860s, was tailored to the needs and tastes of the "lady." Replacing those cramped and uncomfortable ships christened "sea-coops" by Harriet Beecher Stowe, the steam palace boasted palatial decor in its common areas, numerous baths and toilet rooms, electric lighting, and in short, all of the latest amenities. Significantly, the steam palace particularly catered to women. Boudoirs were decorated in soft blue and gold, their portholes made of stained glass and their tables laden with flowers "blooming even when the sea is gray and sullen," as one traveler wrote.[39]

Why this solicitousness for the ladies? The accommodation of steamships to feminine needs expressed the Victorian ideology that defined Woman as the weaker sex, delicate and requiring male protection. The creature comforts of the steam palace aimed to close the gap between the hardships of an ocean crossing, on the one hand, and women's physical frailty, biological mission to bear children, feminine tastes, and "natural" preference for domesticity, on the other.[40] Behind many of these women, moreover, were economically and socially ambitious men who, in Thorstein Veblen's analysis, depended on women to carry on "the business of vicarious leisure, for the good name of the household and its master."[41] Women's travel signified the financial success of men, particularly in the Gilded Age and after, when the newly rich sought additional means to display their monetary prowess.

At the same time, entrepreneurs in the expanding economy of the United States understood that, like other products in a capitalist economy, women must circulate in order to be financially profitable. Charged with the cultural and social life of the nation and with the disposition of leisure time for their families, traveling Victorian women often brought men and children with them, and they all translated into money for steamship and tour companies. This is not to say that steamships were kept afloat by profits taken from the saloon trade. The shipping of cargo, from the mails under government contract to foodstuffs, was crucial to the steamship business, and speed was the major player in the decisions of governments and commercial enterprises to engage one steamship line rather than another in the fiercely competitive naval industry. Nevertheless, the prestige of entire fleets such as Cunard and Inman and White Star was considerably enhanced by the glow cast over the lot by a single flagship offering advanced comforts for passengers. Such a ship made for good advertising and better receipts from cargo as well as from the ladies.[42]

The marriage of the ideologies of gender and capitalism was consummated when the traveler disembarked on foreign soil. Prohibitions against female travel for travel's sake have been linked historically to ideas of the feminine, connected in turn with women's sexual vulnerability. From the very origins of sightseeing in the sixteenth, seventeenth, and eighteenth centuries, as Judith Adler finds, "It has never been irrelevant whether a traveler set out in a male or female body, and for centuries moral treatises warned of the dangers which travel posed to women."[43] The body of the traveler had been relevant as women traveled into the American wilderness and sometimes suffered captivity. The body was relevant again as women traveled to the prairies of the Midwest to homestead, only to experience yet another form of captivity in minimal homes far from relatives and friends they had left behind.[44] The body of the traveler continued to be relevant, of course, when women ventured abroad. It was understood that women were subject to a host of perils large and small, either invited or avoided by their comportment and appearance. Women who traveled alone or in groups without men were subject to suspicion, expected to take measures to ensure their virtue and the appearance of virtue. They were in any case referred to as "unprotected."

Enter commercial enterprises such as Cook, Baedeker, and Murray, ready to guide and guard the ladies in their travels anywhere and everywhere. The young Mary Thorn Carpenter's account of travels in Egypt in 1894 registers the ubiquity of Thomas Cook & Son, who "conquered tourist Egypt" and "made investigations concerning this strange creature, the tourist," for fifty years.[45] Women constituted a considerable portion of Cook's clientele, making it profitable for Cook to find accommodations, transportation, and information to reduce the "travail" of travel for the fair sex.[46] Women's travel required not only physical conveniences but special, ideologically driven accommodations that commerce was pleased to supply.

The creature comforts that defined the "steam palace" and spilled over into other travel services, domesticating travel and securing safety for Henry James's "frail vessels," worked hand in glove with Victorian ideologies of Woman to authorize women's travel and generate profits. What technology and economics made possible, ideology made probable and profitable. This is not to say that Victorian women were merely victims of a false consciousness, the dupes of captains of industry and commerce.[47] Rather, women's travels were occasioned and motivated, as we have seen, by desires that women recognize and proclaim, such as vacationing, study in the school of travel, health, and professional pursuits; and women made strategic use of the culture's imposition of gender constructs on their movements, as subsequent chapters of this book will show. Nevertheless, the numerous and complex factors at work in the culture to facilitate the phenomenal rise of women's travel included the cooperation between the ideologies—the value systems—of capitalism and gender. This cooperation fueled the global ambitions of the Victorian woman.

Burgeoning numbers of female travelers, consuming the paraphernalia of travel as well as the thing itself, created healthy markets beyond those of transportation, touring companies, and accommodations. Artifacts such as steamer trunks, clothing, farewell gifts, stationery, travel books, and travel guides were profitable, of course, in the commodity culture of Victorian America, and useful to both men and women. Serving as encouragements to travel, books and guides were a kind of promotional literature parallel to documents written to draw settlers to the West by assuring them that homesteading was both possible and promising.[48] But gender-specific practice prevailed in the production and marketing of the accouterments for foreign travel. There were, for example, publications specific to men, informing them about equipment useful to travel in particular places. Men traveling to Lebanon were counseled by Henry H. Jessup, an American missionary in Beirut, to bring an overcoat, a white umbrella, a drinking cup, straps, strings, papers, drawing paper, geological hammer, compass, spy-glass, pamphlets for pressing flowers, and a full supply of clothing.[49]

Once women traveled in numbers sufficient to constitute a substantial market, female-specific subindustries flourished. As the century advanced toward its close, trunkloads of printed materials grew out of and were as-similated back into the discourses of femininity, advising women on such matters as dress, packing, and behavior while abroad. Florence Hartley's *Ladies' Book of Etiquette and Manual of Politeness* (1872) includes chapters on "Traveling" and on "How to Behave at a Hotel" because a lady should remember that "to be truly polite, remember you must be polite at *all* times, and under *all* circumstances." One of the prodigious number of popular travel books by Thomas W. Knox includes, in addition to advice on "Traveling with Camels and Elephants" and "Traveling with Reindeer and Dogs," a chapter entitled "Special Advice to Ladies, by a Lady" (1881). The Women's Rest Tour Association, an organization itself the product of women's travel, advised in *A Summer in England* (1891) that women "for-swear shabbiness" in clothes worn on the ship because, "unless entirely lacking in the natural feminine desire to look your best, you will then deeply regret masquerading as a guy." To avoid this, the adviser continues, women should "take for travelling a new, stout, plain, and pretty dress. . . . If any woman questions the need of beauty in such a serviceable gown, let her remember that the consciousness of being well and appropriately dressed will double the pleasure of her trip."

In 1900, Mary Cadwalader Jones, Edith Wharton's sister-in-law, justifies the publication of yet another advice book because, she writes, "Year by year an increasing number of women travel in Europe, often in parties which do not include a man" (a subject examined in chapter 4 of this study). She builds her recommendations for wardrobe and luggage on a domestic metaphor: "Travelling is something like cooking; the better a cook is, the fewer utensils she needs outside the necessary tools of her trade; and the more you go about, the less you will care to accumulate things."[50] Although such conduct books were first of all practical, informing anxious or prudent travelers of their needs and wants while abroad, they were also agents of ideology. In such gender-inflected conduct books, as in the gendering of the steam palace, the economics of publishing and the culture's ideology of Woman serve one another's interests.[51]

Conduct books have historically served ideology. They belong to an old literary practice that passed through several transformations, from courtesy books directed to a male aristocratic audience in the sixteenth, seventeenth, and eighteenth centuries to etiquette books directed to a genteel female audience in the nineteenth century. Such books aim to impose order on potential disorder and to encourage civility in social relations.[52] Addressed to women, they take on the additional task of telling women how to make themselves desirable to men. Conduct books specify, according to Nancy Armstrong and Leonard Tennenhouse, "what a woman should desire to be if she wishes to attract a socially approved male and keep him happy." In turn, such books tell men what sort of woman is desirable.[53]

In Victorian America, what made a woman attractive and marriageable to an approved male? How did a woman keep a man happy? The domestic arts were touted as the key, and the Cult of True Womanhood with the doctrine of separate spheres, elaborated well before the Civil War, constructed domesticity as the consummation of Woman's desire. The definition of women as narrowly domestic creatures coincided, as well, with new economic conditions in which capitalism and an industrializing economy slowly replaced the cottage-based family economy of the eighteenth century and earlier. Men's labors outside of the home became the source of family income, while women's work was increasingly contained within the household. The ideological glorification of domesticity conveniently eased adjustment to these new conditions and provided women, deprived of many of their earlier functions, with a sense of purpose, a purpose rendered both as the ground of their desirability and their avenue to the procurement and retention of an acceptable mate. At the same time, and convenient to the ascendancy of the middle class in the 1830s, the construction of domesticity as women's art and purpose served to distinguish the genteel woman from other, undesirable categories of females inimical to an egalitarian nation: the idle, aristocratic woman on the one hand and the laboring, lower-class woman on the other. Conduct books elevating domesticity and linking it to desirability served as agents of these ideological moves, easing the culture's way into new facts of life and creating, incidentally, a new category of labor.[54] Catharine Beecher's *Treatise on Domestic Economy* (1841), for example, shows women how to be desirable wives and how to satisfy their own presumably womanly desires through child care, health, hearth, husband, garden, kitchen, and myriad other household concerns.[55]

The expansion of women's travel occurs in these economic and ideological conditions. It occurs when cultural forces would tether women ever more tightly to the arena of the home and secure the separate spheres envisioned by such as Catharine Beecher as anchors of order and stays against the fragmentation and confusion of a burgeoning, industrializing nation. As Kathryn Kish Sklar puts it, "Gender roles were an effective way to channel the explosive potential of nineteenth-century social change."[56]

Travel, however, seems to work against gender roles and the cultural forces that would ensure their continuation. Having historically been thought of as dangerous to social structure, order, and system, travel threatens to throw a wrench in the domestic works.[57] Historically, men were the adventurers into foreign lands. Women travelers, particularly when they went abroad at their own behest and independently rather than "accidentally," made incursions into male territory and male prerogatives even as they departed from their own. Women's travel threatened the separation of spheres and the differences between the sexes. Furthermore, travel was potentially reductive, if not destructive, of female desirability as constituted in relation to domesticity. The culture must, therefore, recuperate women's travels. Even as it allows women to travel and consume the commodities profitable to business enterprise, the culture must draw women back into the orbit of values signed by the domesticity that women's travels disrupt. Enter conduct books of travel, one of the culture's efforts to control disorder and to order the new phenomenon of women traveling in numbers. The task of recuperation was yet more urgent in post-Civil War America, when chaos and fragmentation seemed imminent and when the presumed guardians of family and social order, women, were departing the home shores in escalating numbers.

Undertaking to reimpose rules of order on this seemingly disorderly scene, reminding women of their particular importance in the unfolding of Providential history, and standing in for husband, family, and neighbors at home, conduct books of travel offered women methods of self-surveillance. Even as the Women's Rest Tour Association offers practical advice when it recommends that women pack a "plain" and "pretty dress," it simultaneously advises women, a half century after Amelia Bloomer, on how they can maintain their femininity while living out of suitcases. As the Women's Rest Tour Association's writer put it, a woman would not want to be caught "masquerading as a guy." She must not, that is, engage in cross-dressing as Annie Smith Peck had done, creating a brouhaha by wearing a transgressive tunic and knickerbockers when she scaled the Matterhorn in 1895.[58]

To whom is it useful that women do *not* masquerade "as a guy?" It benefits men, whether husbands or fathers or brothers, who are assumed to allow and to sponsor women's travels and who profit from a gendered geography that distinguishes male from female territories. Woman's dress is an important sign of male status and pecuniary class. The more ornamental and cumbersome a woman's clothing, the more financial successful the male. "The high heel, the skirt, the impracticable bonnet, the corset, and the general disregard of the wearer's comfort which is an obvious feature of all civilized women's apparel," Thorstein Veblen explains, put in evidence the "master's ability to pay."[59] In addition to serving as a sign of the pecuniary status of men, the dress of the traveler, a woman temporarily undomesticated and released from her domestic round, must signal her ongoing allegiance to her sphere and her men, perhaps cast in doubt by her geographical designs. Following the advice of conduct manuals, care in dress creates and maintains a woman's desirability and the reputation of the men who sponsor her.

Yet another important historical aspect of conduct books is their relationship in the nineteenth century to women's sexuality. Conduct books have always tied women's desirability to sexuality. Conduct material, as

Mary Poovey points out in her study of the proper lady, assumes "the voraciousness [of] female desire" as it addresses measures to curb it. These measures include the denial of all appetites, signaled by modesty and self-effacement in all things, from dress and speech to the angle of one's gaze. It is true, of course, that women were vulnerable to sexual harassment and violation in the nineteenth century as now, and codes of conduct and manners served to protect women as well as to constrain them. Yet conduct had meanings beyond prudence. Demeanor and manners testify to chastity or its absence, and chastity is woman's defining virtue and the bottom line in the desirability sweepstakes. Piquing a man's desire by delaying its gratification, female chastity simultaneously prompts the male to marry and presents him with a respectable woman with whom to seal the bargain. Chastity is a matter of morals, encoded in manners; and conduct books take both morals and manners as their province.[60]

The conjunction of sexuality and conduct books sheds light on texts of travel behavior. Particularly when traveling solo but in other circumstances as well, women must at all times appear to be modest and virtuous—or, in a word, desirable. In the lore of the Victorian era, the traveling woman never knows when the chivalrous help of males may be needed. Proper dress and comportment, even as they absolve her of any suggestion of sexual allure, will elicit the interest and sympathy of the male. Dress and comportment will show her to be the sort of woman proper males have learned to desire and protect. This is the backdrop that makes especially meaningful the statements of Elizabeth Bisland in "The Art of Travel," a chapter in a two-volume advice book called *The Woman's Book: Dealing Practically with the Modern Conditions of Home-Life, Self-Support, Education, Opportunities, and Every-Day Problems* (1894), effectively a revision of Catharine Beecher's earlier work. "There is, in reality, nothing to prevent a woman from seeing every civilized, and even semi-civilized, country in the world without other protection than her own modesty and good sense," Bisland writes, because "the very defencelessness of a lonely woman appears to put every man upon his honor." And should it occur that men are not put on their honor? If women have painful experiences, Bisland continues, "in nine cases out of ten it is due wholly and solely to their own fault. . . . The garment of modest purity is as magic a defence today as when Una wore it."[61]

The function of conduct books in reining in the behavior of traveling women becomes even more clear in the light of what the historian Mary Ryan calls the "gendering of geography" that occurred in Victorian America. Women's travels to foreign lands are part of a larger picture of the years between 1825 and 1880, when women moved into public spaces. Women's travels reiterate on a global scale the movement of women into public spaces at home in the United States. The same fears and the same efforts to corral women that emerged with urbanization and women's presence in city streets are visible in the advice given women who travel abroad in the larger sense of the word. Ryan identifies 1840 as a benchmark in the gendering of geography. Before 1840, social geography did not precisely specify the spatial boundaries between male and female, public and private. The household was still a center of production and of professional and business practice; domesticity and business overlapped. Women's comings and goings were marked by class and sexual, not gender, distinctions; women of the better classes were granted patriarchal protection, while poor women were sexual prey. But between 1825 and 1840, places of political activity and amusement slowly became male preserves, and the phrase "public man" came to connote civic honor while the phrase "public woman" came to be associated with harlotry.

After 1840, fissures between the private and the public became visible. Alive with people from all occupations, classes, and ranks, city streets came to be perceived as a sexual battlefield, with the rhetoric of sexual danger reaching extravagant proportions by the 1870s. It was men, however, who were understood to be sexual prey to the advances of dangerous women of the lower classes in the streets. Endangered women, those of the better classes, were envisioned as prey to unwanted attentions, defined (euphemistically) as insulting to their sensibilities rather than threatening to their bodies. The motley character of public spaces and streets became associated with what was perceived as an undesirable pluralism. To combat the seeming disorder of this threatening ethnic excess, gender boundaries were drawn, carving at least a symbolic order out of perceived disorder. The doctrine of separate spheres, dividing the whole of life by gender, from activities in and out of the home, to the vote, to the designation of special rooms for women on steamboats, was imposed on public space. Designated city spaces were feminized, assuring women safety from the hurly-burly of the street. That safety, significantly, was to be found in department stores and restaurants, luring women into commodity culture.[62]

Conduct books of travel participate in this gender-saturated climate, advising women on modest demeanor as they draw them to the well of consumerism. When a Miss Manners of the Victorian era, Florence Hartley, advises women travelers on wardrobes, she assists them in consumerism as well as in modesty. Prescribing special walking costumes, including shawls and bonnets, garments of rich material, "snowy white" collars and sleeves, and "neatly-fitting, whole, clean gloves and boots" in her *Ladies' Book of Etiquette and Manual of Politeness* (1879), she offers them because a lady's "dress, carriage, walk, will all be exposed to notice; every passer-by will look at her, if it is only for one glance; every unlady-like action will be marked." Yet her recommendation of special walking costumes at the same time abets the progressive insertion of women into a consumerism nourished by the demands of a woman's special place in the social order. Profits increase together with the requirements for a proper woman's wardrobe. Indeed, ideology, conduct books, and capitalism travel together.

The city streets of the world were perceived as extensions of the streets of the United States. When Elizabeth Bisland advises women on solo travel, she identifies strategies to protect them from the unwanted attention of the motley crowd, to guard women against the unseemly looks and leers to which women going about in public were subject. "The woman who is cool-headed, courteous, and self-reliant," Bisland asserts, "can travel around the world in every direction and find no word or look to daunt or distress her."[63] Although Bisland casts the danger in terms of "word" and "look" (as did American periodicals and newspapers when they described dangers to women on American city streets), there is surely a sexual subtext in her advice. Why is that subtext unspeakable? Why is sexual vulnerability left to the traveler's imagination? Decorum and gentility are of course at work here. But discursive restraints encode class divisions as well. The unspoken speaks; the female traveler to whom Bisland speaks is quietly identified as of the "better," genteel classes, distinct from the sexually passionate creatures of the under classes.[64] What Bisland says constructs women's conduct and desires, and what she does not say constructs and maintains class distinctions.

Beyond conduct books, women's travel created other opportunities for publishers: a market for newspaper and magazine articles on travel generally and on women's travel specifically. Travel materials simultaneously satisfied and shaped public demand for news from abroad and for stories of adventure and feats—rendered yet more sensational if undertaken by a woman. After magazine publishing began to be a profitable industry in the 1840s and 1850s, magazines such as *Harper's New Monthly*, with a sizeable female readership, worked out a success formula that included travel accounts. After the Civil War, magazines and their readers multiplied as rapidly as women travelers.[65] Because the ideology of gender, centering women in the home, made the travel of women abroad seem different, a deviation from the norm, it made traveling women more newsworthy. Women themselves understood the connection between adventures, gender, and profits, and proceeded to exploit that connection for their own ends. Annie Smith Peck, for one, traveled to Mexico in 1897 to ascend El Popo, previously unscaled by a woman. To finance her expedition, she approached Arthur Brisbane, editor of the New York *Sunday World*, and proposed to plant his newspaper's banner on its peak (as Fanny Bullock Workman later planted a placard reading "Votes for Women" in the Karakoram). Persuaded, Brisbane contracted with Peck for her story of the ascent. Peck, meanwhile, walked away with an advance to cover her travel expenses to Mexico and the gear for her climb. And Brisbane? He proceeded to fill the *Sunday World* with ads announcing Peck's adventure and highlighting its dangers and difficulties.[66] Emphasizing gender, the press cast women travelers as a species of the "man bites dog" story, making good script to attract readers and advertisers.

Doing more than simply writing about traveling women and explorers, the newspaper and magazine establishments themselves initiated and then exploited feats of women travelers, creating the material from which copy was then produced. The stories of Nellie Bly and Elizabeth Bisland are exemplary of the link between traveling women, newspapers, magazines, and profits. Joseph Pulitzer, publisher of the New York *World*, sent Bly abroad in 1889 to beat the fictional record of Jules Verne's Phileas Fogg and his eighty-day circumnavigation of the globe. Pulitzer's gamble was a wild success: a week after Bly's much-ballyhooed departure, the circulation of Pulitzer's newspaper was up from 268,230 to 270,660, and "a month after Bly's departure, it had hit a whopping 273,090."[67] Intensifying the competition and thus the chance of profits, John Brisben Walker, editor of *Cosmopolitan Magazine*, dispatched Elizabeth Bisland two hours after Bly's departure to challenge Bly's feat (and Pulitzer's) and write about it. The success of Nellie Bly's stunt is inscribed in its spin-off: contests, board games, lectures, and children's books, as well as plenty of wet ink in various newspapers and periodicals.

Why were these exploits so profitable? The terms in which they were reported suggest that the spoils were generated by gender. The *World* praised Bly because "her grit has been more than masculine . . . a tribute to American pluck, American womanhood and American perseverance," and Bisland was lauded in the *San Francisco Chronicle* as "an energetic and plucky little woman."[68] Songs and jingles about Nellie Bly played on gender in the manner of this one:

> "Oh Fogg, good-by," said Nellie Bly,
> "It takes a maiden to be spry,
> To span the space twixt thought and act
> And turn a fiction to a fact."[69]

The incongruity embedded in the notion of little women coupled with big feats, an incongruity constructed from gender ideology, was a moneymaker.

Bly herself attributed interest in her travels to the fact that she was not just any girl but an *American* girl who had set the record for speed in world travel.[70] Her consciousness of national identity, like that of the *World* journalist who three times over associates Bly's grit with her nationality, is typical. It returns us to the impact of Victorianism on women's travel and its authorization. The mission and morality of the United States, together with issues of identity, made travel matter in the nineteenth century for both men and women, but not for men and women alike. Rather, questions of morality, identity, and mission weighed differently on women and men for reasons of the place of women in American history and for reasons of women's economic situation from the 1820s forward. It is important to an understanding of women's travel (and subsequent writing about it) to recall that—although the identity of the American woman as a citizen was, from the inception of the republic, a vexed issue because of the now-familiar conflict between republicanism and citizenship, on the one hand, and essentialist ideas of Woman on the other—American womanhood functioned from the eighteenth century onward as the emblem of American culture and of the elusive notion of "Americanism." The women of the United States were apostrophized as being "powerful as the New World," the "carrier[s] of a triumphant destiny," the "incarnation[s] of the essence of an entire continent," the embodiments "in so eminent a fashion [of] the intangible quality of 'américanisme.'"[71] They were "America" italicized, emblems of antebellum America and its millennial promise.

Catharine Beecher outlined the connection between gender difference and American destiny in this way: to the people of the United States, she wrote, "is committed the grand, the responsible privilege, of exhibiting to the world, the beneficent influences of Christianity, when carried into every social, civil, and political institution," and "to American women, more than any others on earth, is committed the exalted privilege of extending over the world those blessed influences, that are to renovate degraded man, and clothe all climes with beauty."[72] American women, that is to say, had a particular and important place in the master narrative of world history. In the next chapter, I examine the colonialist and imperialist implications of this mission in women's travel writing. Here I wish to emphasize that across the nineteenth century, Woman was used as the symbol of the republic. She was personified by classical goddesses honored in public ceremonies before the Civil War and by the silhouette of the Goddess of Liberty or Columbia in the 1860s and the 1870s.[73] Even as the travels of the American woman in foreign lands advertised to a home audience the affluence of her male sponsors, her travels spoke to an international audience, as well, about the nation's affluence generally and the achievements of American civilization, the City on the Hill for whom the American Woman served as measure and point of reference.

Her measure, in turn, was taken by reference to the ideologies of Woman and the status of the female "other." Fortunately for women, travel was connected to the study of history and geography, subjects the ideologies of Woman approved. As Nina Baym has observed, the study of history was thought suitable for American women from the beginnings of the republic, and by the 1830s it was thoroughly conventional to advise women to learn history, a subject long since installed in female academies.[74] Women's excursions into the history and geography of the world through the agency of travel stood to benefit the nation in particular ways because of the sphere and mission assigned to women: to inculcate virtue and good citizenship in the children and men in women's charge. Because such excursions clarified the mission and position of the United States in history, travel served as a valuable adjunct to the American woman's role as citizen and mother, making women's travels acceptable in principle.

The changing economic conditions in which American women found themselves in the first half of the nineteenth century and beyond made the increasing accessibility of travel and women's mission a fortunate coincidence. We recall that beginning in the 1820s, women were progressively more tightly attached to a narrowed concept of domesticity, detached from economic productivity. The historian Sklar, analyzing the lifework of Catharine Beecher, points out that women's status deteriorated when the household lost its place as the basic unit of economic production; previously esteemed for their economic contribution, women suffered from dependency roles. "An ideology of self-sacrifice could mask some of the losses women felt about their status in the first half of the nineteenth century," Sklar writes, "but it supplied inadequate nourishment for their crippled sense of self-esteem." [75] Travel moved into the void created by the new relationship of women to productivity. It carried women before the Civil War on an important, proper, and purposeful womanly mission into history. After the Civil War, travel transformed the consumption of leisure into the production and fulfillment of womanly duties to husband and family, whether by continuing to pursue history or by displaying the financial triumph and prowess of her spouse.

Moreover, the American woman, to the Victorian mind, was made remarkable by her difference from the women of other nations, witness her position in American society as articulated by Alexis de Tocqueville in 1835: "You will never find American women in charge of the external relations of the family, managing a business, or interfering in politics; but they are also never obliged to undertake rough laborer's work or any task requiring hard physical exertion." [76] (The putative disconnection between manual labor and American women [read white, Anglo-Saxon, Protestant, and middle class] had an enormous influence on women travelers' readings of their foreign sisters, as chapter 2 will show.) Tocqueville's perception of the role of the American woman was echoed thirty-four years later, in 1869, in Catharine Beecher and Harriet Beecher Stowe's dedication of their book of domestic science, *The American Woman's Home: or, Principles of Domestic Science; being a Guide to the Formation and Maintenance of Economical, Healthful, Beautiful, and Christian Homes*, "To the Women of America, in whose hands rest the real destinies of the republic, as moulded by the early training and preserved amid the maturer influences of home." As historian Paula Baker points out, across the nineteenth century and into the twentieth, the doctrine of separate spheres was not simply embraced but glorified; the most powerful argument against women's public initiatives, whether in abolition or temperance or the professions or suffrage, was the argument that they threatened the existence of separate spheres.[77]

The nineteenth century offers remarkable examples of the continuing allegiance to separate spheres and the tensions it provoked. Mary Clemmer Ames is one of them. The highest-paid newspaperwoman of her day, she attacked political corruption, exposed drunken congressmen, championed woman suffrage, and supported the newly emancipated black population in the 1860s. Nevertheless, Ames criticized women correspondents who dared invade the congressional reporters' galleries, maintaining that the "true woman" belongs in the home.[78] Kate Field, author of five books and numerous articles in magazines and newspapers in addition to two books of travel (discussed in chapter 4) is an intriguing instance of the inner conflicts provoked by domestic ideology. At the age of seventeen, Field wrote, "Oh, if I were a man! I pity myself, indeed, I do. There is not an ambition, a desire, a feeling, a thought, an impulse, an instinct that I am not obliged to crush. And why? because I am a woman, and a woman must content herself with indoor life, with sewing and babies." Two years later, in August of 1857, she wrote this in her journal: "I sometimes think it is a great misfortune that I was not born a boy, for then any and every employment would be open to me, and I could gain sufficient to support my mother and self." Writing in 1872 to an aunt who was fretting over Kate's single state (and who eventually disinherited her because of her ambition to be a lecturer), Kate Field claimed, "I have had several escapes from matrimony, for which I thank God. A life of ambition is a terrible grind, you say. And how about most marriages? Are not they terrible grinds?" Yet despite these sentiments, according to Lilian Whiting, her biographer of 1899, Kate Field "insisted always on marriage and motherhood as the only complete fulfillment of the ideal of womanly life."[79]

Such psychological turmoil, however, did not dislodge the doctrine of separate spheres. The power and influence women derived from the doctrine continued to be for many, as they were for Tocqueville, the stroke of genius that makes the superiority of American women who are, in turn, the source of the power and prosperity of the United States. The American "difference" is the woman's difference twice over, first from men and then from all other women, her peers in gender but her inferiors in status, making her an excellent ambassador (unofficially, of course) to the nations. In short, the discourses of femininity[80] that circulated in Victorian America managed, paradoxically, to domesticate travel. Departures from home were recuperated for domestic purposes, and domestic purposes authorized and even encouraged the very emblems of American domesticity to leave home.

As the nineteenth century progressed, the discourses of femininity came to include a public role, albeit contested, that eventually took shape in the "New Woman" of the Progressive Era and prepared the ground for what became, by 1900, the college graduates and other women confident of their public place because of the work of earlier generations of women.[81] Public spaces, as we have seen, included those open to travelers. The movement of women out from domestic shores and into international spaces may be construed in several ways. Sandra Gilbert and Susan Gubar's construction allows for an extremity of liberation. If women were "imprisoned in men's houses," severely confined within domestic as well as national boundaries, as Gilbert and Gubar say,[82] then it follows that women were likely to experience an exhilarating sense of liberation when they traveled and seized for themselves that freedom of movement historically allowed only the male. A second reading of women's travel, that of Mary O'Brien, brings into play another aspect of women's situation that travel altered. According to O'Brien, traveling women transcended "the contingencies of biological being" to which they were historically held hostage. Travel set women moving through time and space as men had historically done.[83] Leo Hamalian offers a third reading of women's travel: "For most women, immobilized as they were by the iron hoops of convention, the term 'abroad' had a dreamlike, talismanic quality. It conjured up a vision composed of a whole cluster of myths, half-myths, and truths—of sunlight, of liberty, of innocence, of sexual freedom, of the fantastic and the healing, of the unknown and the mysterious—all those concepts that stood in direct confrontation to domesticity." Hamalian asserts that "when women did buy tickets to sail on ships to India or to ride the Orient Express to Baghdad, their real destination, more often than not, was a restorative idea rather than a place on a map."[84]

Women travel writers typically marshal tropes that cast travel as a liberating activity. Elizabeth Bisland writes of "the great Cunarder [swinging] free from the docks, bearing me away to the delights and mysteries of foreign lands"; Mrs. A. E. Newman finds Britain to be "Eden restored"; Harriet Trowbridge Allen writes of "the newness and delightful strangeness" of Rouen; and Lucy Bronson Dudley defines arrival in Liverpool and debarkation on English soil as a rebirth, with passengers emerging "from their chrysalis state."[85] Ella W. Thompson's description in 1874 of her sense of travel merits quotation at length for its revelation of the power of travel, even the thought of it, to liberate a woman from the burden of domestic responsibilities. Thompson writes:

> I want to say, to begin with, that the writer of this book is one of "the few, the immortal few," left of her sex in America, who would rather have an India shawl any day than the suffrage; but in dark moments, when both have seemed equally unattainable, it has occurred to her that most women's lives are passed, so to speak, in long, narrow galleries, built about with customs and conventionalities more impervious than stone. Sometimes they contract to a hot little kitchen, and the owner might as well be a Vestal Virgin, and done with it, her whole life being spent in keeping up the fires. . . . Plenty of doors lead out of these galleries, but only those marked "Church," "Visits," and "Shopping," move easily on their hinges.
>
> Most of us . . . cast longing eyes at the door marked with the magical word "Europe," and it has opened freely enough when the husband said the "Open, sesame"; it is only of late years that women have made the amazing discovery that they can say it themselves with like success, but it is well to keep the hinges well oiled, and the rubbish cleared away from the threshold. When my turn came, I felt as if I had been taken into a high mountain and been promised all the kingdoms of the earth, and had at once accepted the offer.[86]

Thompson frames her remarks in the contentious debate of her time over woman's place and rights, over India shawls and the suffrage, and situates herself as a conventional woman. Thompson then connects women's travel not simply with a sense of freedom, but with the aspects of women's lives that make women covet the freedom of travel. Travel lifts the weight of domestic responsibilities and interrupts the dull round of routine, and it is particularly sweet when, having made "the amazing discovery" that the door to Europe can be opened by them, they have acted on their own desire and by their own choice rather than that of husbands.

Yet the picture of women's travel and reactions to it is more complex than fantasies of freedom and of open doors and extended vistas suggest. The picture admits of at least two other, less romantic interpretations. First, the "release" of women into international waters may have been, paradoxically, an agent of domesticity even as it was a strike against the separate spheres to which the sexes were assigned in the ideology of Victorian America. The numbers of women who departed from American shores after the Civil War with such seeming freedom and the (sometimes grudging) blessings of their countrymen may have been complicit in a conservative desire to return women to their homes, to revise women's post-Civil War victories and to redefine them as defeats. If domesticity exists and has meaning only in the presence of its opposite, the marketplace (the outside world), and if the marketplace works to reinforce domesticity and domestic individualism, then travel, ideologically considered, is not entirely what it seems. Travel becomes a disciplinary agent. It reinforces the difference between and thus the production of domesticity as well as its opposite. In this scenario, the experience of travel itself, underscoring the opposition between the outside world and the comforts and security of the home shores, stands to heighten the importance of home and domesticity.[87]

A second interpretive possibility, still within the understanding of "home," suggests that women's travels may have worked to strengthen the structure of society, the separation of spheres. If "home" is "an eminently retrospective gesture," needed and indeed even thought only "when home has already been left behind," as Georges Van Den Abbeele contends; and if "tourism assumes a return to the home, and a change in attitude toward it, in which the home becomes chosen rather than a fate," as Eric J. Leed maintains, then travel works against itself.[88] The political uses of certain commonplaces that circulate around travel (for example, the idea that going abroad makes us appreciate home) are unveiled. The cooperation of

American culture in women's foreign travels may signal a view of travel that, like the American frontier for men, functions as a kind of safety valve for restless women. Travel set in relief the privileges of home at a time when narrow constructions of domesticity were under seige. The additive of the perceived difference between the women of the United States and their foreign counterparts, a difference in favor of the United States, prepares the stage for backlash. The superior situation of the American female, observed repeatedly in the cultural contrasts made visible in travel and broadcast to the nation upon the return of the native from abroad, stood to amplify the privileges of the woman fortunate enough to be an American. Travel stood to make the inequalities in women's status as citizens, against which many women took up arms as they sought the vote and entrance into the professions after the Civil War, seem inconsequential alongside the privileges conferred upon white, middle- and upper-class women in the United States. Travel rewrote "home" in new and more appealing terms.

III

Public response to women's travels abroad registers the desire simultaneously to encourage and constrain women's global ambitions. Public response embeds the complexities, apprehensions, and ambiguities in the culture's attitude toward the phenomenon of traveling women, demonstrating once again the gendering of travel in nineteenth-century America. Public reactions sometimes supported women's initiatives and sometimes impeded them, interjecting into the physical "travail" of travel a psychological dimension: the question of the propriety of travel for women, and in what circumstances. Throughout the nineteenth century, travel for reasons of health or in pursuit of knowledge and culture, like that of Emma Willard in the interests of Troy Seminary, and travel tied to a husband's pursuits, like that of Sophia Hawthorne joining her husband in the consulate at Liverpool, was sanctioned. Missionaries to foreign lands, like Agnes McAllister who directed the Garaway Mission Station on the Kroo Coast of West Africa in the 1880s, were cast as "Christian heroine[s]." [89] Such women as these traveled for "womanly" purposes, in keeping with conventional ideas of women's place and role as domestic creatures charged with the care of men, the education of children, and the promulgation of Protestant, Anglo-Saxon, and middle-class virtues and values. Accordingly, "womanly" travel escaped the censure leveled by Lydia Maria Child at travel as mere "public amusement."

When wealth and the numbers of traveling women escalated dramatically after the Civil War, similar, favorable judgments on women's travel persisted—if travel was decorously pursued. These judgments were sometimes registered by affluent, upper-middle class men, anxious to broadcast both their economic success and their manly, self-abnegating labors in the demanding world of business. John Straiton, for example, proudly prefaced his wife and daughter's book of travels in India, Asia Minor, Egypt, the Holy Land, Turkey, and Greece with this: "It is still quite novel for two American ladies to go half-way around the world, as these have done, on a journey of intelligence, recreation, and health. Business men in our country can seldom take the time for foreign travel, and being myself unable to get away, I was willing to let them find their own way abroad." Straiton writes, "The journey gave the materials of enjoyment and instruction for life; while the splendid health in which they returned was partial recompense to those left at home for their ten months of absence."[90]

The court of public opinion, however, was not invariably kind and receptive to traveling women or comfortable with their exploits. In the later nineteenth century, when the female traveler who ventured into international spaces was often a type of the New Woman, women's travel was a magnet for diverse and complicated reactions. On the one hand, through clever marketing that played on stereotypes of Woman, the public in the last quarter of the century was drawn into the exploits of journalists like Nellie Bly and Elizabeth Bisland—lauded, lionized, and applauded for circumnavigating the globe in record time. On the other hand, some segments of the public continued through the turn of the century to be uneasy about what they perceived to be excessive numbers of female travelers. Envisioning American womanhood as an emblem of American culture and reading the American woman as Alexis de Tocqueville had done, as tea leaves foretelling the millennium and the nation's destiny, the public continued to associate the private, domestic role of the American woman with, to repeat Tocqueville's words, America's "extraordinary prosperity and growing power."[91] The remarks of Lavinia Johnson in the *Utica Herald* in

1859 clearly link female domesticity with millennial promise. "When man and woman learn to treat each other reverently, each to honor the work of the other not as they mark it out—but as it is apportioned by the hand of the omnipotent," writes Johnson, "the millennium finally reigns."[92]

In the last quarter of the century, a secularized, positivistic version of inevitable, historical progress associated with Spencerian sociology sometimes displaced millennialism. The residue of perceptions similar to Tocqueville's remains as late as 1882, in the midst of extensive public debate about woman's place following upon the inception of the women's movement in Seneca Falls forty years earlier. Lucy Seaman Bainbridge, a religious and social activist who "decided upon a two years' course of study in the school of travel . . . hoping to gain many lessons of life," mimicked the culture's fearful attitude toward traveling women in the voice of a provincial male friend who moaned,

> "Don't see no use for people to go gadden about railroads and steamboats to get more larnin' . . . you mustn't to mind if I speaks my mind very plain to ye; it's my duty. A woman's business is to stay to home and look after things and save. Now there was my dear departed wife Saray 'Liza,—Nobody could beat her at making soap, be it hard or soft, and we never, none of us, used a whole candle till every scrap and bit was all burnt up. . . . Well," sighed the old gentleman, "times is changed! There ain't none of my daughters as savin' as me; their heads are full of notions like the rest. My girls are a paintin' old jugs and saucers, and talkin' about art, and wantin' to go to Europe. Why can't people be satisfied to stay at home and keep to the good old ways!"[93]

What the culture seemed most reluctant to tolerate, however, were female adventurers and explorers. They seemed not simply to transgress the borders of woman's sphere but to usurp the role of men. The adventures of such women were trivialized through the humorous exploitation of Woman's stereotypical foibles. Perhaps the most egregious instance of this is the bit of verse published by the Royal Geographic Society:

> A lady explorer? A traveler in skirts?
> The notion's just a trifle too seraphic;
> Let them stay and mind the babies or hem our ragged shirts;
> But they mustn't, they can't, and shan't be geographic.[94]

When women dared to be seraphic and geographic, they were attacked and put on trial, sometimes by their own sex. Fanny Bullock Workman, for example, challenged Annie Smith Peck's claim to the honor of breaking the world's record for men as well as for women in her ascent of Mount Huascaran. In such an instance as this, the competitive drive of the hard-core explorer, rather than gender, may motivate the attack. Yet gender was a major player in estimates of female achievements. The veracity of Fanny Bullock Workman, but not that of her traveling companion, her husband, was impugned because feats such as hers—climbing the Himalayas and exploring the mountains and glaciers of eastern Karakoram under her own power—struck the Victorian mind as highly improbable for a woman. According to Workman, her critics charged that she "did not really climb the peaks and passes" but was, rather, "hauled to the top by coolies." Asked "by staunch and indignant women-friends to deny [this charge] publicly at lectures," Workman declared it "beneath [her] notice to deny such a trivial accusation."[95]

Critiques and humorous incongruities were cobbled from stereotypes of Woman and the contingencies of travel. When Bisland and Bly set out in 1890 to circumnavigate the globe, Woman's fabled romance with clothing (and the fabulous quantities of luggage that follow) was marshaled on the field of female travel. Observing that "the masculine mind" finds "something strangely exhilarating in the thought of a woman being abruptly torn from her home without sufficient time to put her wardrobe in order," Bisland claimed that to the men who commissioned her feat, "the most delightful feature apparently of the whole affair" was the necessity to "get ready in five hours for a seventy-five days' voyage around the world. Why this should be so a woman cannot easily divine," Bisland writes; "It fails utterly to appeal to *her* sense of humor. It is one of those hopeless warps in the male mind that my sex no longer attempt to comprehend or to straighten, and, finding it incurable, have learned to bear with and ignore it as far as possible."[96]

Discomfort with the impact of widened horizons on women was by no means limited to men. Even women who were themselves in the ranks of the New Woman sometimes expressed a certain uneasiness with the transformations encouraged by foreign travel and exposure to foreign cultures. Ida Tarbell, the fearless investigative reporter and muckraker who exposed the sordid business practices of Standard Oil in a series of nineteen articles in *McClure's Magazine* in 1902, experienced this unease. In her thirties, she traveled to Europe over the protest of some of her best friends. Beginning in 1893, she spent more than a year in Paris working as a journalist in order to study the life of Madame Roland, a political activist who was guillotined in 1793 for her complicity with the Girondins during the French Revolution. Like Margaret Fuller, who admired Roland as an example of "women of a Roman strength and singleness of mind,"[97] Tarbell believed that Roland's life stood as a model for women's fitness for a political role. Yet despite her admiration for Roland, despite her own life decisions, and despite her love of Paris, Tarbell echoes Lydia Maria Child who, sixty-one years before Tarbell, had expressed the fear that travelers "injure themselves and their families." Tarbell writes, "There was a disturbing number of [American women in Paris] compelling me to ask myself again and again if this break for freedom, this revolt against security in which I myself was taking part was not a fatal adventure bound to injure the family, the one institution in which I believed more than any other, bound to produce a terrible crop of wretchedness and abnormality. Had not even the few successes [among American women] I saw about me," Tarbell continues, "been paid for by a hardening of heart, a suppression of natural human joyousness that was uglier even than the case of my poor Miss C [an American woman convicted of shoplifting in Paris]?"[98]

Indeed, conservatives reasonably feared the changes apparently fostered by women's travels. Physical travel across international borders appeared to transform the borders of the mind, as well. Elizabeth Cady Stanton, having traveled to England with her husband in 1840, was appalled at the refusal to admit women to the floor of the World's Antislavery Convention and came home to forge the first wave of the women's movement in powerful alliance with Lucretia Mott, whose acquaintance she first made in London. Margaret Fuller, energized and unfettered in the revolutionary excitement of Italy, came to advocate radical socialist positions that worried and embarrassed her Transcendentalist friends. Harriet Beecher Stowe decidedly widened her horizons through European travel, extending her notion of both "woman" and "artist" while abroad. When she returned home, her biographer Joan Hedrick tells us, her husband Calvin found his "decision-making power sharply curtailed," not simply by Harriet's financial independence but by her "geographical independence" as well.[99]

As the remarks of Ida Tarbell and virtually every other commentator of any gender make clear, the ghost that haunts the machine of women's travel and public response to it is an ideology of Woman rooted in her relationship to domesticity, a set of assumptions and convictions promulgated in the United States about the constitution of the world and Woman's proper place in it. The discourses of femininity that circulated in the course of the century, the continuum of ideas about Woman (and women), extended from the far left (rejecting essentialism and the assignment of women to the private sphere) to the far right (rejoicing in the private sphere) to the center of the ideological continuum (espousing some of the values of each extreme), and various points in between. As historian Anne Firor Scott reminds us, at every point during the Victorian era, from the antebellum years until the turn of the century, each of the positions on this continuum was occupied by both women and men,[100] and sometimes by the same man or woman at different points in life. Sometimes implicitly and sometimes explicitly, but with a consistency that bespeaks the power of gender ideology, the public took the measure of women's travel, its value and its meaning, as it took the measure of women, their value and their meaning, by reference to one or another point on this spectrum. Travel mattered in nineteenth-century America for both men and women, but it mattered particularly for women and their observers because of gender. The matter of gender, having prohibited or radically circumscribed travel for women before the Victorian period, now made the foreign travel of women a matter for discussion and display.

IV

Technology, economics, and the marketplace, together with conceptions of the history and mission of the United States, joined the discourses of femininity circulating in nineteenth-century America to make women's travel possible, important, marketable, and profitable. Having traveled, American women transformed their adventures abroad into a prose that wrote "home" from the vantage point of abroad. Seizing the advantages and confronting the impediments to the pursuit of the craft of travel writing in their particular situations, they did the work of inscribing their experiences abroad. Women proceeded to insert themselves into the historically male world of the travel book, the subject of the next chapter.

Chapter Two

Literary Inroads

Genre, Gender, and Difference

Toward the end of the eighteenth century a change came
about which, if I were re-writing history, I should describe more fully and think of greater importance than
the Crusades or the Wars of the Roses. The middle-class
woman began to write.

—Virginia Woolf, *A Room of One's Own*

At the turn of the century, Esther Chaddock Davenport published a book
of travels called *Going on Me Own: The Trifling Summer Adventures of a
Woman Abroad* (1900). On the flyleaf of a gift copy of the book, her daughter Ada wrote: "I don't know why mother went abroad nor why she wrote
about it, but she 'went' and she 'writ.'" The mother's choice of title, the
daughter's inscription, and the existence of the book itself capture the attitude of many nineteenth-century American women toward travel and
its transformation into prose. Like many women, Esther Davenport drew
attention in the title of her book to gender coupled with independent
travel, with "going on me own." Again like many others, she cast her "adventures" in the diminutive, defining them as "trifling." Daughter Ada's
inscription reiterates the sense of inconsequence embedded in her mother's
title. Ada pretends that she didn't ask and Esther didn't tell about the going
or the writing. Ada represents Esther as going abroad haphazardly and then

simply tossing off a little book about it. Despite the nonchalance and coy-
ness encoded in the language of both women, the book was published and
the daughter thought well enough of it to offer it as a gift. Esther and Ada
use language to mount a performance on the stage of travel and travel
writing.

The mother and daughter's performances tell a typical story of nineteenth-century American women who, having invaded the historically
male territory of travel in significant numbers, then transformed travel
into a passport to the historically masculine domain of the travel book.
Having escaped what Leo Hamalian calls "the iron hoops of convention," [1]
they then constructed linguistic expressions of freedom and creativity in
books of travel which, like the genre itself, are "an implicit celebration of
freedom . . . a poetic ode, an ode to Freedom," as Paul Fussell describes
those written by male travelers.[2] These "odes" proliferated in step with the
technologies of travel and print as both the century and economic prosperity advanced. Of the more than 1,700 books of foreign travel published
in the United States by Americans before 1900 (exclusive of newspaper and
magazine articles and unpublished diaries and journals), 195 of them were
women's work.[3]

This body of work entered a generic field with which the American
public had a love/hate relationship. The popularity and the marketability
of travel writing in America, documented in the records of lending libraries
and book sellers, attest to the American romance with travelogues. In the
first half of the nineteenth century, travel writing was important economically and philosophically, useful to merchants and international traders in
an expanding, industrializing economy. As we have seen in chapter 1, it was
useful, as well, to other citizens who, engaged in the now-familiar American quest for identity, found in travel accounts the difference from the
"other" that shaped the meaning of "American."[4] Furthermore, travel accounts helped to assuage the sense of cultural fragmentation created by the
diversity and rapidity of change that accompanied economic and industrial
expansion. As Ronald Zboray explains, accounts of travels offered a promise of stability and "models for individual characters, usually the writers,
mastering alien environments much more foreign than that of early capitalism, and yet much more comforting because they usually reinforced the
values of a traditional precapitalist world."[5]

The American romance with travel writing continued into the second half of the nineteenth century.[6] Whereas some 323 books of travel by Americans were published in the United States before 1850, at least 1,439 were published from 1850 to 1900. Even the most tedious of them found readers. The *New York Times* greeted the travel account of Mark Twain's fellow traveler to the Holy Land, Mrs. Harriet Griswold, with the observation that "the world would not have been greatly the loser if *A Woman's Pilgrimage to the Holy Land* [Griswold's account] had never been written." The *Times* was correct—and yet Griswold's account sold 20,000 copies.[7] The market for books of travel was sustained not only by affluence and escalating numbers of Americans boarding steamships, but by interest in world events. The colonization of Africa, the formation of the Republic of Liberia in 1847, and abolitionism in the United States, for example, saw American accounts of travel to Africa rise from five before 1840, to ten between 1840 and 1860. In the next thirty years, between 1860 and 1890, and coincident with the Civil War and the travels in Africa of Henry Morton Stanley of the *New York Tribune*, twenty-four accounts were published, and in the decade of the 1890s, another twenty-one. Historical events and economic initiatives again cooperated with travel writing in the case of China. Having published three accounts of travel to China before 1870, American women published sixteen in the thirty years between 1870 and 1900, when missionary activity and the lure of Asian and particularly Chinese markets to shippers and manufacturers in an industrializing America were on the rise.[8]

The sheer quantity of travel writing, however, occasioned ritual laments. As early as 1817, a reviewer opined that almost everybody who "happens once in his life to wander from the precincts of his own native village, thinks it his duty to enlighten the public with a narrative of his adventures." Twelve years later, in 1829, a reviewer bemoaned the numbers of sailors and naval commanders who, "not content with discovering countries and winning battles, steer boldly into the ocean of literature." In 1841, Catharine Maria Sedgwick wrote that European travel is a field "so thoroughly reaped that not an ear, scarcely a kernel, remains for the gleaner." In 1870, a reviewer claims to register "a new mental protest against another addition to the absolutely innumerable books of European travel." These laments are ritualistic and strategic; they are the straw men that announce a display of new material. Despite protests of yet another travel account, the one under review is of course claimed as notable either for its virtues or its vices. Nevertheless, the notion of travel writing as an overworked genre was influential in the real world of publishing. Helen Hunt Jackson, for example, journalist and novelist, best known for championing Native Americans in *A Century of Dishonor* (1881) and *Ramona* (1884), was advised by the editor of *Hearth and Home* in 1871 to take heed because travel letters were a "'drug on the market.'"[9]

The rhetorical prognosis for the genre continued to deteriorate until the close of the century. In a preface to an account of travels around the world in 1897, a publisher comments on the difficulty of attracting readers. "Americans now cross the ocean in palatial steamers to see for themselves what was once attainable only through the medium of books," he writes. "The columns of the daily press report current events from every part of the globe almost as soon as they occur. Therefore, to publish a book describing the scenes and incidents of a six months' tour in foreign lands seems almost absurd."[10] A book of travels published in Victorian America joined what Eric Savoy aptly calls a "literature of exhaustion"—or at least what was rhetorically so characterized.[11]

The genre's history and nature stood to exacerbate the problems of generic exhaustion and a supersaturated market. A hoary tradition encrusted with conventions, the travel genre invited formulaic and sometimes tedious writing. Nineteenth-century books of foreign travel are replete with what Neil Harris calls "ritualistic expressions of the appropriate": comments on the sea crossing, the difficulty of handling foreign language, the dishonesty of porters, the atrocities of bandits, the bustle and decay of cities, the pride of being American, the ache of homesickness, the joy of returning home.[12] Travel books assiduously carry the reader to cultural shrines, monuments, churches, museums, harems, khans, the Pyramids, and various of nature's monuments such as the Alps and the Black Forest and the Dead Sea. Travel books are compendia of obligatory talk about obligatory sites inscribed and prescribed in guidebooks and canonical literature. Conventional attitudes emanate from predictable subject matter and rhetorical strategies, all contributing to the hardening of the genre as the century proceeds, and making it progressively more difficult to transform travels into seemingly new and provocative texts. As a critic put it in

1857, "The subject of European travel is so hackneyed that only first-rate ability is competent to make a new book on the subject interesting."[13] Travel writing suffered from what James Buzard calls the "belatedness" problem, the perception that much of the world, but especially Europe, had already been written about. While this perception was not new to the nineteenth-century traveler, it reached crisis proportions during that century.[14]

Enter the traveler and writer who is female, bringing in her train the matter of gender. Victorian attitudes toward women who would assume a public voice and publish their adventures abroad offer both an opportunity and a complication in the fortunes of Victorian travel prose when written by women. On the one hand, women were literary practitioners from the beginnings of the republic, participating with community approval in a range of literary activity, from newspaper editing to competitions for literary prizes.[15] The ground was prepared to receive women's travel accounts. Situated in this milieu, allusions to gender in women's texts or in reviews of them, particularly those that are disparaging, are safely construed as figures of rhetoric.[16] Gender turns out to be a performance, and the players may be the travel writers themselves, strutting their stuff on the stage of travel, or reviewers criticizing the performance from the gallery. But on the other hand, the surge of women travelers and their accounts of foreign adventure occur, as the previous chapter discussed, at a historical moment when the meaning and boundaries of woman's sphere were contested and increasingly indefinite; and when the definition of the domestic sphere was being stretched to encompass ever more public terrain, to the expressed consternation of many Victorians. This creates an ambiguous context in which the line between "mere rhetoric," or performance, and description, or the transcription of actual perception, is sometimes difficult to discern. Nathaniel Hawthorne's infamous remarks about "scribbling women," for example, are rhetorical, drawing on stereotypes of women as gregarious gossips, but they are also referential, pointing to Hawthorne's response to the popularity of woman's fiction, a popularity that outstripped his own.

Whether opaque or transparent, a matter of rhetorical play or actual perception or both, the reception of women's texts of travel across the century embeds allusions to gender and incorporates the public debate about woman's sphere. Reviewers juxtaposed the market, the public sphere, with

the culture's domestic ideology of Woman in the process of assessing accounts of travel by women. Take, for example, a review from 1845 and
another from 1874 that, though separated by thirty years and the Civil War,
seem contemporaneous because the terms of their arguments and the basis
of their fears are similar. Each review constitutes the union of women and
publication a threat to womanliness. In 1845, an anonymous reviewer
praised the poet Lydia H. Sigourney's *Scenes in My Native Land* because it
proves "that American women can be intellectual without leaving the
proper sphere of their sex." In 1874, a reviewer of Ella Thompson's *Beaten
Paths*, while applauding her charm and brightness, admits to an urge to
eliminate "some of the wittiest passages of the book. . . . Things in the
cold black and white of literature are different from things airily laughed
at in company that one knows familiarly. By and by the ladies will learn
this,—or their critics will learn to judge them more generously." On some
occasions, diction encodes a gendered critique. In 1872, for example, an
anonymous reviewer found Helen Hunt Jackson's *Bits of Travel* to be
spoiled by too much "vivacity." In an especially insidious gendering of the
travel book market in the later nineteenth century, cultural arbiters accused
women of touring solely in order to write tour-memoirs, implying that
the disease of "cacoethus scribendi" had found its way from the world of
Catharine Sedgwick's story of that name to the world of women's travel
writing. While the "familiar charge" of traveling to write memoirs was
applied to travelers of both genders, it was, according to James Buzard,
leveled against women in particular "on the basis of their proverbial gar-
rulousness and exhibitionism." [17]

Apparently undeterred by such charges, women travelers inserted and
asserted themselves in the storied tradition of travel writing. Why they did
so and how they made use of the conventions of the genre is the burden of
this chapter, excavating what lies buried in the double voice, one proud
and the other coy, of Esther Chaddock Davenport's title and her daughter
Ada's inscription.

I

Invigorated and made vocal by travel, women travelers inserted themselves
into the literary world of travel in increasing numbers as the century

evolved. In addition to articles in the periodical press, women published some 27 books of foreign travel before and 168 after the Civil War, most of them encompassing travel in several lands. Many of these were the work of women who did not routinely aspire to print. While it is not surprising that women who were engaged in other writing practices—poets and novelists such as Lydia Sigourney and Caroline Kirkland and essayists such as Margaret Fuller—would publish their travels, and while it was the professional work of journalists like Kate Field and Mary Krout to write on assignment, there were other, "miscellaneous" women, otherwise absent from the annals of history, such as Abby Morrell and Adelaide L. Harrington and Esther Chaddock Davenport, who were somehow prompted by travel to come before the public in print. Why did such women pursue what was for them the exceptional and public activity of publishing travel accounts? The commonsense answer to this question is that writing about one's travels was, in the nineteenth century, akin to the showing of slides and videos in our time: a way to relive, share, and magnify what is for many people an important and often singular experience. Caroline Kirkland put it this way in 1849: "The desire to go again [to Europe] is stronger even than the desire to go at first; and the next best thing is to live over again what so much delighted us, in attempting to describe it to others" (HA, 1:8). Ideological, commercial, and literary facets of Victorian life offer additional answers to the "why" of publication by traveling women.

The same Victorian *Gestalt* that enabled women's travel authorized the writing ambitions of the female traveler, as well. Like the male, she was motivated by Victorian didacticism, self-righteousness, and ethnocentrism to publish a book of travels. The Victorian American, generally persuaded of his superiority and of his duty to serve as a model for the world, "saw himself as uncorrupted and morally superior," as Paul R. Baker puts it, in religion and morality. The American thought that the American family, treatment of women, work ethic (making begging and religious orders seem so reprehensible to Americans), system of commerce, and above all, the American system of government justified his feelings of superiority. Perceiving himself as better than his foreign counterparts in honesty, sincerity, devotion to business, social relations, and religious practice, he was pleased to give lessons but not to take them.[18] He was an agent of colonialism.

This self-righteous sense of national superiority was magnified in the case of women. As we have earlier seen, women had responded to the founding question of the identity of the American woman and her political and civic responsibilities by carving out positions and functions connected with republican motherhood.[19] Granting moral authority to women, American culture had early licensed on gender grounds a circumscribed female activism in matters attached to virtue and morality. Women developed a sense of purpose and vocation *as women*, assigned a moral mission to teach and to work for reform in the world outside of the home.[20] Nina Baym's analysis of women historians in antebellum America can be instructively extended to women who wrote travels, an annex of history. Accepting "the narrative promise that women's historical day is close at hand," women historians read history "as especially significant for their sex," Baym writes, and Protestant Christianity as the only ideology that, valuing intellect and spirituality over physical strength, "opened at least some kinds of public and political space to women." On these grounds, Baym continues, "White, Protestant, Anglo-Saxon United States women felt fully authorized by their culture to speak for history because they felt so fully that the end result of the historical narrative was, precisely, themselves."[21]

Convinced of their authority and superiority, and feeling the incremental power of certain historical events as the century evolved, Victorian women made their way to publishing houses. As the century advanced, woman's sphere was gerrymandered.[22] Women pushed further into the public domain, their voices increasingly occupying the podium and print media. Women's public initiatives were encouraged by the escalating public debate over women's rights and emancipation; the expansion of women's education and women's colleges (with graduation sometimes followed by an addition to the concept of "finishing," a trip such as that of Jane Addams in the previously male school of the European tour); the proliferation of various women's organizations; and the emergence and visibility of the New Woman, modifying conventional female roles, asserting and enlarging women's right to a career, to a public voice, and to public power.

Together with women's historic activity in the institutions of literature from the beginnings of the republic, these currents contributed to a cultural ambiance in which women, equipped with an expanding sense of selfhood and potential, would undertake the publication of their experiences abroad. From the 1850s forward, women increasingly became creators as well as curators and receptacles of public culture. Publishing travel books, women laid further claim, in the words of Carroll Smith-Rosenberg, "to the long-standing rights of bourgeois men"[23] and, addressing many of the same issues as men, made their voices heard. Women's books of travel were extensions of women's battles for rights, understood as battles for a place in public discourse, in this case public discourse about foreign lands and their testimony to America's millennial place and progress.[24] The didactic destiny of the American woman was arguably more manifest than that of the "lords of creation" and their later incarnation, the captains of industry, because to her was ascribed an elevated place, special power, moral insight, and an exalted mission to make use of these on behalf of humankind.

The travel book, historically a repository of political commentary (examined in chapter 4), offered itself as a vehicle for the didactic destiny of American women. In the 1840s and 1850s, travelers such as Jacob Abbott in *A Summer in Scotland* (1848) and George Wilkes in *Europe in a Hurry* (1853) had launched counterattacks on critics of America such as Basil Hall, Charles Dickens, and Frances Trollope. Women travelers join in this battle of the books. Thus Harriet Beecher Stowe urges, in *Sunny Memories of Foreign Lands*, that travelers "admire" and "love" as well as "carp and criticize." "There is not an unfavorable aspect of things in the old world which has not become perfectly familiar to us," she writes, "and a little of the other side may have a useful influence."[25] The travel book remained an arena for ideological and political combat through World War I.

Throughout the nineteenth century, women entered the arena with increasingly global designs. The rationales women supply for their accounts of travel trace the movement of women into increasingly comprehensive and public discursive domains. Before the Civil War, female travelers typically cast themselves as handmaidens to the personal comfort and the intellectual and moral enrichment of other individuals. If they speak at all for a cause in the body politic, they do so in passing. Thus Caroline Kirkland modestly claims in 1849 to write "to give you a simple, personal narrative," she says, and to suggest "what may be advantageously accomplished by the traveller" (HA, preface). Diffident and homely motives are articulated across the century, as when Harriet E. Francis (1828–1889), wife of an American minister to Greece, Portugal, and Austria-Hungary, gathered her travel letters into *By Land and Sea: Incidents of Travel, with Chats about History and Legends* (published posthumously in 1891) for her grandchildren. But with increasing frequency during the last quarter of the century, ambitious, public, and overtly political reasons for writing join reasons of personal helpfulness. Adelaide Rosalind Kirchner writes *A Flag for Cuba* (1897) for the political reasons her title announces: to appeal for Cuba's independence shortly before the Spanish American War; and the journalist Mary Hannah Krout writes *Hawaii and a Revolution* (1898) to encourage the United States to annex Hawaii. Some women professionalized the American woman's global mission. Elizabeth Banks, a journalist, echoing the earlier, local work of Nellie Bly on behalf of causes such as prison reform, took her muckraking skills to England. She insinuated herself into successive roles as a domestic, a flower vendor, a female companion, and a laundress, and wrote an exposé of the deficiencies of British society entitled *Campaigns of Curiosity* (1894). American women advanced from domestic to municipal to global housekeeping.

Banks and others mimic the practice of nineteenth-century American women writers in other genres who saw themselves as instruments for good, who felt, as Joanne Dobson says, "a mandate to speak for moral betterment, either that of the reader or that of the world" in order "to effect conversion in spirit or in behavior, or to alter conditions in the world."[26] In her study of travel writing and transculturation, Mary Louise Pratt identifies such activity in a foreign culture as a "branch of the civilizing mission" and a political practice conducted by the "exploratrices sociales." "Social reformism," Pratt writes, "might be said to constitute a form of female imperial intervention in the contact zone."[27] Pratt finds these interventions in the colonizing of the Americas, but such interventions move in other geographical directions as well. For American citizens, the "contact zone" was the Scottish borderlands and the Appian Way and North Africa as well as the wilderness areas of the Yucatan. Wherever they were, many American women conceived of intervention, especially in the shaping of public opinion, as right and proper.

Perhaps the single most energizing factor in the decisions of Victorian American women to write their travels, however, was the opening of journalism to women, especially after the Civil War. From early in the nineteenth century, women were active in publishing and in newspaper work, crusading for social justice and female emancipation. The names of early women journalists, some familiar and some obscure, are often linked with travel writing. Anne Royall, for example, who published her own newspaper in Washington D.C. from 1831 to 1854, published ten volumes on travel in the United States between 1826 and 1831; Sara Jane Clarke, or "Grace Greenwood," who in the 1840s wrote for the New York *Home Journal* and the *National Era*, as well as editing *Godey's Lady's Book* for a time, published *Haps and Mishaps of a Tour in Europe* (1854); and Margaret Fuller, correspondent for the *New York Tribune*, wrote travel letters for that newspaper in the late 1840s. After the Civil War, Mary Abigail Dodge, or "Gail Hamilton," made a name in journalism and wrote travels, as did Kate Field and Mary Hannah Krout (discussed in chapter 4). The expansion of women's place in journalism shows in figures taken from the *Congressional Directory*: whereas four women were listed in 1870 as eligible for the Capitol press galleries, twenty were listed in 1879. By 1889, women journalists had made such an impact on the profession that the *Journalist*, a professional journal in New York City, devoted an entire issue to profiles of fifty women editors and reporters. On that occasion, the editor pointed out that although a newspaperwoman earns her living by wielding a pencil rather than sewing on buttons for the "lords of creation," she is no less a woman for that. The number of daily newspapers in the United States quadrupled between 1870 and 1899, and women were an integral part of the newsroom.[28]

Journalism created what Richard Brodhead calls "scenes of writing" that slowly opened wider and wider to women, enabling them to envision themselves as journalists and to imagine journals and newspapers as outlets for their writing.[29] Two-way streets for women who traveled, newspapers and periodicals offered opportunities to publish travel articles; and women wrote travel articles to clear a path into newspaper and periodical work. In the 1880s and 1890s, with a growing audience of women and burgeoning advertising directed at women shoppers, women's opportunities for press and periodical writing increased. Women sometimes used these opportunities to publish articles about their travels or, like Nellie Bly and Elizabeth Bisland, traveled and wrote about it on assignment from their editors as we recall from chapter 1. Journalism was a great resource, and female journalists used travel writing as an entrée into it, making their way in the profession. Moreover, the existence of numerous outlets for travel writing stood to encourage women with a travel tale to tell to seek a publisher, even if they were not professional journalists.

Contrary to those already-noted ritualistic expressions of dismay, the literary marketplace, including the periodical press and newspapers, was hospitable to travel writing in the 1800s. Early in the century, the *North American Review* routinely published several major articles annually about travel books.[30] Beginning in the 1830s and the 1840s, travels and letters from foreign correspondents were a staple of the penny press. Shelley Fisher Fishkin has found in a two-week period in March of 1842, for example, that the *New York Herald* carried letters from England and Horace Greeley's *Tribune* carried letters from China and news from Mexico. In the 1850s, seizing upon an interest in distant places stimulated by the upsurge in domestic travel by railroad and foreign travel by ship, newspapers significantly increased their use of letters from traveling correspondents in far-off places.[31] Magazines such as *Harper's New Monthly* and *Atlantic Monthly* offered lengthy monthly travel articles, often accompanied by sketches of women in various picturesque poses such as lounging on shipboard or visiting harems or, parasols in hand, riding in jinrickshaws drawn by coolies. In the book trade, the publication of travel books burgeoned in nineteenth-century America in the last half of the century, as we have seen. This was the market in which the female traveler found herself and the market in which she showed herself as capable of "doing literary business" as her sisters who wrote fiction.[32]

Indeed, the wherewithal to enter the business was near at hand. Assiduously writing home from abroad, travelers had often written the equivalent of a book of travels by the time they returned to American shores. Journals kept en route and letters dispatched from Italy and Egypt to family and friends at home supplied first drafts from which to work. In prefatory remarks, women persistently represent their decision to publish as accidental rather than premeditated, a decision pursued only at the urging of friends. Sarah Haight's remarks are typical: "It was with extreme reluctance that the author of the following letters, consented, in the first instance, that they should appear before the public, even in the columns of a newspaper;

but she found herself obliged to yield to the earnest solicitations of her friends, and permit their publication." [33] Statements such as Haight's, while conventional and theatrical, contain nevertheless this element of truth: that travel books often existed in holograph by the time the traveler returned to the home shores. This fact made short the road from a New York or San Francisco pier to a publishing house.

Three further encouragements set women to the task of publishing their travels: the nature of the genre, its standing in the pantheon of literary forms, and Victorian attitudes toward the literary amateur. Historically, travel books are remarkably elastic and discontinuous affairs. They are repositories of the topical and the trivial, and of history, art, anecdotes, and quotations from other books and other travelers. They are, in effect, literary carpetbags in which travelers pack all that they need for their travels and all that they collect along the way, to be unpacked and preserved in a potpourri of forms, from letters to journals and diaries, to poems and dialogues, to essays and narratives. [34] Sometimes they are chronicles and memoirs of travel, structured by geography and the chronology of the traveler's journey. Sometimes they are essays structured ethnographically by topics (such as schooling or women or religion in a foreign culture—an organization favored by missionaries). Sometimes they alternate between chronicles and essays. [35] As William W. Stowe explains, travel books are "a genial form of narrative . . . a meeting place for various narrative voices, literary styles, levels of speech, and kinds of subjects, combining disparate modes of discourse without necessarily generating any tension among them or forging them into a 'higher unity.'" [36] The "genial form" and the authorized absence of a "higher unity" may have encouraged "miscellaneous" women, those I defined earlier as women largely without literary aspirations, to publish in the genre. The ready-made structure of the itinerary of travel itself, in the instance of chronicles, may have motivated such women to write a book. There is also, of course, the warrant in the travel genre for culturally authorized and conventionally female forms such as the letter, the diary, and the journal. Because these are forms in which women are historically practiced and believe themselves to be competent, the writing of travels may have seemed a welcoming rather than forbidding pursuit. [37]

In short, the publishing of travels was inviting to women. In addition to women's historical warrant, in America, to participate in literary enterprises, the publication of travels put a woman's reputation at little risk, even among a conservative readership, because of the perceived status of the genre. Without pretense to literary grandeur, accounts of travel "merely" report, with attempts at accuracy, the "facts" of travel and of foreign lands. The travel book is one of those "lesser forms" in the autobiographical tradition, and autobiography was thought to require, in the words of Jane Marcus, "keen observation rather than divine creativity." As autobiographical writing is a "harmless activity" requiring "only talent, not genius," so its kin, travel writing, is innocuous. To boot, "men were less likely to criticize women" for engaging in autobiographical writing of any kind, including, then, travel writing.[38] When these aspects of the genre meet the ideal of "genteel amateurism" that, compatible with middle-class ideals of womanhood, held sway in antebellum America and was honored across the century, the road along which the seemingly less bold female traveler "happens" into the publication of a book is staked out. Even those politically conservative, post–Civil War females who favored a domestic feminism that encouraged women to reach out into the public domain precisely because of women's special qualities[39] could respectably occupy a seat in the modest vehicle of travels. Travel writing makes room for the amateur passenger before the 1860s and, thereafter, for the expert as well.

II

But how does gender intervene, we must ask, and what difference does it make when a text of travel is written by a woman rather than a man? The interventions of gender and difference in the writing practice of nineteenth-century American women travelers are sometimes obvious in titles and in protestations of subject matter. In more than a tenth of the travel books published by Victorian American women, writers and publishers cooperate to make a display of gender in titles or subtitles or printing characteristics—witness Mrs. E. A. Forbes's *A Woman's First Impressions of Europe* (1865); Lucy Yeend Culler's *Europe Through a Woman's Eye* (1883), where the title in bold face and upper case letters is repeated in the last line of the text; May French Sheldon's *Adventures in East Africa or Sultan to Sultan: The Narrative of a Woman's Adventures among the Masai and Other Tribes of East Africa* (1892); and missionary Agnes McAllister's *A Lone Woman in Africa* (1896).

Furthermore, women travelers make subject matter a gender issue in their texts as it was in their culture. They rationalize what they do and do not include in their accounts by invoking the Victorian division of subjects and interests along gender lines. In 1839, Sarah Haight wrote, "I think I hear you say, away with all such *bas bleu-ism* [talk of charters, history, and tribal commanders], and talk to me rather of shawls and robes, turbans and slippers, pearls and emeralds. Talk of Circassians and Georgians, harems and baths, sherbets and sweetmeats, pipes and coffee" (LOW, 124–25). And Catharine Maria Sedgwick wrote in 1841, "Do not fear that I am about to give you a particular description [of docks and warehouses]. . . . Our 'woman's sphere,' does not extend to such subjects" (LA, 52–53).

Mining in 1882 the vein that Sarah Haight had mined forty-one years earlier, Lucy Seaman Bainbridge writes of her adventures in China: "Life everywhere is made up of little things. This is especially true with women; hence if I write of trivial matters, leaving to others of the opposite sex the broad, comprehensive opinions of peoples and politics, it must be remembered that the writer is looking at the world with a woman's eyes. After years of dealing with butcher, grocer, and the milkman, it is a matter of real interest to a housewife how these things are managed round on the other side of the world" (RWL, 164). As if the process of writing brought her to revise her definition of the trivial, Bainbridge later validates women's presumed interests by equating them with those of businessmen: "It is a woman's nature to delight seeing inside of other people's homes. There's nothing wrong in it, any more than for merchant X. or Y. to peer into the depths of his neighbor's store to see how trade is going on. Carrying out this women's curiosity during our stay in Maulmain, every Christian home was visited" (RWL, 469). In one way or another, these remarks protest the writer's womanliness, as in Ella W. Thompson's text quoted in chapter 1: "I want to say . . . that the writer of this book is one of 'the few, the immortal few,' left of her sex in America, who would rather have an India shawl any day than the suffrage" (BP, 9–10). Yet what do such interventions mean? These protests are honored in the breach as women record and comment on whatever they please. Again, public rhetoric to the contrary, all issues were women's issues in the nineteenth century. Whatever else they may be, these obvious evocations and invocations are performances of gender. They are staged to carve out a place for women's work in an allegedly overworked genre and to project a "womanly" woman who, although she may pretend to engage in a transgressive act, is in fact behaving herself.

Apart from such insertions, the similarity of nineteenth-century travel accounts across gender lines is striking. Having followed the same guidebooks, such as Murray and Baedeker, and having dutifully visited the same obligatory sites, such as the Louvre and the Pyramids, women and men alike regularly construct in their accounts of travel virtually the same attitudes about their experience of the world. Antitourism, romantic nostalgia, fixation on the past to the sometimes derisive neglect of the present, and the inevitable comparisons of "abroad" with "home" are customary fare.[40] Yet despite the apparent "sameness" of itineraries, topoi, and attitudes, women's travel writing recurrently differs from men's. Though it is risky to generalize about so eclectic a practice as travel writing, it is fair to say that taken as a body of work, women's texts of travel make gender visible at certain sites as women work their way into the world of travel writing and around the constraints of gender. At particular intersections of genre and gender, fissures open to allow a glimpse of gender at work. Sometimes the traveler explicitly writes gender difference into the text. Sometimes the gendered discourses of Victorian culture to which women's writing was inescapably subject deposit traces of difference. Whatever the means, gender at times erupts and becomes significant beyond its insertion in the text as a subject. Gender erupts at four particular intersections: intertextual practices; the convention of the apology, including tropes; obligatory talk about the commonplaces of travel such as modes of transportation; and textualizing of the "other." Examining these textual moments in the generic practice of both men and women, I will first show the apparently "same" in their texts, and I will then show the intervention of gender that makes the difference.[41]

Travel accounts are full of historical and cultural information taken in part from observation and in part from historians, novelists, poets, and other travelers. A recurrent practice, therefore, in the travel writing of both men and women in the nineteenth century is the invocation of intertexts, or recourse to predecessor texts. Because Americans male and female were reading history, it is no surprise that it would find a place in records of travel to historic sites. Yet there are additional reasons for the prominence of history in accounts of travel. History and the travel accounts of others, together with travel itself, provide a pretext to write. Travelers invoke predecessors in allusions to, dialogue with, and sometimes copious quotations from travel books, works of literature, and histories (sometimes complete with bibliographies and lists of references). This kind of intertextuality occurs in accounts of travel in the United States as well as abroad; Margaret Fuller, for example, invokes George Catlin, John Murray's *Travels*, Henry Schoolcraft's *Algic Researches*, Mrs. Jameson's stories, Washington Irving's books, Thomas L. McKenney's *Tour to the Lakes*, and a collection of Indian anecdotes and speeches in her own *Summer on the Lakes*. Intertextual practices speak to the accuracy of David E. Johnson's observation that "travel begins and ends in the book; it takes place in the interval between reading and writing."[42] In some books of travel, dialogue with other texts reaches the proportions of what I call a meta-travel book convention, the installation in a travel book proper of a book about the difficulty of writing travels. The foreign culture, its landscapes, works of art, cities, and monuments— already, even exhaustively, textualized—are overlaid with poetic and historic allusions until the tradition lends itself to analysis in Roland Barthes's laboratory of the text as "a multi-dimensional space in which a variety of writings, none of them original, blend and clash." Whatever degree of poststructuralist, Derridean inescapability some might ascribe to these "tissue[s] of quotations drawn from the innumerable centres of culture," as Roland Barthes might describe travel accounts,[43] the nineteenth-century traveler deliberately invoked predecessors, producing new text by alluding to other, older texts.

The purposes for which Americans traveled abroad are the fundamental reason they allude so frequently to predecessor historians, writers, and travelers. Predecessors clear an avenue into foreign lands. Their books are the tools of intelligent travel. Nineteenth-century Americans, earnestly traveling in search of history and the past, conscientiously consulted libraries of material to assist their understanding. This equips them not simply to travel, but to write about it. Nineteenth-century travel writers sometimes focus on contemporary life in foreign lands, of course, particularly when contemporary life includes revolutions or other events that amplify the sound of history lumbering toward the millennium. To be abroad during revolutions, to be an eyewitness to history like Margaret Fuller during the Italian Resorgimento and Edith Wharton during World War I, was to observe history in the making. Travelers in the United States, too, whether visitors like Alexis de Tocqueville or Gustave Beaumont or Louis Xavier Eyma, or Americans like Margaret Fuller or Caroline Kirkland writing about Michigan, envisioned the future—history—in the making.

As noted earlier, in antebellum America a master narrative was at work; history was God's work progressively and inexorably unfolding, event by meaningful event.[44] By the turn of the century, remnants of millennialist thinking remain in secularized, Spencerian form, slipping toward imperialist thinking. In *In Morocco* (1920), for example, Edith Wharton praises the "civilizing" work of the French in an Algeria they sought to colonize. Yet most travelers avoid travel in countries in the throes of conflict. For the typical traveler abroad, present time is merely the channel through which, unfortunately, she must pass. Like the weather, the present is the prevailing condition the traveler must tolerate in order to arrive at her destination, the historic past.[45] The rendition of the historic past, in turn, is taken from predecessor texts that invade the traveler's writing practice.

The work of Joseph and Elizabeth Robins Pennell, Bayard Taylor, and Harriet Trowbridge Allen typifies the intertextual dimension of travel writing. Undertaking a global imposition and totalizing revision of predecessor texts, the Pennells, who eventually became widely known and even more widely published travelers, not only revise Chaucer in their *Canterbury Pilgrimage* (1885) and rewrite Laurence Sterne in their *Sentimental Journey through France and Italy* (1888), but include prefatory comments to draw attention to the revisionary nature of their work. Bayard Taylor, the most popular travel writer in mid-century America, invokes and corrects predecessor travel writers in *Journey to Central Africa* (1854). "It is remarkable that both [James] Bruce and [John Lewis] Burckhardt, who travelled by land from Berber to Shendy, failed to see the ruins," Taylor writes. Although Bruce speaks of broken pedestals, Taylor continues, "he does not mention the groups of pyramids which are so conspicuous a feature in the landscape." Taylor credits his curiosity about the temple of Djerf Hossayn to "the enthusiastic description of [Bartholomew] Warburton, and the disparaging remarks of [Sir John] Wilkinson," and then allows that both are "correct, in great measure." When it suits him, he recounts stories and alludes to Greek myths evoked by particular sites.[46] Harriet Trowbridge Allen, too, uses hearsay, myth, literature, and other books of travel as the building blocks for many of her observations in *Travels in Europe and the East* (1879). She remarks that "I have had my own ideas of Moorish architecture and decorations from Irving's glowing descriptions" and takes great pleasure "in tracing the steps of Mr. Irving, using his exquisite tales of the Alhambra as my guide" (TEE, 475, 493). She claims that "the life-like portraitures of Prescott and Motley" have brought Spain particularly alive for her (TEE, 476). She is a happy woman by the time she leaves Spain, not because she has visited Spain in her own person but because her imagination, a repository of Washington Irving, John Motley, William Prescott (and other predecessors, no doubt), has shown her the way. "For once my dreams have been realized," she writes, "and I have seen Spain as I have imagined it" (TEE, 494).

Such intertextual practices point to epistemological and narratological aspects of travel and travel writing with serious consequences. Substituting for the traveler's own construction of the world even as they assist her in making meaning, intertextual practices are part of the epistemological paradox that we read well and with pleasure what we know how to read, and what we know how to read depends on what we have already read.[47] In the case of travel, the world is the text, and the meanings the traveler constructs are dependent on the world as textualized by others. Edith Wharton articulates this epistemological dilemma when, landing at Iseo, she finds that "there is no telling . . . how much the eye receives and how much it contributes" to her vision of the lake of Iseo.[48] Earlier than Wharton, Sarah Haight, wife of a wealthy merchant and a society matron known for her lavish entertainments, was confronted with "turbaned Turks and veiled women, queer Armenians, and chattering Greeks," all "so novel and unique" to her that she "could scarcely believe it to be reality." Therefore, like many other travelers, she turns to the tales of the Arabian Nights. She invokes a narrative in which a woman literally preserves her life by telling stories, even as Haight now preserves a portion of her life between the covers of her book of travels. Yet even as a "page of Hadji Baba" (LOW, 1:26) enables her to make sense of the scene, it undermines in the same stroke, ironically, a commonsense purpose of travel, to see the world for oneself.

Sarah Haight and her compatriots manifest what the critic Edward Said calls a "textual attitude," or recourse to what one has read about something distant or unknown. According to Said, "People, places, and experiences can always be described by a book, so much so that the book (or text) acquire[s] a greater authority, and use, even than the actuality it describes."[49] Textual attitudes explain how it came about that, as the historian Cushing Strout remarks, Europe has always meant for Americans a set of ideas, values, and institutions as much as a specific geographical place. Europe has always been the history of an idea rather than a fact in an atlas.[50] The set of ideas developed from texts and creating a textual attitude is part of the semiotics of travel. Contrary to commonsense understandings of the purposes of travel, some travelers do *not* set out to see a sight empirically; rather, they undertake to find the congruence of a sight with the idea of it, with a type that derives from earlier travelers.[51] Thus Caroline Kirkland, for example, remarks on her visit to Kenilworth that "it is absolutely necessary to the spirit of the thing to be able to sit with the eyes shut, and recall the associated ideas, and then to have leisure and quiet to fit them to the actual scene. In cases where Scott has given life to the past for our imaginations, this is peculiarly necessary, for he makes the place where a part of the thing said or done so completely, that when we see the one we can never be content until we have added the other" (HA, 1:41).

The traveler's reliance on predecessor texts creates, however, a greater irony and another epistemological dilemma. Pre-texts promote blindness as well as vision. When Sarah Haight resorts to a page of Hadji Baba to assign meaning to an otherwise incomprehensible scene, she makes explicit the role of discursive formations, which, even as they enable a vision of other lands, become "agents of blindness."[52] Ushering in versions of the past constructed by others, intertexts elbow out the present. They contribute to the "meanwhile" problem, or the textual fate of contemporary life in foreign lands.[53] Predecessors can turn texts and travelers, male and female, away from the places they have come to see. Travelers turn, instead, to what they did *not* see and make a rhetorical display of it. In a world in which it is difficult to write something new about sacralized sites, travelers sometimes work up a perverse travel drama around what they did *not* visit, confounding the expectations invested in travel and travel writing.

Take, for example, Harriet Trowbridge Allen writing about the Holy Land. Claiming first that it would be irreverent "to hurry through places so fraught with the most sacred associations," and therefore better not to visit them at all, she then claims she is "glad" to leave Syria unvisited. Why? "Travel is such a disenchanter that I should be afraid to go there," she claims. "I would rather have the vision in my mind surrounded by the mystery and grandeur which only my imagination can bestow, than to see it, and realize it, and find it what it is" (TEE, 458–59). Allen prefers *not* to see the Holy Land. Rather, she prefers her imagination of the place, nourished by reading and armchair travel, to the world she has come out to see as an actual traveler.

Visiting Syria apparently threatens the life of Allen's imagination, a repository of intertexts, because of the offensiveness, the impossibility, of the present. "To go there and find the ignorance, superstition, and filth which are inseparable from the East—to have pointed out to us by ignorant *ciceroni* [local guides] places around which thought lingers solemnly and with awe," Allen writes, "would be painful in the extreme." Nor is it only the contemporary Middle East on which she turns her back. In Paris and Versailles, as well, Allen only has eyes for the past, focusing on the "sadness and horror" of the fate of "poor Marie Antoinette," that "doomed queen" who, together with "stately trains" of other noble figures, is now gone. "How easily imagination supplies the present void!," Allen writes (TEE, 458, 6–7). The void is contemporary life, empty of the past glories cataloged by others. She cannot imagine contemporary, continuous life, impoverished, fallen from its former grandeur, and therefore unrepresentable. On the other hand, of course, the poverty of the present heightens the splendor of the past, the object of Allen's travels. An actual site, though impoverished in time present, sparks the traveler's imagination.[54] The *un*importance of the present in comparison with the past, then, is paradoxically crucial to the traveler's journey into the past.

In the case of the American traveler, two additional semiotic frameworks, overlooked by scholars of the genre, foster a conflict with continuous life: the association of the United States with the conceptual categories of present and future, and the association of the rest of the world with the past. The American travels the world, as we have seen, for lessons in history and confirmation of America's millennial progress. As Julia Ward Howe puts it in her 1868 travel book, "The prophetic nation [America] is working out and fulfilling the prophet's future."[55] We see this not only in women's accounts of foreign travel, but also in women's books of travel in the United

States, as when Margaret Fuller writes in 1844 about "the picturesque beauty" of Illinois, "so new, so inspiring."[56]

Equipped with schema to construct the meaning of other lands almost exclusively in terms of their past, the traveler from the United States is able to make sense of them only *as* past. Furthermore, equipped to construct the meaning of older nations as unimportant except as steps in the march of history toward the fulfillment of God's millennial plan sweeping forward in the United States, the continuous, present life of foreign lands inevitably seems inferior. As Sarah Haight so uncompromisingly puts it, "The modern city of Alexandria is scarcely worthy of your attention" (LOW, 1:89). Here is the "meanwhile" problem at its most intense. Present time is simply banished—and vanishes, leaving only a trace—from the traveler's larger interests, the past as that which must give way to the future, to the United States.

Yet travel writers put the "meanwhile" problem and its accomplice, intertextuality, to narratological use. They translate them into opportunities for drama that testify, in turn, to the rhetorical nature of travel writing, its opacity rather than its transparency. Like other conventions and rhetorical strategies, the "meanwhile" problem and intertextuality, whatever referentiality they may have, are also metaphors. Travel writers figure contemporary life in foreign lands as an obstacle to be overcome, an element in a serial ordeal that magnifies the courage and heroism of the traveler's persona. They do this, we must remember, at a time when travel, travelers, and their accounts were relatively abundant, and when travel writers must therefore distinguish themselves and their work from the pack if they are to find an audience. The traveler who tolerates the vicissitudes of the present for the sake of attaining the sacred monuments and moments of the past, the grail, is indeed heroic.

Further, travel writers enlist predecessors to reshape into an asset what Eric Savoy calls "the *burden* of prior travel writing" that militates against and even prevents originality.[57] Catharine Sedgwick, for example, undermining the notion that women lack a sense of humor, uses predecessors as objects of satire, creating humorous effects. Claiming to be "tired of repetitions of descriptions," she says, she will provide "the following summary of epithets. For castles: 'beautiful, brooding, baronial, crowning, elevated, lofty, high, grand, magnificent, superb, sublime, lordly, mounted, mouldering, murky, perched, spring up, suspended, overlooking, watching, protecting, guardian, smiling, frowning, threatening, lowering, hovering, hung, towering, decayed, dilapidated, crumbling, ruinous, picturesque, lonely, light, airy, massy, heavy.' Villages: 'pitched, perched, planted, imbosomed, lapped, cradled, nested, sheltered, hidden, concealed, cribbed, ensconced, peeping, terraced.' We had the modesty to call them *synonymes*" (LA, 234). Moreover, predecessor accounts are made to testify to the writer's status as an authority among authorities. As we have seen in the case of Bayard Taylor, the invocation of other travel writers encodes the intelligence and preparation that ensures the reliability and value of this traveler's account.

Putting intertexts to perhaps an even more clever use, some travel writers make them demonstrate not simply authority but superiority to previous travelers. In this way, they fashion the act of travel writing itself into an epic. The writer slays the dragon, other travel books, and replaces them with the writer's own text, making way for yet another travel book in which much of the talk is about travel talk. Mark Twain, for example, claims in the preface to *The Innocents Abroad* that his purpose is "to suggest to the reader how *he* would be likely to see Europe and the East if he looked to them with his own eyes instead of the eyes of those who traveled in those countries before him." In the text proper, he then goes on to satirize various forms of textualized travel that stand between his readers and their own eyes. He berates the oral tradition, the "old Travelers" who "prate and drivel and lie"; the scholarly tradition, the ancients who are noteworthy because "the information [they] didn't have was very voluminous"; the artistic tradition, "the old Venice of song and story." He seizes upon the meta-travel book convention, a running commentary on travel writing, to satirize his companions, pictured in "the semblance of a writing-school" at work "under the swaying lamps," writing "for two or three hours diligently in their journals"—earnestly launched and then abandoned in the course of their travels.[58]

Characteristic of Victorian travel writers, Helen Hunt Jackson wrestles with pre-texts, turning them into a pretext to write. She takes out after the uselessness of phrase books and repeatedly plays with guidebook practices that, she claims, circumscribe her practice even as she rejects theirs. Guidebooks are staged as agents in a drama in which Jackson must compensate for their omissions. She must mention the towels drying in the sun at the Baths of Caracalla because "the historians" make no mention of them.[59] She berates guidebooks for lacking the very information the traveler wants: "The few rare bits of knowledge that I do hanker after never *are* in that unpleasant red book"; and she is "quite surprised" by the rare occasions on which she and her Murray do agree, as when they both find that the cloister of San Pietro in Montorio is "proper to be admired" (BT, 168, 173). Guidebooks also dictate certain exclusions: she is "under bonds never to write about ruins" because that is what the guidebooks always do (BT, 151). Tempted to *include* "a little guide-book about Torcello," she resists the temptation because "I remember that I promised never to do guide-book at all" (BT, 206). She prefers, in fact, not to be "tormented with its [the guidebook's] husks of information," because "it doesn't make the least difference to you which room [in the Baths of Caracalla] was the 'Cella Frigidaria' and which the 'Cella Calidaria'; and as soon as you settle that, you can be happy" (BT, 167). Like Twain and other travel writers who play with predecessor accounts, Jackson makes a display of her writing skills and fashions a besieged and harried but nevertheless determined persona, a writer and traveler managing against the odds to display geniality and originality at a time when there seemed less and less to display. Such use of intertexts extends and redirects the conventional dramatic interest of travel writing from the challenge of travel itself, associated with discovery and adventure, to the challenge of textualizing travel in a world "always already" textualized.

The epistemological and narratological similarities in the travel accounts of men and women do not answer, however, this crucial question: is the convention of intertextuality the same when marshaled and manipulated by men and women? Does the apparent sameness of male and female practice disguise a difference?[60] When the nature of conventions is taken into account, and when women's texts of travel are situated in their Victorian, rhetorical context, the answer to this question is yes. There is a difference. Generic conventions, as Robert Scholes reminds us, may be indexical. Having a phenomenal or existential connection to what they signify,[61] they may simultaneously point inward to generic practice and outward to the phenomenal world. In the phenomenal world of Victorian America, we recall, women's place in travel and its discourses was subject to rhetorical diminishment; women's propriety in writing and broadcasting their views to the public was ritualistically contested; and women's books of travel, as we have seen, were subject to gender-inflected reviews. What Linda Alcoff calls the "positionality" of men and women in the institution of writing was different.[62] Men, as a class, were incontestably fitted to write and publish their views, whereas women, as a class, were the "challenged." The male, *homo viator*, both wrote and traveled by an ancient birthright, thoroughly assumed and assimilated.

The female, however, maneuvers on a different terrain, even if only rhetorically. She proves and constructs her right both to travel and to write. Her maneuvers bear out Julia Kristeva's position on sexual difference as "at once biological, physiological, and relative to reproduction." Sexual difference, Kristeva says, "is translated by and translates a difference in the relationship of the subject to the symbolic contract which *is* the social contract; a difference, then, in the relationship to power, language, and meaning."[63] As a consequence, predecessor texts incorporated into women's work resonate differently than those incorporated into men's. When the normative male invokes predecessors, a single voice, that of literary convention, is presumed to speak. When the marked female calls on predecessors, however, the discourses of femininity offer the additive of "femaleness." In this context, Victorian readers bring this "femaleness" to the text and construct meanings accordingly. But what is more important, as my analysis will demonstrate here and in later chapters, the texts of women travelers often embrace this cultural context. Women travel writers are like their counterparts in the world of journalism who, as Ishbel Ross says, "had to go in for dizzy self-exploitation before they could make themselves heard at all."[64] They deliberately inject "femaleness" into their rhetoric.

The work of Helen Hunt Jackson and Sarah Haight typifies the presence of difference, of the additive of "femaleness," despite the apparent sameness of male and female intertextual practices. Like most travelers of her era, Jackson associates Venice with John Ruskin. But unlike most, she does so oppositionally. Operating intertextually and attempting to prove her dutifulness to her traveling fathers, she observes that she was "praiseworthily conscientious [a virtue that may itself be gendered in the feminine when inscribed in a woman's text] in attention to all that Ruskin tells us is admirable" (BT, 196–97). But her conscientiousness is not rewarded. The Doge's Palace, she writes, "may be imposing; I suppose Ruskin knows; but somehow it won't impose on me, and I can't get it to" (BT, 197). Jackson's text thus declares its infidelity to the text of the father, Ruskin's text of Venice.[65] Infidelity can be perpetrated, of course, by a male, but in the balance of Victorian culture in which the Hydra of gender is always already heaped in the scales of meaning, the weight of infidelity differs when it is the textual act of a woman.

Sarah Haight's visit to Palestine typifies another such lode of gender in the fissure created by intertextuality. Haight creates a drama in which, as in the texts of Mark Twain and Helen Hunt Jackson, the writer-protagonist is almost defeated by her splendid forerunners-antagonists, now cast as a challenge to be met by the travel writer, now proof of her heroism as she invokes and deflates her forerunner in a mock-epic struggle. Doing combat with Alphonse Lamartine's *Voyage en Orient* (1835), Haight's writer-protagonist almost loses herself in a confusion of ideas spawned by this formidable contemporary. But she finally recovers and returns to herself, to her own ideas. Haight writes,

Doubtless you have perused the highwrought effusions of Lamartine, and dwelt in ecstasy on his glowing iambic. Long before I reached the shores of Palestine, I was in raptures with his beautiful *fancy sketches*; and while I followed him through the mazy groves up to the giddy summit of his Parnasus, "Le souffle impétueux de l'humaine pensée, Equinoxe brûlant dont l'âme est renversée," shook my every nerve, my thoughts became confused, and my imagination intoxicated; until at length the *divine* heroics of the "poet" overcoming my remaining powers, "Poussant tour à tour les plus forts sur la cime, Les frappe de vertige et les jette à l'abîme," prostrated all my hopes, and shipwrecked all my delightful anticipations. I was seized with despair at the prospect of my poor intellect not being able to appreciate, nor my unworthy heart sufficiently to venerate, the sacred places I was about to visit.

Since I have been wandering over holy ground, my ideas have recovered from the effects of the thunder of this modern Jupiter. More fortunate than Phaeton, I find the car of my imagination has escaped unbroken, the steeds of enthusiasm unharmed and sound, the reins of judgment not lost. (LOW, 2:49–50)

This traveler's irreverence before canonized sources magnifies her conquest of her competitors. It also magnifies Haight's boldness and daring.

She, a woman new to travel and travel writing, presumes to join a decidedly hoary tradition. She maneuvers among male authorities as did Margaret Fuller, who, in *Summer on the Lakes*, inserted herself into the library of male understandings of the American Indian.[66] But perhaps most tellingly, this travel writer transmits confidence in her own ideas and judgment by defining herself against Lamartine, by linguistically breaking free of this overwhelming and powerful male. She displaces a giant, replacing him with a new authority, a female authority, Sarah Haight. Her faithless text is delivered to an audience saturated with the discourses of femininity, an audience in possession of two a priori ideas likely to shape their reading: the idea that, in writing matters, the woman is bold who competes with a man; and the idea that, as Caroline Kirkland said of her own travels, it requires "audacity . . . to offer one's poor thought of these great and beautiful things, after all that has been well said about them" (HA, 1:vi). Haight is, indeed, doubly audacious.

III

The dynamic set in motion by intertextual practices is similarly at work as travel writers manipulate the apology, or the disclaimer, a second conventional feature of the nineteenth-century text of travel. Sometimes freestanding and sometimes embedded in evocations of intertexts, apologies are another site at which gender becomes visible. The apology is ubiquitous in nineteenth-century practice. Washington Irving enlists it in the account of himself in *The Sketchbook of Geoffrey Crayon, Gent.*, claiming that "my heart almost fails me at finding how my idle humor has led me aside from the great objects studied by every regular traveller who would make a book." Margaret Fuller enlists it in *Summer on the Lakes*, asking if "all the little" she has to write "can interest" the reader.[67] Henry James, too, works the apology together with intertextuality and the "meanwhile" problem. He claims that Venice presented the writer with a challenge: "Venice. It is a great pleasure to write the word; but I am not sure there is not a certain impudence in pretending to add anything to it. . . . Venice has been painted and described many thousands of times. . . . There is nothing new to be said about it certainly." Predictably undeterred, the indomitable James converts the impossible into his main chance. He perversely introduces the matter of Venice's overdetermination, the "belated-ness" problem, into his text both for the sport of circumventing it and to justify yet one more text of travel, his own. Transforming the "meanwhile" problem into a conceit, he boldly declares, "The old is always better than any novelty. It would be a sad day, indeed, when there should be something new to say." [68]

Female travelers also make use of the apology along a spectrum of dis-claimers that range from the torturedly earnest, to the playful and theatrical (like James), to the diffident. In the preface to her book about China, the missionary Henrietta Shuck projects an intense and timid persona, fright-fully reluctant to come before the public. Shuck writes, "Whatever be the imperfections of the following miscellaneous notices, it is deemed inexpe-dient to burden their publication with many apologies. Their preparation was originally undertaken for the special perusal of young friends and ac-quaintances in Virginia, nor am I now certain that they will have a much wider circulation. They may, however," she continues, "meet the eye of some who are familiar with China and the Chinese; these will probably find nothing new, but for the benefit of such, let it be understood, they were not intended." [69] Shuck first diminishes her book by referring to un-specified "imperfections." She next labels "the following" as "miscella-neous" and "notices," a doubling of diminishments. Then, ignoring the load (or is it the lode?) of deprecation already embedded in her prose, she continues, "it is deemed inexpedient to burden their publication with many apologies," signaling her acquaintance with the apology as a conven-tion even as she interjects the notion that her preface is unconventional. Disclaiming a "manly" desire for public influence or profundity of insight, she dons the garment of humility, claiming that, having written these "no-tices" for young people, she is not so vain as to anticipate "a much wider circulation." Yet a touch of her suppressed desire escapes her control; per-haps her work will "meet the eye of some who are familiar with China and the Chinese." Having in that phrase exposed her desire, she must imme-diately re-repress it: readers who are knowledgeable about China "will probably find nothing new." Yet if they do not, says the serpentine Shuck turning back on herself yet once again, "for the benefit of such, let it be understood, they were not intended." The degree of ambivalence and dif-fidence Shuck expresses here about writing for publication bears witness to the epic battle raging between her desire to appear in print and her need to repress that desire.

More often, however, the field of battle is less painful and more playful, as in the case of the trope. Drawing on the domestic sphere to explain the loose shape and structure, the absence of a higher unity, in an account of travels, women travel writers use tropes as disclaimers in alternative dress. Tropes drawn from the domestic sphere often play on the apology and the fit between the rhythm of women's daily lives and travel. Like home life, travel and journal keeping move by fits and starts, subject to delays and interruptions. Women inject domestic metaphors to explain the form of their accounts, but also to flavor them at the copious table of travel books. Two examples suffice to document the practice. Helen Hunt Jackson calls one of her travel entries "a kind of washing-day-dinner letter. You'll eat it," she says, "because you can't get any other, and you won't be hungry as if you had eaten nothing; but don't we all hate Monday dinners?" (BT, 244). Mabel Loomis Todd, editor of Emily Dickinson's poetry, claims that her book about the Amherst Eclipse expedition to Japan "necessarily makes divers small branchings in its course, like a sort of ornamental needlework much affected by our grandmothers," and she asserts, "I have, as it were, feather-stitched my way to Yezo and back again."[70] Yet the very existence of the transgressive travel book itself marks the apology as empty, as a performance. Coy self-deprecation, in short, is largely a rhetorical strategy. It introduces into the discussion the possibility of pitfalls in order to underscore, for the reader's admiration, the skill with which the pitfalls are avoided, even as it insinuates an element of courage on the writer's part, facing down difficulties and doubts.

Like the drama fashioned around predecessor texts, the apology inscribed by both male and female travelers displays writing dexterity and creates the persona of a writer conquering obstacles. But in travel writings by women, the additive of "femaleness," the positionality of women within the institution of writing and the potential indexicality of convention, creates rhetorical affects that differentiate the male from the female apologia. The texts of Mark Twain and Helen Hunt Jackson, again, demonstrate the difference. Simultaneously underscoring and dismissing the convention of the apology, Mark Twain simply declares, in his preface to *The Innocents Abroad*, "I offer no apologies for any departures from the usual style of travel writing that may be charged against me." Nor does he perform deferential gestures toward predecessor travelers and writers. On the contrary, he goes on the attack, as we have seen, insulting and accusing others of stupidity and lying.

Helen Hunt Jackson, on the other hand, rolling the convention of the apology into her meta-travel book, uses it self-reflexively. She criticizes her lack of industry in writing: "But I have been so stupid, I have sat dreaming away over the mountains and have not written out the stories I have heard and the people I have seen" (BT, 260). Yet when she is industrious, she apologizes for this as well, on the grounds of quality and quantity: "This letter is sure to be the worst I ever sent you, dear souls," she writes (BT, 244). "But I write to you too much about pictures. I remember I used to think it the most stupid reading in the world, other people's notions of pictures which I had not seen" (BT, 274). She accuses herself of the sins Mark Twain ascribes to others. Helen Hunt Jackson's play on the apology, like that of other women travelers, may be an authentic murmur of a gendered insecurity in the use of the father's tools; or it may be strategic; or it may be a performance mounted for rhetorical affect. It may reveal an actual lack of confidence; it may cleverly evoke amateurism to maintain an aura of the feminine as a woman goes about doing a man's business; or it may be theater acted by Woman on the stage of Victorian America. All of these are responses to women's position in the institutions of writing. All of these make the difference that invades the same in women's practice of the apology, as women go about their business of shaping the public's notions of foreign lands.

IV

Fissures offering a glimpse of gender at work sometimes open at a third intersection of literary convention and gender, the textualizing of modes of transportation, or what I call the vehicle convention. Extending vehicles rhetorically beyond their practical use to travelers, that of carrying them hither and yon, travelers male and female often transmute them into important players and rhetorical occasions. Vehicles are made to serve as signs of the peculiarity of foreign ways and the fortitude of the traveler tolerating their discomforts, whether ocean vessels, camels, donkeys, jinrickshaws, diligences, or railway coaches. Mark Twain turns vehicles into devices of comedy, making fun with the pilgrim Blucher's donkey in order to make fun of Blucher. The ass, incapable of taking orders because he knew no English, "scampered zigzag across the road . . . scraped Blucher against carts and the corners of houses . . . [and] finally came to the house he was born in and darted into the parlor, scraping Blucher off at the doorway." [71]

When a female is on the road in any sort of vehicle, gender is her traveling companion; "femaleness" sits by her side. Gender may occur in content or in form. When Elizabeth Robins Pennell, for example, builds a rhetorical display around her tricycle, she injects gender into the content of her ado. She reports the gendered amazement of an innkeeper at Empoli who registers surprise not only at the novelty of a three-wheeled velocipede, but amazement at an even greater novelty: "That a *Signora* should ride, the *padrona* added, ah! that indeed was strange!" [72] Helen Hunt Jackson, on the other hand, works gender into the form of her account. She embeds in a hansom ride an unabashed pleasure in violating gender proscriptions. At Liverpool, she and "P.," her companion, "jumped into a hansom, and drove at such a pace . . . P. had always been afraid to get into a hansom, from a vague instinct that it was not the thing to do it; but, emboldened by my vagabond indifference, she yielded to her long-suppressed desire, and off we dashed . . . I think myself that it is not just the thing for 'dames seules' to drive about in, but I'm very glad we did it" (BT, 132–33). On another occasion, recording a trip in an *einspanner*, she exploits the vehicle convention to create a sense of freedom and independence. "Fancy me dashing along for a day and a half all alone in one of them," she writes. "Really, the things one does in Europe would seem extraordinary at home" (BT, 266–67).

A sense of freedom is not, of course, the preserve of the female and her texts. Americans of all stripes found in travel an escape from Victorian conventions and restraints, and a sense of larger liberty. John Tomsich identifies the desire to escape as in fact the deepest motive of genteel travel literature. [73] Yet if this was true for the male traveler, how much more so for the female, the symbol and enforcer of gentility, the figure whose womanliness could rise or fall with genteel status. Perhaps for this reason, Helen Hunt Jackson does not allow the thrill of the carriage ride and the *einspanner* to remain simply generic; she does not construct it solely from the openness and speed of the vehicle that, like the donkey on which Mark Twain places his companion Blucher, is equally available to both sexes. Rather, she organizes the liberty of the ride into a display through an emphasis on gender: the riders are "dames seules" in the one case and Jackson is "all alone" in the other, each an oppositional practice that intensifies the pretense of freedom peculiar to women who throw off the shackles of propriety. In handling the vehicle convention, females intentionally make gender visible while males go about their normative ways.

V

The fourth generic practice that draws the difference in male and female texts is the representation of the "other." As observed in chapter 1, travel, whatever else it might be, was an American exercise in "othering" for purposes of self-definition. But how is it that "othering" manifests itself in the practice of writing? In *Discourses of Difference*, Sara Mills identifies several strategies through which indigenous people are constituted as "other" to the traveler: the description of people as "a list of features" rather than as individuals; the relegation of people to a time distant from that of the traveler; and the practice of "portraying other nations in terms of abhorrent smells and filth."[74] American travelers, male and female, engage each of these "othering" practices. Bayard Taylor, for example, describes the Nubian tribe of Mahass as a list of features, "tall, well-formed men, with straight features and high cheekbones, but the lips were thicker than those of the Arab tribes of Ethiopia. The latter are of almost pure Shemitic blood, and are descended from families which emigrated into Africa from the Hedjaz, seven or eight centuries ago."[75] The missionary Agnes McAllister, too, represents African women and children in ethnographic terms, as a series of "wrists" and "waists" and "ankles" decked out in "small bells" and anklets, and "brass rods . . . put on halfway up to the elbow" (LW, 153–54).

Traveling in Morocco at the end of World War I, Edith Wharton evokes a time far distant from her own, describing Morocco as a "rich and stagnant civilization" and the present as "a perpetually prolonged past." Through judgment-laden diction, she constructs not just the poverty but the inferiority of Moroccans in her description of the windows of their houses: "*slit[s]* stuffed with *rags* and *immemorial* filth, from which a lean cat would suddenly spring out, and scuttle off under an archway like a witch's familiar" (emphasis added).[76] Even though the people of the United States were themselves a colonial people, the rhetoric of their travel accounts "colonized" the people of other lands, much as it colonized Native Americans in accounts of domestic travels. What Nina Baym finds in history written by women in antebellum America occurs in travel accounts across the nineteenth century and into the twentieth. "The expansionist ideology of American Manifest Destiny," Baym explains, "transformed republicanism into imperialism." Americans envisioned the United States as the nation destined to oversee and provide a model for the formation of republics the world over. Protestantism, republicanism, millennialism, and racism walked hand in hand toward a divinely ordained future, the millennium. Roman Catholicism, understood by many antebellum Americans as a version of Roman paganism, was an obstacle to the divine plan.[77] Thus it occurs that so many American travelers are vitriolic in their "othering" of Italian clergy, not to mention Bedouin tribes and African indigenes.[78]

In the midst of what might be called an imperialist rhetorical "sameness," the question of difference remains. Women perceived themselves to be ahead of men, as we have seen, in the march of civilization, a march that led away from physical supremacy toward the supremacy of the virtues and traits ascribed to Woman and incarnated, or so bourgeois Victorians hoped, in women. But when men and women wrote the "other" into their frequently imperialist accounts, is there a difference in addition to that of women's presumed superiority? The answer divides by gender, both the gender of the traveler and the gender observed *by* the traveler. The construction of men and women, by men and women travelers, differs.

I will first address the "othering" of indigenous males by male and female travelers. Typically, indigenous males, if at all constituted as a threat (rather than a mere annoyance, as in the case of beggars) are cast in terms of masculine prowess and danger to the traveler's life and limb. Thus when Bayard Taylor, for example, has "Adventures among the Shillook Negroes," as he names a chapter in *Journey to Central Africa* (1854), adventures in the masculine, heightened by race and racism, are indeed the case. When he arrived "to examine" the fearsome Shillooks, Taylor recalls that "a large body of men, armed with spears, appeared in the forest, coming toward us at a quick pace." Taylor is met by their leader, "an old man excessively black in complexion." In the meantime, "other warriors had come up and taken their seats around [Taylor]." The leader greets Taylor with this: "'Tell us what you want; if you come to fight, we are ready for you.'" Taylor narrates a typical story of male adventure, reiterating the ferocity of the natives, "all armed—the most of them with iron-pointed spears, some with clubs, and some with long poles, having knobs of hard wood on the end."[79]

Not danger to life and limb, but danger to sexual integrity is the likely issue in the encounter of a woman with indigenous males. The subject of sex, a particularly problematic topic in an age of gentility, is surrounded by discursive restraints that structure women's travel writing as they earlier structured captivity narratives. In addition to the matter of race, omnipresent although a silence of the text, the construction of an incident in Agnes McAllister's 1896 book of African experiences is a classic of discursive restraint imposed on a sexually evocative event. McAllister describes a scene in which men prepare a bed for her. To her dismay, they remain in the room after the work is completed. "I lay very still for a time," she writes, "in hope they might come to the conclusion that I was asleep, and be induced to go out." She does not, however, declare fear of sexual violation. Rather, in what may be a displacement of her fears, she attributes her discomfort to the temperature of the room: it was hot, yet the men, she knew, would courteously stoke the fire while they remained in the room because "the natives do not like to sleep without a fire for light," she explains (LW, 153–54). If the room is to be cool, whether literally or figuratively, the men must be shown to the door.

Female vulnerability, codified in conduct books, fiction, and the press, was a rhetorical and actual obsession in Victorian America. Women travelers go to great lengths, as I will show in chapter 4, to confirm the existence of male chivalry and female security in virtually every part and port of the world—if women but behave properly. This caveat, this insistence that women's propriety governs men's behavior, is another mark of the feminine. Women must behave properly or suffer the consequences, and the "consequences" mark failure to behave properly. In the act of denying female vulnerability and fear of the male, especially although not exclusively the male of another race, women's texts encode both, inscribing the male as always "other" to women. Caroline Paine, for example, describes the "impression the uncurbed, sturdy sons of the desert" make on her. The tents pitched and the camels brought into a circle, "the men stretched themselves outside of the camels, as a protection from marauders. Thus surrounded, we slept securely and sweetly," Paine reports. She adds, however, that before leaving Cairo, a kind friend had assured her "that we might feel certain of being treated with the greatest respect and delicacy by even the lowest of the tribe." "It was to the noble regard shown to the sanctity of our tents by these uncivilized men," she writes, "that we owed much of our comfort and real tranquillity." "Comfort" and "tranquillity" are revealed as code for fear of sexual violation. "We were doomed to experience an unfortunate contrast to all this" in Syria, Paine says, where "ragged, dirty, debased-looking men, inspired us with a feeling quite opposed to the confidence we had in the Bedouins." [80]

When male and female travelers observe women, gender difference invades their prose in yet more complex ways. The male looks on the foreign female from a single window, that of difference. He constitutes her by reference to two differences: she is Woman, always different and never the double of the male; and she is perceived to differ from the American Woman, a difference that in some climates adds race to the "othering" equation. In both instances of difference, she is an idea already textualized, much as other sites and shrines in foreign lands are already textualized. Her inscription in a book of male travels effectively becomes another instance of intertextuality. The male traveler gazes upon foreign women and measures their congruence with the idea of Woman, presumably best incarnated in the women of the United States. If idea and sight/site of Woman do not coincide, the male is disappointed or perhaps even annoyed.

The text of Bayard Taylor, again, is representative in its inscription of black African women. He compares the text of Woman (read Anglo-Saxon, white, Protestant, and genteel) with Shillook women, recording similarities to and deviations from the norm. Reading stereotypes of women in the females of the Shillook, Taylor finds they "were so far overcome by their curiosity" that they dared approach him rather than keeping their distance. Observing them closely, he first reports that "they were nude, except a small piece of sheepskin around the loins, and in their forms were not very easy to distinguish from the men, having flat, masculine breasts and narrow hips." Taylor first fixes on the female traits eroticized in the west, and only later describes uneroticized characteristics of the women, such as their height.[81]

The texts of Nathaniel Hawthorne and Mark Twain are arresting instances of the semiotic process of the textual "othering" of the female. Making "other" the women who are racially and culturally familiar to them, white and Western women, the texts of Hawthorne and Mark Twain show the pervasiveness of gender's objectification of women and the extent of American chauvinism. In *Our Old Home*, Hawthorne writes that the "English maiden in her teens is very seldom so pretty as our own damsels." For Hawthorne, the "English lady of fifty" fares no better. She is "a creature less refined and delicate, as far as her physique goes, than anything we Western people class under the name of woman. She has an awful ponderosity of frame, not pulpy, like the looser development of our few fat women, but massive with solid beef and streaky tallow." Despite such presumed female defects and others he develops at length, Hawthorne observes in an exceptional moment of levity, "You can meet this figure in the street, and live, and even smile at the recollection."[82] Mark Twain is all levity, produced by the sight of a female and her congruence with other texts. He takes up *grisettes*, "another romantic fraud," he says, "if you let books of travel tell it. Always so beautiful . . . Stuff! . . . They were like nearly all the Frenchwomen I ever saw—homely." Later creating the persona of the beleaguered male beset by Woman, always in hot pursuit of Man, he describes a woman who barges into bathrooms, enabling the male pilgrim to play the role of vulnerable female. " 'Beware, woman! Go away from here—go away, now, or it will be the worse for you,' " he exclaims. " 'I am an unprotected male, but I will preserve my honor at the peril of my life!' "[83] Failing to see his double in women because they are always already "other"; able to understand women only as textualized Woman, a predecessor text; and androcentrically confident the "other" exists for his pleasure, the male traveler indulges in sometimes vituperative representations of women if his expectations are not met.

American women, on the other hand, look at the female "other" in foreign lands through two windows: difference and doubling. Difference and doubling produce two textual attitudes in the constitution of the fe-

male "other": ethnographic detachment and a nervous psychological at-
tachment expressed in erratic oscillations between empathy and compassion, on the one hand, and arrogance and disdain on the other. Because
the female "other" differs by reason of nation and culture, the female traveler, like the male, studies her as an ethnographic artifact. In the case of
traveling women, the "same sex" factor facilitates this ethnographic move
because women, unlike men, are granted entrée into female spaces such as
harems and kitchens. Thus positioned to study and textualize difference,
women do so in chapters with such titles as "The Women of India" and
"The Women of China" and "A Visit to a Harem." Even so, the interest
and meaning of such chapters is derived, albeit often in seemingly benign
ways, from the departure of the female "other" from the normative American Woman (again read Anglo-Saxon, white, Protestant, and middle class)
and her rights.

Some travelers wax philosophical about the female "other" while others
wax sympathetic. Anna P. Little, taking her place among the philosophical,
observes about life in Shanghai,

> Women have all their rights, so far as out-door work is concerned; and,
> curiously enough, men seem to monopolize the position of household ser-
> vant, dressmakers, and so forth, which with us are considered as belonging
> to woman's peculiar sphere. . . . The ways of the world differ, as every trav-
> eller soon finds out. What is considered right and proper by the best people
> in one place is considered very wrong and improper in another country.
> Thus in China one man can have a number of wives; and in many districts
> the girl babies are murdered at the pleasure of their parents. In Ceylon we
> were told that the women may have as many husbands as they choose, and
> that a large majority of the children born are boys.[84]

Mrs. S. R. Urbino is among the condescendingly sympathetic. She describes women in a Frankfort market, "mostly old women, sitting in the
street, selling vegetables, etc. Poor things! there they are in the hot sun or
pouring rain. Some of them walk 8 or 10 miles, with baskets of fruit or
vegetables, to the weight of 50 pounds, on their heads."[85]

Other travelers put diction and structure to the task of creating empathy
rather than condescension for the "other." Clara Moyse Tadlock, for example, reporting on "A Turkish Home," describes a "child of eleven, about

four and a half feet in height, who had been married a year." The child's husband, Hafez, "a satisfied proprietor," praises her "fine housekeeping qualities." Tadlock inquires, "'You think so much of learning, have you also taught your wife to read, Hafez?' . . . but the look of entire disapprobation darkening his face answered me before his words. 'No! No! it is not good for her,' shaking his head." Tadlock then draws a comparison: "'But it is a pleasure—we read, you know.'"[86] This exchange is followed shortly with the story of a nine-year-old second wife who, unhappy in her arranged marriage, committed suicide by throwing herself into a well. Tadlock's treatment of the female "other" encodes a sympathetic doubling, an identification of woman with girl-woman, wife with wife, even as it betrays the trace of the superiority of the American Woman, the norm that Hafez refuses to honor.

At times, however, doubling together with difference inaugurates a schizophrenic identification with the "other" that, in its instability, amounts to an identity crisis. The traveler seems to lose her place in a gendered geography. The text fluctuates between the female "other" as the traveler's double and the "other" as difference incarnate. This happens in the text of Susan E. Wallace visiting the remains of the palaces on Seraglio Point, Constantinople, where the harem of Abd al-Hamid II housed several hundred women, all subject to the control of the sultan's mother and guarded by eunuchs. Wallace first constitutes these women of the harem by reference to Orientalism and difference. Steeped in Orientalism, Wallace asks, "But did the musky odalisques wish to leave this walled Eden? Who knows may tell. Oriental women are the only ones I have known who appear contented. There is a serenity in their faces, a repose in their manner pleasant to the pilgrim from the far country we love to call our own, the land of feverish unrest." Wallace's persona, grounded in the American, class-inflected construct of female privilege, colonizes these women, bringing them into being only as they exist in the gaze of "the pilgrim," to whom they offer a "pleasant" interlude.

At the same time, and even as she herself enjoys movement out and about the world, Wallace constructs activity as unrest, setting the active lives of American women at odds with contentment. In effect, she uses the women of the harem to constitute, by contrast, a representation of herself as pitifully harried. The sequence in which this occurs opens with a description of the queen of the harem as "nested" among pillows of silk and lace, "dimpled as a baby of four months. If you can fancy a child thirty years old you have her face." At first blush, Wallace's metaphor seems to offer a critique: the oxymoronic "child" and "thirty" promises to testify against the confinement imposed on women of the harem. Yet a kind of schizophrenia invades the text when Wallace then slips into the rhetoric of Orientalism and "othering," describing the queen as a series of features and her life as a romantic mystery. "In her teens," Wallace writes of the queen, "she must have been beautiful exceedingly—and her eyes—O, those Paradise eyes! Black as death, bright as stars of midnight. Her skin exquisitely fair, a throat of statuary marble, hands that would delight a sculptor to model." Does the meaning here point to admiration or to horror? Horror seems to be the answer when Wallace continues, "But the artist will never behold her. In the gilded cage the bulbul sees no man but her husband and the black slaves." The traveler is not beguiled by the gilding of the cage, by a babylike sweetness in grown women, by a marbleized beauty. Or is she? The schizophrenic movement begun three sentences earlier is reactivated and brought to a climax: "When told of the great things the women of England and America do in church and State," Wallace continues, "the Princess Badoura lifted her pretty eyebrows in a surprised way and said, 'Why you are slaves!' And there was one of the party who thought the Princess was not greatly mistaken."[87] In a peculiar move, Wallace constitutes the Princess Badoura as the double of an avatar of Susan Wallace, an avatar who is the *un*emancipated Woman of the Cult of True Womanhood. Wallace casts herself as a coy, posturing persona, the "one of the party" who agrees that British and American women are the slaves. Wallace stages a romantic yearning for days of yore, when women were women and cages, though confining, were nevertheless "gilded."

The textualizing of the "other" female is not always benign. Doubling seems at times to exacerbate difference, to create an edge. Take, for example, the inscription of peasant women in the text of Mrs. E. A. Forbes. "The cattle are remarkably fine. . . . After the custom of these countries to turn every thing feminine to useful account, the cows are employed in labor quite as much as oxen. A very good type of the civilization appears in a team whose motive power is, conjointly, a woman and a cow," Forbes observes. She then continues, "The women of the peasantry through the continent strike one painfully; there is nothing womanly about them; they look harder and uglier than the men, and it is difficult to see how they could ever have been attractive" (WFI, 224). Forbes first sympathizes with the condition of these women (they strike her "painfully"), recognizing in them her double ("women") even as their class ("peasantry") and locale ("the continent") render them different. But she then slips into a misogynistic, class-driven, culturally constructed disgust with the appearance of these female beasts of burden, now constructed as an uncanny "other," a third gender. They are "harder and uglier than the men," but not quite women, either, because they lack femininity. They have never been attractive. They are neither "womanly" now nor were they at birth.

How is it that doubling produces more disgust than empathy or sympathy? At least four factors work to create this attitude: imperialism, nationalism, racism, and classism. As we have seen, American travel writing by both men and women is a repository of imperialist attitudes and discourses.[88] The once-colonized American now insists on the superiority of the United States even while, ironically, worshipping at historic shrines abroad in a massive effort at appropriation. In the instance of the female traveler, a sense of national superiority is further inflated by a sense of gender superiority. She is doubly superior, first as an American and then as an American woman who believes, with Alexis de Tocqueville, that she occupies a position and is an object of esteem superior to that of any other women in the world.

Thus it occurs that a Lucy Bronson Dudley can insensitively write to privileged readers, "The women here [in France] have the same opportunity of playing croquet, tennis, and golf with the hoe, rake, spade, dogs, and cows, as they do in other countries through which we have passed. I have discovered in the old world three new beasts of burden,—women, cows, and dogs; also two new desserts, green hazelnuts and almonds" (LR, 96). The "hazelnuts and almonds," perhaps gracing a table when the traveler returns to her hotel from a long day of observing the natives, heighten class difference and trivialize and dismiss the conditions in which peasant women live. Meanwhile the phrase "the old world" carries national difference, potentially magnified by the perceived superiority of the American woman. In some cases, the presumed superiority of American women's position is simply asserted. Describing women "dragging heavy carts through the streets, working with the men in the hay-fields" and seeming "more like beasts of burden than any thing else" with their "wrinkled, coarse, and bronzed" faces, Mary Wieting exclaims, "We think our own poor have a hard time of it, but the wife of the poorest laborer in our own country lives like a queen, compared to the condition of these poor creatures here."[89] The provincial, class-bound Wieting writes this, ironically, at a time (1888) when American women had already plodded westward in wagon trains in blazing sun, and when women of the laboring classes were working long days in close and dangerous factories.

Social class is the unspoken, the unspeakable, but the most powerful component in the "othering" of women in other lands. Class either eases identification with the "other" or obstructs it. The road to doubling is made straight by class similarities: Susan Wallace, for example, engages in her peculiar doubling in the instance of a woman who holds the position of a Muslim princess; and Emma Willard, encountering women of the patrician class in the entourage of the Marquis de Lafayette in 1833, recommends "valuable improvements [for American women] from the instruction of French women in regard to dress, which, after all, is no unimportant affair to a woman."[90] The road to doubling is obstructed, however, by class difference. In the face of the lower classes, travel writers often mask class in gender pieties, displacing the fundamental source of difference from class to gender. Feelings of scorn or pity, disgust or compassion evoked by scenes of wrenching labor are rhetorically anchored in gender matters, in the maltreatment of the female sex. When Mrs. E. A. Forbes mixes cattle and women, and when Lucy Bronson Dudley combines "women, cows, and dogs," they lay their shock and dismay on the doorstep of womanhood: how can Woman be treated this way? As if poverty and excruciating labor are unthinkable only for the fair sex, let men live and labor as best they can, women travel writers refer their disapproval to gender norms and their violation. Moreover, they absorb all American women into a single class, a privileged class, their own class, a middle-class, white enclave. The rage in their texts at the sight of women at work like cattle and dogs is rhetorically driven, not by the violation of human rights but of gender rights.

What is behind this displacement of class on gender? Between 1830 and 1860 in America, class dynamics become subsumed in gender ideologies,[91] a condition that continues into the twentieth century in texts of travel. Gender is made visible while class is made invisible. As we have seen, class and everything else about women are subsumed in gender in the texts of Hawthorne and Twain as they extravagantly essentialize women and textualize Woman. Class is again subsumed in gender in male texts that register shock at "disrespect for the sex," as the historian Paul Baker observes, when women are seen doing the work of men.[92] The category of "sex" absorbs social class. Kathryn Kish Sklar attributes this to the complexities of an urban society in which the mingling of men and women in the industrial workplace "blurred the lines that separated men from women. Victorianism was an effort," Sklar finds, "to retain the old ideological goal of domesticity by continuing the belief that society's fundamental social divisions were the 'natural' ones of sex, rather than the pernicious ones of class."[93] The romance of America does not admit class stratification.

Moreover, women were already identified as a class—Woman—classified only by gender. When a woman violates the norms of her gender class—when she is large or ugly or leathery, when she is not "classy"—the male can speak of her only as what she is not: she is not Woman because her conduct and appearance do not meet the norms that constitute Woman. Like male travelers, women travelers create a version of class-as-gender. Forbes, Wieting, and the others foreground gender ("woman" is the subject of their sentences) and, if they mention class at all, they subordinate it ("peasant" is an adjective modifying the main noun, Woman). Thus the problematics of class difference are consumed in difference in gender status, as they were in the newspapers and conduct literature discussed in chapter 1. Women of the genteel classes are assumed to be virtuous women, whereas women of the lower classes are assumed to be sexual, dangerous, and barely women at all. Women travelers carry this set of assumptions abroad and, continuing to conflate class and gender, draw the difference between "other" women and the "queens" of America, the women who are, as Abby Morrell said in 1833, "the happiest of their sex."[94]

But how and why is it that in women's travel writing, the invisibility of class, masked by gender, acts like the worm in the apple, finally consuming any empathy that doubling might produce? How does the mask of gender account for the callous smugness of a text such as Lucy Bronson Dudley's, mingling the labors of peasant women with "hazelnuts and almonds"? Although a disagreeable and smug disposition may account for some of it, we must still inquire into the role of material conditions in shaping the mentality that informs Dudley's prose. The matter of class mobility in the United States may be complicit in this mentality. David Leverenz explains that class mobility in the nineteenth century created a paradoxical class consciousness. The ability of Americans to move up and down the class ladder puts them on guard, lest they fall rather than rise, Horatio Alger-like, in the world.[95] If we situate men's and women's inscriptions of the women of other lands in the conditions of class consciousness formulated by Leverenz, an important difference becomes visible, a difference that may obliterate the potential empathy of doubling and replace it with a sharp, insensitive edge. In the instance of the male traveler, no female, foreign or otherwise, is his double. Whatever sympathy or compassion he may muster results not from doubling but from difference, from chivalric codes of masculinity. Rather than speaking to a shared human condition, the sight of a woman speaks instead to the male traveler's difference from her, his masculinity. Nor does she speak to his social-class condition: the American male maintains or elevates his social class by competition and productivity in the outside world of men. The American male envisions himself as the master of his own destiny. Posing no threat to the class standing of the male, a woman may be the sign but not the source of his success. In short, a woman has nothing to do with a man except as his chosen appendage.

The circumstance of the economically comfortable American woman, however, is different. She maintains or elevates her social class through the manipulation of her gender role, the staging of her femininity encoded in her class standing. Women of the laboring classes, her gender double, embody her worst social fears: a plunge downward on the class ladder. As in the case of Edith Wharton's Lily Bart in *The House of Mirth* (1905), the sufferance of a prosperous male is all that stands between her and poverty. Again as in the fictional case of Lily Bart, that *sufferance* is earned by the performance of her womanly role. Her success is dependent on the perceptions of the male. Absent the perception of her as desirable, she could find herself the double of the foreign female "other" in class as well as in gender. The American woman is able to see herself all too well in women of the lower orders. She is able to see in "them" her worst nightmare. She counters her fear by underscoring "their" difference simultaneously magnifying and securing her superior place.

There may, however, be a rhetorical as well as a psychological dimension to the unempathetic inscription of women from the lower classes in women's prose. The female "other" of the lower classes offers a useful polarity to the woman traveler. In the same way that Susan Wallace, as we have seen, uses the women of the harem to project herself as harried, so the woman traveler can use the female "other" to stage and textualize her own femininity, the quality that makes her attractive to the ambitious male. It is "womanly," after all, to be distressed at ugliness, poverty, and their ancillaries. If a smug insensitivity sometimes marks the prose in which the American female constitutes her "other" sisters, a rhetorical strategy enabled by class (rather than a stereotypical, allegedly natural antipathy between women) may be at work. The inscribing of disgust with the condition of foreign women may be a tool to italicize the womanliness of the female traveler.

VI

In one way or another, women travel writers are always engaged with gender. They work quiet mutations on convention, making gender visible in fissures in their texts. They make displays of gender, sometimes putting it in "whooping italics," as Mark Twain might say, in the titles of their travel accounts and in protests of subject matter. Zealously pursuing literary business and shaping gender into a marketing device, women who travel and write make strategic use of the gender predispositions and constraints and curiosities of Victorian Americans about women's travel.

The one thing women's texts never do with what we call gender is forget it.[96] What Nina Baym says of American women historians is true of women who worked in the annex of history that is travel writing: they "were thinking about women all the time," and "the subject of their work was always women, no matter what they wrote about."[97] Female travel writers are always at work on the subject of women, flirting with the "unwomanly" or pretending to, apologizing in titles and prefaces for doing so, calling on more or less lionized predecessor writers to authorize and advertise the authority of the female travel writer. Travel writing is a performance, and the experience of travel as we have it is not "raw" but transformed: textualized and mediated by numerous cultural discourses. Whatever the actual securities and insecurities to which actual women were subject as they wrote travels in a gender-charged literary and cultural environment, one thing is certain: the discourses of femininity circulating in Victorian America, generating materials and rendering them dramatic, are a major presence in women's texts of travel. It is certain, as well, that these discourses are infused into women's accounts at a time when it was advantageous to do so, when interest in women's difference from men was high and the sacralized sites of other lands, especially Europe, were progressively more familiar.

Nineteenth-century American women took hold of the potential of travel and the generic tradition of the travel book to produce "works" in Patricia Yaeger's meaning of the word, as places in which the commonplaces of the culture are confronted, appropriated, destroyed, and reconstructed. Like the fiction analyzed by Yaeger, women's texts of travel are works that "do the work of reinventing culture."[98] The culture written and reinvented in women's texts of travel abroad is the culture of the United States and what was understood as its core, the home and the women charged with its well-being. Writing abroad, women were rewriting home and their place in it. Their texts of travel, representing a portion of a traveler's life, are autobiographical writings. They are cultural works that undertake to tell the story of one woman, inevitably implicated in the story of Woman already written by the culture. The next chapter examines women's use of the travel genre as an autobiographical occasion.

Chapter Three

Autobiographical Occasions

The Fashioning of Selves in the Texts of Abby Morrell, Sophia Hawthorne, and Martha Coston

> In a humanistic tradition in which *man* is the measure
> of all things, how does an appendage go about telling the
> story of her life?
>
> —Barbara Johnson, *A World of Difference*

In 1889, Mary Elizabeth Wieting published a presumptive biography of her husband entitled *Prominent Incidents in the Life of Dr. John M. Wieting, Including His Travels with his Wife around the World.* At first glance, her work seems entirely conventional. Choosing as her subject the life of her respected husband and adopting the third person pronoun, she declares to have "written this history as a tribute of affection to him who has preceded her into the Great Unknown," adding that "she has written a somewhat extended history of their tour around the world in 1875 and 1876, which was a source of much pleasure and profit to them both, and to which Dr. Wieting always referred as one of the pleasantest episodes of his life, from which he returned with a vast fund of practical knowledge" (PI, 3–4). In her prefatory remarks, she casts herself as a self-effacing wife and shows her awareness of genre and her command of the convention of the apology, with its rhetoric of diminishment. "This volume presents itself to its little world—not in the character of a biography alone, nor yet a complete history of travel," Wieting writes, "but partaking of the nature of the two, without aspiring to the dignity of either" (PI, preface).

This apparently conventional beginning is rendered curious, however, by what follows in Wieting's text proper. After devoting the first 15 of more than 200 pages to her beloved spouse, Wieting peremptorily declares, "The writer of this book, having been the Doctor's enthusiastic and much interested companion on this expedition, takes the liberty of telling the story of their travels for herself, asking the reader's pardon for the introduction of the big letter 'I,' thus rendering the relation purely narrative and descriptive" (PI, 15). The biography of John Wieting is transformed into the autobiography of Mary Wieting, traveler. Except for a single mention in passing, the good doctor does not reappear in the text until the day of his funeral. Even on this solemn occasion, his bereaved widow eulogizes him in generous quotations from the press rather than from her own hand. She then reflects philosophically on immortality rather than personally on her loss. From this alleged biography of a man and his travels, the reader learns little about the man. The reader does learn, however, a great deal about Mary Wieting and her reactions to travel. *Prominent Incidents in the Life of Dr. John M. Wieting, Including His Travels with his Wife around the World* might more accurately be named *Prominent Incidents in the Life of Mary Wieting, Including Her Travels with her Husband around the World.*

Wieting's use of biography and travel as an autobiographical occasion announces the complexity of the nineteenth-century female traveler's relationship to travel writing as an annex to autobiography. Wieting seizes the occasion of travel to write a portion of her life, but she inoculates her text with the persona of the culturally approved, devoted wife. She attempts to appear to conform to what Bénédicte Monicat, writing about nineteenth-century francophone women travelers, calls "the rule of decency," the norm that makes it difficult for women "to write publicly about themselves," to be "properly" the subjects of their own discourse.[1] Trying to have it both ways, Mary Wieting and other women travel writers make use of the culture's template of Woman even as they contest and exceed its boundaries.

The presence of the culture's template of Woman means that the culture's biography of Woman is invariably a presence in women's texts of travel. Margo Culley's observation about women's autobiography aptly describes women's writing of travel-as-autobiography as well: "The autobiographical act itself contests WOMAN."[2] Woman is made visible, she comes to public notice, in her relationship to the "rule of decency," a rule tailored to the conduct of life in the domestic sphere. Travel and writing about it, bringing [masculine] knowledge of the world with them, are conducted in the public sphere. Making the "rule of decency" difficult to keep and, for some, tempting to break, travel and writing about it cast Woman in the limelight, where variations on and deviations from the rule become visible as well. Paradoxically, the woman travel writer enlists the biography of Woman, the culture's "always already" Woman, to set the stage from which the traveler projects other voices and other selves, or what Sidonie Smith calls the "polyphonic possibilities of selfhood" that autobiography releases.[3] A woman's account of travel is thus transformed into three narratives: one of travel, one of Woman, and one of the traveler's other selves.

Occurring in a hybrid genre that challenges taxonomies, women's writing of travel-as-autobiography, protean and complex, resists categorization. To order the unruly autobiographical dimension of women's accounts, I have arranged them in a tripartite division that the texts themselves invite: writing as self-construction, writing as self-destruction, and writing as self-revelation. In writing travels as self-construction, the traveler fashions new voices and versions of the self. The travel account of Abby Morrell typifies this form. In the process of travel and writing, Abby Morrell discovers the constraints that gender, or the "rule of decency," impose on women, and she shapes an alternate self who differs from the rule. In the second form of writing travel-as-autobiography, self-destruction is the goal. What might be called a Western variation on *purdah*, self-destruction takes place behind the scenes while the culture's ideal of Woman is performed center stage. Seeking to suppress rather than to fashion or express other voices, the writer attempts to conceal and ignore them. The travel account of Sophia Hawthorne belongs in this group. Attempting to immolate a subjectivity that nevertheless haunts her account of travel, Sophia Hawthorne not only prefers the persona of Woman but designs her text to foreground Woman and hold that ideal up for public admiration. The third form of writing travel-as-autobiography, self-revelation, is the converse of Sophia Hawthorne's autobiographical efforts. Adopting the mask of Woman to cover and make palatable disruptive acts beyond the "rule of decency," travel writing as self-revelation seeks to amplify, for public recognition, voices and versions of the self silenced in the culture's biography of Woman. The narrative of Martha Coston takes this form. It aims to make public a woman who, dressed as a lady, succeeds in the male world of international business.

The differences in these excursions into autobiography are largely attributable to the different historical situations from which they emerge. Born in 1809, Abby Morrell was a postrevolutionary woman living in that period of U.S. women's history in which republican motherhood was the ideal, women's political consciousness was being reshaped, and female seminaries produced a new generation of literate women, aware of their capabilities and aware of women as a group. She is of the generation in which, building and expanding on the variety of institutions launched during the American Revolution, women began to test the waters and explore their various possibilities and perspectives. They began to earn income by participating in what economic historians call a fledgling "putting-out" system producing goods in their homes for sale to a central dealer. They began to work in textile factories; to teach school; and to conceive of marriage as companionate rather than patriarchal.[4] Abby Morrell married a seafaring man and traveled in the late 1820s, an era in which women were relatively bold and experimental. Although born in the same year as Abby Morrell, Sophia Hawthorne was launched into travel when the Cult of True Womanhood was at the height of its ideological influence, validating more narrow definitions of domesticity and femininity when such definitions served new economic conditions. Sophia came from the genteel Peabody family, married a genteel man, traveled abroad in the domestic 1850s, and reluctantly published her travels in 1870. Her travel account bears, as we shall see, all of the earmarks of the cult to which she pledged allegiance. Martha Coston, born in 1828, worked beside her husband and traveled after the Civil War, when the United States was increasingly alive with women's issues and women's initiatives. Although Coston does not care to admit it in her tale of travel, her exploits were enabled by the historical conditions that shaped her ambition and emboldened her imagination.

I

In 1833, Abby Jane Morrell published her *Narrative of a Voyage to the Ethiopic and South Atlantic Ocean, Indian Ocean, Chinese Sea, North and South Pacific Ocean, in the Years 1829, 1830, 1831*. Her narrative provides an exceptional starting point from which to scrutinize the practice of women writing travel-as-autobiography because her account is stamped with two hallmarks of women's travel writing, the constructs of Woman and of American. Both travel and writing become schools for Abby Morrell in which old frames of reference are dislodged, to be replaced by new ones. New understandings of gender, of nationality, and of herself develop in the text, eventually installing a female version of "the [male] American," manifesting the characteristics of adaptability, self-reliance, perseverance, resourcefulness, and resilience.[5]

Abby Morrell's account of travel bears witness, as well, to travel writing as a process of self-exploration: not the exploration of some essential, unitary "self" waiting to be uncovered but, rather, of inchoate potential and possibility that new experiences bring into being. Writing about British women travelers, Mary Russell observes that "it is only in recent years that people have been able to recognize the existence within themselves of many differing and conflicting aspects of their personalities, some of which are characteristics more commonly found in the opposite sex." Reminding us of Western culture's rigid assignment of human characteristics to one or the other sex, and pointing to such women as Eleanora Duse who claimed to have a thousand women within her, Russell continues: "It is not altogether surprising therefore that when women, by virtue of their travelling, find the freedom to express another side of their character, one which hitherto has perhaps been unexplored, they sometimes feel confused about where exactly they fit in."[6] Russell's statement can fairly be supplemented by another observation about the woman traveler: when she undertakes to write a book of travels, she engages in the process of constructing what travel liberated in her, ordering confusion into versions of self in the act of writing.

Abby Morrell was one of many women in the nineteenth century who sailed the seas with their husbands in clipper ships, whalers, and steam packets.[7] Her travels were not without precedent, but they were nevertheless exceptional. She was twenty years old when she set out to sea and less than twenty-four when she wrote her narrative. She traveled with her husband, Benjamin Morrell, on his sealing vessel, the *Antarctic*, a small topsail schooner of 175 tons used for the trade and seal-hunting ventures at which he amply succeeded.[8] Abby Morrell traveled for two years short of five days, setting sail on 2 September 1829 and returning by way of Europe to New York on 27 August 1831. She saw places infrequently visited by Western women: New Zealand, Manilla, Cape Horn, and St. Helena, crossing the Equator to the Azores. According to her own account, she was the first American woman to visit some of the places she describes.

The voyage itself was grueling. Abby Morrell reports that seasickness reduced her to a baby; and fever drew her up "like a cripple," bringing her close to death even as it killed several members of the crew (NV, 18). Her husband's narrative of the same voyage presents her condition much more dramatically. Benjamin reports that "the fever had left her a perfect cripple, being quite drawn out of shape; as her limbs could not be straightened, and her ankles were drawn nearly up to her body."[9] He recounts, as well, Abby's fear of death and burial at sea, her body becoming food for sharks. Sickness aside, other perils human and natural beset the voyagers, savagely attacked by Philippine natives, and becalmed at sea shortly after crossing the Equator. In addition to withstanding the same trials as the men, Abby Morrell suffered sexual harassment at the hands of the American consul at Manilla, "a man of respectable acquirements, and of courteous manners," she points out. He contrived to keep her in Manilla in the hope of seducing her while her husband went off to the Feejees.

Her account of her reaction to the consul's harassment conforms to a now-familiar pattern: she thinks first to protect her husband, then doubts herself, and finally incommodes herself to avoid trouble. Although the consul's motives are "as plain as day" to her, she writes, "I dared not express myself freely to my husband, for fear of the consequences from his quick sense of injury, and his high spirit as a brave man."[10] She then doubts her own judgment: "My youth and ignorance of the world made me fear that I had put a wrong construction upon the consul's demeanour." Finally, she is compelled to conform her activities to his wishes. She is "determined to steal a march on him, and go on the voyage to the Feejees, at all hazards," but the harasser intervenes and forces her to remain in Manilla. He "scattered slanders" about the Morrells, writes Abby, "in order that I might feel myself so shunned and ruined as to fly to him for protection; but I had made up my mind to die there before I would even speak to him." His slanders succeed, nevertheless, in restricting Abby Morrell's liberty: although she does not "fly to him for protection," she must fly to assured respectability, to the quarters of friends in Manilla, relinquishing her wish to live in her own quarters (NV, 51–53). Her husband's comment as they depart Manilla registers both the stress she apparently suffered and the relief that followed once out of danger. "Her spirits, so long depressed, were now buoyant as the air," he writes, "and she flitted about the vessel like some ethereal form from a higher sphere."[11]

Why would a young woman undertake such a taxing voyage, leaving home and a child behind? Abby Morrell offers her reader (and herself) conventional reasons for her voyage. At the age of fifteen, she had married her widowed cousin Benjamin, seven years her senior. She then immediately found herself alone for a period of two years while Benjamin plied his seafaring trade. She was next alone during his European voyages; again alone in 1828 when he sailed for the South Seas; and alone a fourth time when she gave birth to her first child. In short, she was simultaneously single and married during the first five years of her married life. Finding unbearable what she calls "the distress of separation," she writes, "I then came to the determination that if he ever went to sea again I would accompany him." Benjamin at first "would not hear a word of it," Abby says, "but when I insisted, as far as affectionate obedience could insist, he detailed to me all the evils of a sea-faring life. I remained fixed, and he at last reluctantly yielded; and when he had agreed to it, he put the best side outwards" (NV, 17–18).

Benjamin Morrell, however, became not only reconciled to but appreciative of his wife's presence on board ship. In his account of the voyage, he characterizes Abby as an energetic, spirited woman, a woman who may have chosen to travel simply for the adventure of it. Benjamin registers amusement "with the curiosity, vivacity, and activity of my wife, who was almost constantly on deck, with her drawing apparatus, sketching different views of the islands as we passed them; and the hundreds of native-built boats, bound to and from Manilla, some of which were striking specimens of clumsy naval architecture, and still worse rigging." [12] Abby Morrell's own account shows that she made the most of travel, stretching her powers of observation and imagination. Like the fictive Ishmael of *Moby Dick*, Abby Morrell records her own observations of the sea and its elements together with the reports of others. In the process of writing, she assumes a scientific voice. Fascinated by ambergris, she "examined this wonderful substance very attentively," noting its color and its perfume, providing alternative accounts of its nature and origin (NV, 83). In New Zealand, studying ostriches and gathering statistics on their height and feathers, she corrects the record: "Modern writers have stated that the ostrich incubates her eggs, and has as great a regard for them as any other bird; now this assertion appears to me unfounded. The ostrich cannot set upon her eggs; there is no joint in her legs that will allow her to bring her body upon her nest" (NV, 137). Exposed to shells, she develops and indulges in her narrative a passion for conchology.

The voice of the scientist, amplified as the voyage proceeds, is preceded by another voice that speaks at the start of the narrative but infrequently thereafter, the voice of a mother who voluntarily leaves her child for two years for the sake of a stimulating and rewarding but nevertheless trying and perilous voyage. Morrell declares a wish to be with her spouse as her reason for travel, despite its domestic cost. In this she joins other women of her time. Examining the diaries and letters of early-nineteenth-century wives of seamen, peddlers, and other traveling workers, the historian Carl N. Degler has found expressions of a greater love for an absent husband than for the children at home. According to Degler, such women, emotionally dependent on their absent husbands, threatened to join them in their travels.[13] Degler's findings lend historical support to Mary Russell's assertion, in her study of women's travel accounts of the nineteenth century, that "the idea of maternal bonding was not then invested with the same importance as it is today." [14] In the late nineteenth century, the British Lady Anne Blunt and the American Fanny Bullock Workman fit this pattern, leaving children behind as they pursue their interests.

Early in the nineteenth century, Abby Morrell did the same, offering an example of the range of attitudes toward motherhood expressed before the ascendancy of the Cult of True Womanhood, when what Nancy F. Cott calls "the emphatic sentence of domesticity" was imposed on women.[15] The locking of mothers and motherhood into domesticity was not only a construction raised on biology and economic convenience, but a reaction to and critique of women like Abby Morrell who conducted their lives according to the more hardy eighteenth- and early nineteenth-century ideas of womanhood that preceded the reign of domestic ideology. Abby Morrell's decision to leave her son in the care of her mother for two years, while she joined her husband at sea, bears witness to the latitude of women's activities in the 1820s and underscores the genesis of the gap that opened between the ideology of domesticity and the actual lives of women.

The way in which Abby Morrell presents the matter of her children in her account of travel is particularly significant. As early as the sixth page, she declares that "nothing will satisfy a mother in regard to her offspring, but her own care," and, she points out, "I had left my boy behind me, and distance seemed to make me more anxious for his welfare" (NV, 18). This raises the expectation that motherly anxieties, sorrows, yearnings, and reflections as she sails about the world will warrant space in the narrative stretching before the reader. That expectation is dashed. Abby Morrell's child commands very little space in her account. Morrell is so absorbed in travel and writing that in 230 pages of text, she mentions her son only three times more, and then only in passing. The first fleeting mention occurs as she proudly reflects on being an American. Writing out of her sense of republican motherhood, her important role in the shaping of American citizens, she looks forward to the day "when my own dear boy might be an active man among them [Americans], and the prospective view of that period, generally long to those who have children, did not seem to me at this moment half so long as I had been absent from my country and my child" (NV, 186). The second reference to her child occurs as her journey draws to a close. Although she "had left [her] child a short time to him, a long one indeed to [her]," she nonetheless "thought [she] had learned enough to balance the pain of this absence," she writes, "in the attainment of that discretion which a mother should have in bringing up a child" (NV, 222–23). The separation, that is, was worth it.

The third instance in which Abby Morrell mentions her child is especially telling. The occasion is the docking of the schooner in New York and reunion with family, a reunion that might warrant joyful comment on her child, his growth and manner and appearance, after a two-year separation from him. In Abby Morrell's order of textual priorities, however, pride of place is given to her stepfather and an aunt who had died during her absence. Then, eschewing what could have been an affecting scene, she says only this of her child: he was "alive and well" (NV, 229). In an afterthought, she adds that nine days later she gave birth to another son—a pregnancy decorously undeclared in the course of her narrative. She no more dandles this second child nor dawdles over his birth than she did over her first child. Instead, she again turns immediately to herself as writer. But as if the shore and its social institutions immediately draw her into their orbit, she justifies the act of writing by coyly subordinating it— and her self as writer—to her motherly role. Objectifying and subordinating herself to her son, she writes: "His mother's Journal may, in some future day, be read by him, and he may be stimulated to put some of my plans in a train of experiment." Concluding her account, she notes that business took her husband shortly thereafter "to the south, and wishing me to accompany him I did so" (NV, 229), leaving now not one but two children behind.

What are we to make of the scarcity of Abby Morrell's textual attention to her children? In the context of travel writing, it may be surprising that she mentioned her children at all. Women did not necessarily write about their children in accounts of travel, witness the diaries of women on the Oregon Trail in which children are rarely mentioned, and then only in sickness, danger, and death. In her numerous books of foreign travel, Fanny Bullock Workman never mentions the daughter she left behind in a boarding school. Fanny's friends were in fact very surprised to learn that she had a child.[16] From the perspective of generic practice, Abby Morrell tattles on herself, as it were, flagging something that need not be mentioned in an account of travel, particularly travel that took place without children in tow. Therefore any mention of her children is a revealing autobiographical moment.

The construction of Abby Morrell's account invites several readings of these moments. Abby Morrell does not choose to tell whether she pushed aside motherly thoughts and longings during her voyage of two years or whether she had few such thoughts and longings. But occasional reference to her child is part of a rhetorical design occasioned by and bearing witness to the murmurings of the cult of domesticity abroad in the culture's discourse. By 1833, a woman whose activities exceeded the boundaries of the domestic must contend with the culture's attitude on the subject. And women, as the publisher's "Advertisement" declares, are Morrell's anticipated readers: the volume will be "read with pleasure, especially by readers of her own sex and country." Taking the measure of her target audience, Morrell makes two rhetorical decisions. First, as if judging that a mother's longing is common whereas a woman's seal-hunting adventure is not, she devotes her account to uncommon subjects: the places and peoples of the Ethiopic and Indian Oceans. But second, she interjects her child to assuage her audience. Her rhetorical plan is exposed in the defensive gesture of justifying her decision to leave her child. Benjamin Morrell makes no mention whatsoever of his children in his account of travel, but in hers, Abby Morrell insists on "the attainment of that discretion which a mother should have in bringing up a child." Inescapably becoming a player in the culture's developing conversation about women's place, she rationalizes her travel. Leaving a trace of a discourse that contests a mother's discretion, Abby Morrell makes a plea for mothers: "It is by the kindness of Heaven that mothers do as well as they are found to do; for most of them in the early part of their days can have only the philosophy of the heart to direct them, not that of the head." She then recuperates her travel, framing it in conventional understandings of women as helpmeets: "My adventurous course was not a source of pride to me,—it was not for any specific purpose that I became a voyager, but simply to be a companion of my husband" (NV, 223). This womanly statement may be construed as testimony to the power of gender expectations in the life of even so adventuresome a woman as Abby Morrell. It may be read as well, however, as a clever exercise of rhetorical skill in navigating the waters of gender norms, defining ever more narrowly the meaning of domesticity and the range of women's "appropriate" activity.

There is a third way, however, in which to construe Abby Morrell's references to her child. She may have mentioned him in order to address an audience of one: herself. Perhaps surprised at the degree to which the novelty and thrill of travel overshadowed homely and motherly concerns, she may have been trying out voices to account for this phenomenon. Travel having occasioned an act of autobiographical writing, the autobiographical act may have become an occasion to create a spokeswoman for her conduct as a traveler who is mother, wife, scientist, humanitarian, and writer. The evolution of Abby Morrell's reasons for writing traces transformations in her thinking. In her preface, Morrell declares her initial plan, to write simply to tell of her adventures. "When I took up my pen to prepare my journal for publication," she writes, "I intended to make nothing more than a plain narrative of the events of my voyage, interspersed with such general remarks as might suggest themselves to my mind" (NV, 168). Eventually her "plain narrative" took unanticipated shapes. It registered a sea change brought about first by travel and then by the process of writing. The first shape is that of a document to ameliorate, as we recall, "the condition of American seamen," a noble reason for publishing her adventures. This document becomes, in turn, a discourse on gender and nationality as Morrell's ideas become entangled in notions of Woman and patriotism, creating a record of the conflict between the limitations imposed by the laws of gender and the freedom promised by American identity. The problem of female citizenship comes to shape the text,[17] and Abby Morrell's travels in foreign locales become excursions into the place of women in the homeland.

The schools of travel and writing teach Abby Morrell the limitations of female citizenship and republican motherhood, not to mention the constraints of the cult of domesticity that Morrell's *Narrative* implicitly contests. Travel and its transformation into prose expose the inadequacies of the gender system and the "rule of decency" that would govern women's words. At the start of writing her adventures, Abby Morrell understands that while she is authorized, as an American woman, to exercise influence on public matters, there are nevertheless some subjects that belong to men, including military matters. "Decency" would silence her on such subjects, outside of a woman's province but about which she wishes to speak. Therefore she walks cautiously in territory staked out as male. "It may be thought strange," she writes, "that a woman should take up a subject so foreign to those which generally occupy the attention of her sex. It was, however, deeply on my mind that, *being a woman, I was in some measure better qualified to offer a few suggestions* on this subject [the condition of seamen] than any one engaged in the navy or the merchant service. . . . [The public] might at least expect sincerity from me." Abby Morrell takes advantage of the moral authority ascribed to her sex. Wishing to speak about defense, she feels obliged to "[beg] the reader to understand that *I know, or think I do, which is perhaps of quite as much importance,* a good deal about the subject of defence, from hearing an almost perpetual conversation about the capability of defence of one place or another in parts of the world where there were no guns or castles, as well as in those which were strongly fortified" (NV, 168, all emphases added). Assuming authority even as she apologizes for it, Morrell proceeds to lecture the world, when it suits her, on "masculine" matters of government, law, and commerce. She calls for government support for private exploratory ventures (NV, 164); for legislation to impose quarantines (NV, 172); and for settlements in the South Pacific to benefit commerce (NV, 224).

In the process of writing, Abby Morrell comes to see that insofar as gender and "decency" have foreclosed women's experience, they have crippled women's reach. Perilous travel and the pangs of separation from loved ones, she finds, have enabled her, like the men in Stephen Crane's open boat, to be an interpreter. She can now more fully appreciate certain scenes in the *Lusiad* of Luiz Vas de Camöens, fully accessible only to "those who have parted with friends to go on long and perilous voyages," she claims (NV, 140). Moreover, Morrell learns that travel displaces the fears and sorrows of separation, the interpersonal emotions that are said to absorb Woman, and replaces them with larger feelings and concerns. She reasons that the home setting to which homebodies are consigned conspires with the familiar routines of daily life to preoccupy the mind with thoughts of absent loved ones. New adventures and unfamiliar territories, on the other hand, preoccupy and absorb the mind and emotions of the traveler. Thus the sorrow of separation, Morrell writes, is "lost in a nobler [emotion], which incorporates the pride of science and individual heroism," made accessible to women through travel. "Woman, more than man," she writes, "delights in glory . . . she feels *the national glow* that would sink every thing at the thought of honor" (NV, 141, emphasis added). She comes to feel, that is, like a "manly" patriot.

Abby Morrell learns that womanly "decency," having denied women broad experience, also denies them what she calls "the feeling of nationality." Morrell writes,

> At home we females think but little of national glory, or rather not much of the means of supporting it; but when abroad *we become interested in every thing connected with commerce or naval power.* A woman in these distant seas would be as proud to point to a fine frigate or a seventy-four from the United States as she would in dwelling on the fame of Washington, or any other distinguished man of our country. *The feeling of nationality comes over us when abroad, but we leave it for others to support when we are at home.* A female feels herself lost in the great mass of her countrywomen, but when abroad she represents them all; and she must be dull indeed if she does not understand this situation. I was the first American woman who had visited some of the places I have described, and being a subject of curiosity, no one could be indifferent to such a situation; it is not, however, to me a matter of vanity. *Our men have been everywhere, but our women have not wandered much from home.* (NV, 144, emphasis added)

Exposed to "commerce or naval power," and unlike British women travelers who, according to Karen R. Lawrence, "tended to mistrust the rhetoric of mastery, conquest, and quest that has funded a good deal of male fictional and nonfictional travel," Abby Morrell develops a "manly" taste for America's imperial destiny.[18] Linking pride in national accomplishment and pride in American womanhood, she tallies the loss incurred by the female citizen confined to the domestic round. She accuses the constraints placed on women of a kind of treason, of working to diminish patriotic fervor, the birthright of every American. In effect, Abby Morrell's narrative traces the growth of nationalism in her thoughts of home from abroad. Travel appears to develop if not give birth to the nationalistic sentiments that characterize women's travel writing across the century.

In the experience of travel and its translation into prose, Abby Morrell discovers how arbitrary and debilitating are the gender divisions that parcel out education to men and women on the lines of gender. Having been introduced to the dangers of the sea, she writes, "I am surprised any one would go a mile from land a second time without knowing enough of the science of navigation to find a port when he wished. Woman as I am, I never would sail another voyage without some knowledge of this science; enough to make ordinary calculations cannot lie very deep when so many pretend to it" (NV, 142). Contrary to the doxa of the culture that insist on the difference between men and women in intellectual and other arenas, and particularly in the sciences, Morrell finds that the borders of experience, rather than those of sex, stake out the borders of the mind and curiosity. Even a woman can learn the science of navigation if exposed to it. Moreover, such knowledge proves easy to acquire—as must be the case, she implies, if so many men pretend to it. Her text allows that men have exaggerated the difficulty of some things in order to inflate themselves, and they have self-interestedly fenced off certain territories for themselves as they fence women in.

Yet how useful to her, she discovers, a more adequate education would have been. Abby Morrell goes out to observe strange worlds and phenomena without the formal education afforded men. She travels without having ready-to-hand the intellectual habits and conceptual categories that [male] education offers. This is the lack from which she suffers, the lack that impedes her learning and writing. Morrell remarks,

> The great difficulty we women feel in collecting information, is the want of order and classification of our thoughts; and we therefore labour much harder to arrive at true conclusions than those who have a regular pigeon-hole in which to place all sorts of information. . . . I doubt whether a scientific observer would have had more thoughts than passed through my teeming brain; but *he would have known how to arrange them*, and have drawn conclusions tending to establish known truths, or elicit new ones; while whatever observations or conclusions I might make were liable to be dispersed for *not knowing where to preserve them*. (NV, 223–24, emphasis added)

Morrell assigns value to the position of outsider: "The unstudied and unpractised mind, however, observes many things that might escape the notice of the best educated" (NV, 224). Yet she discovers that she lacks the training to take full advantage of her opportunities as a world-wanderer. Like Catharine Sedgwick who, lamenting the poverty of her formal schooling, declared, "I have all my life felt the want of more systematic teaching,"[19] Abby Morrell discovers that same "want" when travel presents her with material to catalog and interpret.

In the light of the indictment of the gender system that develops in the course of the narrative, Abby Morrell's dedication of her book is at once sincere and diversionary. Anticipating Alexis de Tocqueville, Morrell dedicates her book "To my Countrywomen, the happiest of their sex, born in a land of liberty, educated in a knowledge of virtue and true independence, single by choice, or wedded with their own consent, friends to the brave, and patrons to the enterprising." Yet even as she calls upon her countrywomen to assist her in her cause, the amelioration of the lot of American seamen, she draws their attention to the contradiction between gender proscriptions and the rights of Americans. Her written text, then, like the life-texts of many women, includes both a declared and a muted and potentially revolutionary purpose.[20]

Drawing near home shores once again, Abby Morrell "began to question myself as to what purpose I had spent my time during this long and to me interesting voyage." She understands that, though "not prepared by education or habits to make the most of my situation," she felt herself "a much graver matron than when I embarked, and had more settled and, as I thought, more rational opinions for the government of life; I had suffered much, but enjoyed more; I had laid up a stock to reflect and reason upon during my future days" (NV, 222). Travel had transformed her. According to her husband, Abby "was hailed as the heroine of a romance in real life" upon her return.[21] It seems that travel and the status it conferred on her provided the autobiographical motive as defined by Georges Gusdorf: "I count, my existence is significant to the world."[22] This sense of significance motivated her to write a narrative of self-exploration, of psychological travel, as she wrote a narrative of world-exploration, of geographical travel. Abby Morrell shared, in 1833, the sentiments of another traveler, Eleanor Smith Bowen (Laura Bohannan), who wrote a century later, "I have written simply as a human being, and the truth I have tried to tell concerns the sea change in oneself that comes from immersion in another and savage culture."[23]

II

On 6 July 1853, twenty-two years after Abby Morrell had returned from her far-flung voyage, Sophia Peabody Hawthorne, together with her husband Nathaniel and their three children, steamed out of Boston Harbor on the *Niagara*, a paddle-wheel steamer of the Cunard line, headed for

Liverpool. Sophia was an accidental tourist. She traveled in the wake of Nathaniel's appointment by Franklin Pierce as American consul to England, a post in which he served for four years until 1857, when James Buchanan won the presidency of the United States. Following Hawthorne's resignation from his post as consul, the family traveled to Italy, visiting Rome, Florence, and Siena, eventually returning to England by way of France and Switzerland. When they set sail on their return trip to America on 16 June 1860, the Hawthornes had been abroad for seven years.[24]

Both of the Hawthornes, Sophia as well as Nathaniel, were diligent writers. During her sojourn of eighteen months in Cuba in 1833 and 1834, Sophia had conducted a voluminous correspondence, later reassembled by her sister, Elizabeth Peabody, and "bound into three volumes as a Cuba Journal, a family keepsake."[25] When as a newlywed she lived in the Old Manse, Sophia and Nathaniel kept a mutual journal for which, in the words of their son Julian, "first one and then the other held the pen in lovely strophe and antistrophe."[26] Sophia also kept an extensive notebook during the Hawthornes' years in England and Italy. Randall Stewart evokes a charming picture of these determined, disciplined journalers in Italy: "After the day's sight-seeing and sketching, after tea and the children's bedtime, Hawthorne and his wife and Ada Shepard [the Hawthorne children's governess] sat down at the large living room table to write. There was 'a profound quiet,' Ada reported, 'broken only by the busy, active scratches' of their pens."[27] According to another Hawthorne biographer, James Mellow, Nathaniel Hawthorne had seen "much of the great world," from which he drew material for such works as *The Marble Faun* and *Our Old Home*, while "Sophia had fulfilled her yearning to see the cultural shrines of Europe—the great palaces, the grand museums."[28] The evidence shows, however, that Sophia's exposure to the great world did more than fulfill her cultural yearnings. Her exposure was the foundation for the journal and letters that eventually became her *Notes in England and Italy*, published twelve years after her travels and eleven years after her husband's death.

Sophia's account is a textbook case of the writing practice of many "miscellaneous" American women as earlier described, women who did not ordinarily aspire to publication. Traveling, keeping journals en route, and publishing them after the trip's conclusion, these women often did little to moderate the formulas of travel writing, to transform convention, to make the travel book tradition bend to their own rhetorical initiatives. Sophia Hawthorne deliberately and diligently works to place herself among these genteel amateurs. *Notes* includes an array of the conventional practices of the travel writer. It opens with a perhaps truthful but nevertheless predictable disclaimer: her notes "were never meant for publication," she writes, but friends "have repeatedly urged me to print them, from a too partial estimate of their value; and I have steadily resisted the suggestion, until now, when I reluctantly yield." [29]

Like other travel writers, she seeks the congruence between sites and predecessor texts, as when she writes about the Burns' Monument: "We went up on the roof and there my longing eyes at last rested upon 'the banks and braes a'bonnie Doon.' And I saw 'the little birds that wantoned through the flowery thorn;' and I saw the thorn, and heard the birds, as when they almost broke the heart of the poet" (NE, 142). She aligns works of art with ideology as well as predecessor texts. She praises a Holy Family by Francia, for example, because "It is a MOTHER, with a perfect sense of all a mother's responsibilities" (NE, 209); and she praises Guido's *Beatrice Cenci* in contrast with the ubiquitous copies that fail to give "the remotest idea of it" (NE, 212).[30] Visits to museums provoke expressions of Romantic theories of art as a window to the soul and as inspiration— tempered, of course, by New England Protestantism. Enraptured with Domenichino, for instance, she writes, "[I]t seems as if the soul must be pure, and the instrument clean, by means of which the Creator delineates such a scene as is represented here" (NE, 206). Sophia sententiously and conventionally apostrophizes "our old home," England. "What a country is Great Britain!," she exclaims. "Every atom of it is a jewel. History and poetry transmute into precious stones every particle of its dust. One cannot look abroad or plant his foot, but a thousand illustrious shades spring up before him—noble deeds and creations of genius make it fairy-land. And full as it is of riches, it is so small that we can fold our arms round it and love it and enjoy it. Hail Britannia!" (NE, 189). Domesticating the world and pulling it into the orbit of the United States, Sophia's trope turns the Motherland into a child and the former child, the United States, into a mother.

Like the texts of her compatriots, hers is a repository of anti-Catholicism: "I should think Pio Nono would be better employed in preserving such works [of art] from destruction than in writing encyclical letters, for I believe he would save more souls by it," she writes (NE, 312). As for the Catholic clergy: they are "almost invariably repulsive and gross," "peculiarly depraved," and "mostly fat, with flabby cheeks, chins, and throats, of very earthly aspect." As if obsessed with clergy and unable to curb her disgust, she continues: "There is nothing to compare them to but hogs, and they merely need to stoop upon their hands to be perfect likenesses of swine, so that the encounter of one of them in the street gives one a faint sensation" (NE, 480). Again like her republican compatriots, she associates Europe with the past and is repulsed by the ongoing life around her. Contrasting contemporary Florentines with their ancestors, she envisions them as "empty chrysalides—deserted shells. Something has scared away souls," she writes, "and only automatons remain. Perhaps the Medici were the cause of this death and void—the Medici, and then this present race of Grand Dukes" (NE, 468).

What is curious, however, about *Notes in England and Italy* and its autobiographical work is this: it is deliberately and laboriously crafted to appear to be spontaneous, unlabored, and uncrafted. Moreover, it seeks this appearance in order to superimpose on Sophia Hawthorne the culture's biography of Woman, with her travel account as its agent. *Notes* is the performance of a cultural script for which Sophia Hawthorne's journals of travel are the prompt books. As she textualizes her travels, Sophia Hawthorne strives to constitute herself as Woman and to erase those aspects of herself that are other. Her writing of travel-as-autobiography is an act of self-immolation in which she attempts to bury the self Nathaniel called "Sophie Hawthorne" under the "Dove," Nathaniel's name for the other, True Womanly personality of his wife.[31] The burial is interrupted by a revenant, the voice of a younger Sophia Hawthorne who comes to haunt the text of her maturity. The spirit of a countercultural self, this voice resists immolation, as we shall see, despite Sophia's best efforts. Nevertheless, Sophia Hawthorne's text deflects the feminist irony we have come to associate with the texts of nineteenth-century women. Sophia Hawthorne's text does *not* comply overtly in the system (of Woman) in order to engage in subversive, covert inscriptions of a hidden, ignored, and forbidden self. On the contrary, Sophia Hawthorne's writing is designed to activate, instead, what might be called feminist irony-in-reverse. Her writing seeks to reveal, exhibit, and celebrate the version of Sophia's self as Woman, as "Dove," and to conceal, ignore, and destroy the trace of another voice, another self-possibility.

The machinery of *Notes on England and Italy* makes visible Sophia Hawthorne's effort to textualize herself as Woman, to inscribe her traveling persona as a model of the efficacy of the "rule of decency." Sophia uses the artillery of writing conventions to deflect classification among the "scribbling women" she and Nathaniel deplored. Sophia's early personal history contains the onset of her disavowal of the name of "writer." Having kept a journal while visiting Cuba as a young woman, Sophia was, according to T. Walter Herbert, "both fascinated and repelled" when her sister, Elizabeth Peabody, circulated it among friends in Boston.[32] When invited by James T. Fields to contribute to the *Atlantic Monthly*, Sophia famously responded, "I assure you most earnestly that nothing less urgent and terrible than the immediate danger of starvation for my husband and children would induce me to put myself into a magazine or a pair of book covers. You forget that Mr. Hawthorne is the Bellelettre portion of my being, and besides that I have a repugnance to female authoresses in general. I have far more distaste to myself as a female authoress in particular."[33] She refused to publish her *Notes* until, ten years after her travels, stringent financial straits induced her to prepare her notebooks for publication in 1870. These material conditions, together with generic conventions, prompt Sophia to assign a womanly purpose to publishing her work: a desire to bring pleasure to others. She declares that if her notes "will aid any one in the least to enjoy, as I have enjoyed, the illustrious works of the Great Masters in Architecture, Sculpture, and Painting, I shall be well repaid for the pain it has cost me to appear before the public" (NE, preface). Such enjoyment could have been granted the public ten years earlier, of course; Sophia uses convention here to simplify and mask her actual motives, her financial need. In the text proper, Sophia makes it clear that she writes for a private rather than a public audience, often her own progeny. "This I record for my children's sake hereafter," she writes to an invisible audience, for example (NE, 347); and addressing her children, she writes, "Papa, you know, hates to drive, and prefers to wander without purpose" (NE, 67).

(Nathaniel, on the other hand, conceived of himself as a writer accumulating materials to be used later "for the side-scenes and backgrounds and exterior adornment of a work of Fiction" to be offered to the public.[34])

Laying up disclaimers in the preface, Sophia then reinforces them by a perverse preparation of her journal for publication—perverse because she prepares and repairs her notes to flag, ironically, their disrepair. She takes pains to sustain the persona of the reluctant, and therefore womanly, amateur and genteel writer. She constitutes this persona, in part, by making the machinery of editing unmistakably visible. The visibility of the machinery is, in turn, another and perverse instance of masking fact; it serves to underscore and render indisputable the status of her text as an unedited transcript of her travel journals. For example, the erratically epistolary structure of *Notes* enforces the illusion of immediacy and of casual, unreflective prose. She retains epistolary features such as the second person pronoun: "But now we are off to Manchester," she writes, "where I will write you the rest of our experiences" (NE, 25). Devices such as the afterthought reinforce this epistolary "carelessness," as when she reports, "P.S. We have just returned from Boston Abbey" (NE, 13). Footnotes, as well, contribute to the illusion of a virginal text. Rather than emending the body of the text, Sophia inserts such notes as this: "I am mistaken in having supposed this the cippus [tombstone] of the wicked Agrippina, daughter of Germanicus. It was the cippus of the *wife* of Germanicus—who was remarkable for her virtue, in an age of monstrous depravity" (NE, 244). Why did she not simply correct the journal entry? Because she wishes to save for her readers and for posterity the face of the modest, honest Woman, a woman who is also decorous. Commenting on the work of Guido, she writes that "some of his sketches, I must say it, looked like unbaked clay," and then provides a coy footnote for "clay": "I wish to say *dough*, but it seems irreverent" (NE, 245). Seeking to avoid an air of professionalism or artful editing, Sophia wants her work and its publication to appear as an accident that befell her rather than a project she sought. The deliberate, contrived creaking of machinery, clumsily deployed, inscribes a womanly self casually writing letters, or parlor literature (see chapter 5), an entirely appropriate female activity. The impression found its mark. A reviewer for *Harper's New Monthly Magazine* declared that *Notes* "is written in a delightfully gossipy, personal, unconscious sort of way . . .

we found ourselves attracted by the first page, and reading with a peculiar sort of social zest, as if we were talking with a friend of familiar scenes."[35]

In several places in the text proper, Sophia preserves material that an aspirant to the name of writer would emend but that the "Dove" retains. First, she allows interruptions of the main line of the travel narrative to stand. Taking the train of the narrative off on a side-track, she abruptly inserts irrelevant digressions that come to mind "while waiting for their train to fetch them to Mauchline." Second, she retains errors that could easily be excised, witness her remarks about Queen Elizabeth's "Book of Secrets," in which she makes a feeble joke about mistaking the word "fellon" for "fellow." Then, showing a distrust of her joke-telling ability and of her audience, she defensively fends off any appearance of ignorance: "The present way of spelling this word is with one l—felon—and so I easily mistook it" (NE, 60). Finally, she brackets information that a dedicated writer and editor would merge into the text. Concluding the entry from a visit to Siena, for example, Sophia inserts the following ambiguous statement, square brackets and all: "[This ends my rapid survey of our first four days in Siena, when I could make no record in my journal, as events occurred]" (NE, 502). She may count the journal entries themselves, made during her travels, as a "rapid survey," in which case her plea of busyness apologizes for their brevity; or she may have written this "rapid survey" into her account as she prepared it for publication. Either way, the bracketed material serves notice that *Notes* is merely a series of raw, unedited journal entries, a first draft, a private journal that, lacking art and artifice, nevertheless found its way into print despite the author's original intentions.

But what is virtue untried? *Notes* makes visible in another of its features the degree to which Sophia Hawthorne seeks to perform the role of Woman and to immolate other versions and voices of her self. *Notes* quietly declares the existence of a latent but *deliberately undeveloped* talent. Although Sophia *could* do better as a writer, as she wants her reader to know, she has *chosen* instead to follow the "rule of decency." Sophia insists on her knowledge of good writing, purposeful repetitions, and incisive figures. When she describes Lincoln Cathedral, for example, she declares, "I am afraid I have said 'light as fire' once before, in describing York minster, but I can think of no other simile that suits either case so well" (NE, 47).

Furthermore, *Notes* ends with this: "P.S.—My journal was suddenly interrupted by illness—even in the midst of a sentence, and was never resumed; which will account for the abruptness of the close" (NE, 549). Here again is the protestation of virgin journal materials. Yet here again, as well, is the self-conscious writer who is on the one hand publishing unvarnished prose but on the other hand wants to tell others she knows it is unvarnished and knows better than to write an abrupt conclusion. She tells her reader that she is a better writer than her journal shows. Why does a traveling autobiographer seeking, paradoxically, self-immolation want to publicize the possession of deliberately untapped skills? Like the other writing strategies she deploys, Sophia's surreptitious signals of talent highlight her propriety. Far from being forced to comply in the role of Woman, she works deliberately to show her proud and willing compliance in that role. Sophia lets the reader know she could create a perfectly crafted travel account but chooses, instead, her proper place, far from the artifice and dexterity that properly belong to the male in general and to her husband in particular. Consistent with her earlier, decorous refusal to publish with Fields, Sophia's strategies are designed to make visible her rejection of personal ambition to write or publish, making visible in the same stroke her proudly subordinate position to her husband. Nathaniel Hawthorne thus remains, in her words to Fields, "the Bellelettre portion" of her being, while the "Dove" neither pretends to artistry nor marshals it when she could. Sophia Hawthorne enacts what Nancy Cott calls a "central paradox of domesticity, that women were expected to make a *voluntary* choice amounting to self-abnegation" (emphasis added).[36]

Certain exclusions and inclusions in Sophia's text proper become *dramatis personae* in Sophia's performance of Woman. Her tactics become particularly clear when juxtaposed with Nathaniel's practice in *Our Old Home*, drawn from the same travels as Sophia's *Notes*. Sophia retains references to family in her edition/revision of her travel notes. Take, as a typical case, the visit to Lincoln Cathedral. Sophia makes repeated references to her son James, punctuating her prose with his name: "James—was astonished" (NE, 39) and "James—was hungry . . . and went and bought some gingerbread, an acre of it, I should think, 'and munched and munched,' as Macbeth's witches say" (NE, 48). Writing of their ride to Dumfries, Sophia stores up for posterity the words of her children: Rose calls honeysuckle "beesuckle" and James shouts "A ruin! A ruin!" after they passed Carron Bridge (NE, 121). Nathaniel, on the other hand, excised the references to family from his English notebooks when he prepared them for publication as *Our Old Home*.

Sophia and Nathaniel's textualizing of one another as they edit their travel notes for publication is perhaps yet more telling. Take, for example, the record of a choppy boat ride to Old Boston. Sophia writes, "I had plenty of food for long-suffering and patience. I had a chance to be good under difficulties," decorously left unnamed (NE, 52). Nathaniel, on the other hand, having recorded in his notebooks that Sophia was nauseated on this occasion, omits this entirely from *Our Old Home*.[37] Instead, he claims, "the only memorable incident of our voyage happened when a mother-duck was leading her little fleet of five ducklings across the river, just as our steamer went swaggering by."[38] Perhaps most telling of all are Sophia's frequent references to Nathaniel: how, for example, he jumped up and gathered daisies and how "papa mounted the box of the Barouche with the driver" in Mossgiel (NE, 135). Basking in her husband's status as an acclaimed writer, Sophia serves as a press agent for him in her *Notes*, reporting that a book seller in Old Boston, Mr. Porter, introduced the vicar to them after "having whispered who papa was"; that Mrs. Porter, "pointing to a brilliant red-bird," declared that it was "almost as red as the Scarlet Letter" (NE, 61–62); that a house in Old Boston resembles "an enchanting *House of the Seven Gables*" (NE, 69). She records Elizabeth Barrett Browning's comment to her, a jewel in her motherly and wifely crown: "Oh how rich and happy you are to have two daughters, a son, and such a husband!" (NE, 362). And Nathaniel? Although he frequently mentions Sophia in his notebooks, he erases her from *Our Old Home*, gathering her together with the children and himself into a collective "we."

Preparing his journals for publication as *Our Old Home*, Nathaniel Hawthorne revises the self who inhabits his notebooks. Husband, father, and journaler are transformed into writer and authority. Sophia, on the other hand, inscribes her self as wife of an established author and mother of his children. In this way, she molds herself as Woman and insists that she is not Nathaniel's peer, much less his superior. Moreover, by highlighting Nathaniel's genius, Sophia presents herself as an appendage who, as Barbara Johnson puts it in the epigraph of this chapter, goes about telling the story of her life by reference to her man.

There is reason to believe that Sophia's operations on the journals and notes that became *Notes in England and Italy* were as deliberate as Nathaniel's on the notebooks that became *Our Old Home*. As Nathaniel sought the persona of writer, Sophia, too, sought to transform the self of her journals and letters into an ever more faithful copy of Woman. Sophia's editing of Nathaniel's travel notes for publication demonstrates her awareness that writing is autobiographical, creating an autobiographical self who inhabits the work. She sometimes "took great liberties with [her husband's] original manuscripts," Randall Stewart points out.[39] She deleted references Hawthorne made to her ill health; she suppressed "evidence of Hawthorne's legitimately appreciative eye for female beauty" and "prosaic references to their married life." Her work complete, she proceeded to diminish her operations, claiming that "the Editor has transcribed the manuscripts just as they were left, without making any new arrangements or altering any sequence—merely omitting some passages and being especially careful to preserve whatever could throw light on his character."[40] Her laserlike revisions and excisions, that is, protect Nathaniel's reputation and present to the public what she judged to be his best face. In preparing her own journals for publication, what she did and failed to do was done to textualize her chosen reputation, as well. She sought, like Prufrock, to prepare a face, the face of Woman, to meet the faces she would meet.

Her effort to superimpose the culture's biography of Woman on her construction of her own life may explain some of what has been construed as an unpleasant, severe Sophia. It is true that she repeatedly shows herself to be relentlessly ideological and moralistic. The ideology of the domestic creature who calls her husband "Papa" in these *Notes* is at work in the galleries of Rome and Florence when, like steel to the magnet, the "ineffable tenderness of ideal maternity" in a Madonna by Perugino and the "girlish rapture" in Coreggio's famous Adoring Madonna absorb Sophia's attention (NE, 389). She finds in these figures her chosen double, Woman. Doubling again occurs in Sophia's account of Titian's portrait of Mary Magdalen. In this case, however, doubling provokes disapproval. The ideology of the genteel Victorian New England Woman, donning a mask of propriety for some imagined audience, speaks. Sophia turns on the Magdalen as if it/she were alive. "Such a woman would be incapable of repentance," Sophia writes. "She is coarse and earthly in every fibre of her frame, and in every recess of her mind. It is a pity," Sophia continues, "that such a woman should be painted so well. I have no doubt it is a portrait, and I am sorry that Titian knew such a person and contemplated her so minutely" (NE, 392). The domestic creature of decidedly unpleasant disposition, obsessed with cleanliness, conflates cleanliness and virtue, unable to "recover from the dirty cottage [of Burns]" nor see "how anything pure and high and heavenly could possibly grow and flourish in such a noisome atmosphere, with no space for decency, no leisure for order." Then she condescendingly declares, "But God's ways are not ours, and His thoughts are not as our thoughts, and doubtless He has his own shield to guard the innocent heart from wrong; and the soul is not necessarily soiled with the body" (NE, 135). Seemingly mean in financial matters, she parades a stingy self in the text, as when "papa wishes me to corrupt him [a porter who, she admits, was very helpful] with a shilling; but I would not, because I did not put him to any extra trouble" (NE, 106).

Why did Sophia not dissemble this aspect of herself? We have seen her ability to dissemble, her footnotes and brackets, corrections and apologies. She is indisputably aware of prose as pose. Yet she does nothing to soften the aspect of herself exposed by matters of finance, hygiene, or morality. Apparently she finds her attitudes appropriate and perhaps even laudable. She parades in such passages the Victorian virtue of cleanliness and the persona of the frugal housewife, enshrined in the work of Lydia Maria Child in 1833 and complement to the persona of the good wife and mother.[41] It may be, indeed, that more attention to the ideal of Woman and nineteenth-century America's book of virtues would exonerate Sophia Hawthorne or at least soften the charges leveled against her. As T. Walter Herbert says, "Sophia Hawthorne is the most vilified wife in American literary history, after having been in her own time the most admired."[42] Sophia has been used, in fact, as a metonymy for orneriness in American women. In her study of American travelers to Britain, for example, Allison Lockwood associates the carping and querulousness of women travelers with Sophia Hawthorne. "Did they catch the malady, perhaps," Lockwood asks, "from Sophia Hawthorne—from reading *Notes in England and Italy*, published in 1870, which reveals what can only be called a case of 'the cutes'?"[43] Sophia Hawthorne's "cutes," at best unfashionable in our time, were hallmarks of a Victorian, bourgeois, true Woman: fastidious, hygienic, righteous, frugal, and ambitious only for her children and her husband. When Sophia Hawthorne criticizes women writers, certain portraits of females, dirty Italians, and slovenly clergy, she creates the "other" for reasons described in chapter 2: she demonstrates her possession of True Womanhood by drawing back her skirts and reacting as Woman should.

Sophia Hawthorne's autobiographical account of travels undertakes the cultural work of aligning a woman, known by virtue of her husband, with the culture's ideal of Woman in 1867, when conventional Victorian womanhood was under siege. Yet Sophia's performance of Woman is not entirely successful. Despite her earnest labors to the contrary, her text is haunted by a revenant, an aspect of self she chooses to drive into the shadows. The ghost in Sophia Hawthorne's *Notes* is the version of self that, buried since courtship and marriage, stirs upon exposure to Europe, and Italy in particular. Thus, contrary to the cultural work the text places on exhibit, *Notes on England and Italy* unwittingly exposes the expense of spirit exacted by the performance of Woman and the creativity it compromises if not destroys.

"Sophie Hawthorne," the shadow-self of Sophia the "Dove," lives in those passages in *Notes* that record visits to galleries and critiques of art. This version of Sophia is compellingly articulate as she examines and interprets works of art, such as Guido's *Beatrice Cenci* in her "infinite desolation" and "unfathomable grief" (NE, 212); and Raphael's Fornarina that "exceeds my expectations even," she writes, "for, though I thought I should find rich beauty, I did not suppose, from copies and engravings, that there was such purity of expression in the exquisite mouth" (NE, 352). Sophia's reading of Giannicola's Madonna and St. John serves to represent the several stunning descriptions of art works that punctuate her account. Demonstrating her interpretative prowess, she writes,

> It is plain at a glance that they have just come from Calvary, after the Crucifixion, though there is no cross, and nothing represented of the late sacrifice—merely the two figures walking. Mary is a little in advance of St. John. Her hands are tightly clasped, with profound, repressed agony. She looks out of the picture with a pale face that has seen death, and the death of one who is life of her life. There is no distortion of grief, though unspeakable grief is expressed. The head is slightly bent on one side—a certain terror of sorrow is in her wonderful eyes, as if she feared to know how bereft she is, and how awful a scene she has witnessed. . . . A mute

appeal is in her gaze—a desert of woe—the most heart-smiting pathos. Both the figure and face are noble. . . . John turns his countenance toward the Cross, evidently, though none is visible. . . . there seems a marvelous light falling on his features. . . . Like Mary, he is of noble figure and air, and a tender grace sways his movement. . . . He extends his hands toward Calvary, with impassioned, wild sorrow. I think John is not now occupied with his new care of Mary: he is only intent on his own loss, and yet a cord already binds them together. (NE, 316–17)

Sophia calls such occasions as these "my sheaf of memories—my golden sheaf" (NE, 389). Such sheaves substantiate Nathaniel Hawthorne's estimate of his wife's talent: "I have never read anything so good as some of her narrative and descriptive epistles to her friends,"[44] he appended to a letter of Sophia to Fields (quoted earlier) in which she expresses her "repugnance to female authoresses." Nathaniel was correct. The act of writing about art and gallery visits liberates in Sophia an energy and enthusiasm that breaks out of the straitjacket of her ideology. Textualizing her readings of art, Sophia forgets her chosen self—she forgets, that is, Woman. Her defenses down, her mask thrown aside, she unwittingly makes visible in these moments a self quite other than the Woman who calls the clergy of Florence swine, the Woman obsessed with dirt, the Woman who decorously substituted the word "clay" for "dough." The liberated voice of Sophia is confident in her opinions of art, ready to correct art critics and historians, critical of academicians who "get hold of a rule" and "stultify themselves by holding to it, against all the intuitions of genius" (NE, 388). Her account of a day spent sketching in Bolsena is delivered in a voice that escaped immolation. Sophia first describes her surroundings in the harshest of "womanly" terms. Bolsena is so filthy that "no words can ever describe the disgustfulness of the streets and of the people. I do not think they ever touch water. We, of the other side of the Atlantic, have not the remotest idea how dirty a person can be, who has not been washed for nearly three thousand years! This is the state of the Bolsenian, formerly the Volsinian. It is only in Europe that one can see a dirty face, and it is necessary to come to Europe to comprehend it. Description will not avail" (NE, 524). Yet in the midst of their "disgustfulness," the Bolsenians appreciate her work. Their appreciation, in turn, prompts a change of heart in

Sophia. Although she could "scarcely breathe such an atmosphere as they created," she writes that

> this beggarly crowd of Italians gave an impression of refinement and civilization, very old and settled civilization, by their manners and bearing. They were quiet and gentle and exceedingly courteous. They spoke in whispers, and *were deeply interested in my work*, from an innate love of art, woven into their members and being. Their glorious eyes (*which were clean*) shone with delight *at every line I drew which they recognized as true*. I sketched the castle and the town beneath it. . . . I told them I liked their castle very much, and they repeated to each other with pride that I said so. . . . Whenever any one happened to obstruct my view, the rest commanded him to move from the signora's eye, and a vista was kept for me most jealously all the time. I showed them a few other sketches in my book, and at the Campo Tower of Siena they exclaimed, "O bellissima! bellissima!" but always in subdued tones. Not one of them begged money. When I was obliged to leave off, because our hour of departure was come, they all stood aside in a crowd, four or five handsome boys on the outskirts, and as I cordially bade the *beautiful, dirty* creatures "addio," they smiled, and bowed, and waved their hands, like so many princes. (NE, 526–28, emphasis added)

Another dimension of Sophia Hawthorne, a voice that differs from the proper Victorian Woman, comes to the fore. This version of Sophia had at one time been a woman to reckon with. Travel had once before, in her early years, liberated artistic talent in Sophia. In 1833, for reasons of health, her parents sent her to Cuba. There, Patricia D. Valenti says, Sophia was able "to pursue her art in a relaxed manner. Lacking mentors or classes, Sophia developed her skill in portraiture, sculpted, reflected upon her art work, and experimented in some new forms including restoration and decorative art."[45] She had begun to study drawing in 1824 with one of the Palmer sisters of Salem and later studied with Francis Graeter, the illustrator of Lydia Maria Child's *Girls' Own Book*. Sophia's sister Elizabeth, convinced of Sophia's talent, brought a doubting Thomas Doughty of the Hudson River school, skeptical of the reports of Sophia's talent, to the Peabody parlor "to allow Sophia to watch him at work." Finding Sophia to be much better than he supposed, he complimented her on her sense of color and advised her to learn to compose her own landscapes, to develop a style of her own. The list of those who admired Sophia's work included Washington Allston as well as Chester Harding, an artist who, although he otherwise refused to permit his work to be copied, made an exception upon seeing Sophia's copy of a Doughty landscape.[46]

The young Sophia was enthusiastic and even ecstatic when she exercised her talent. Having seen exhibits at the Athenaeum in Boston and in Dedham in 1832, as she was later to visit galleries in Europe, she wrote to her sister Elizabeth: "What do you think I have actually begun to do? Nothing less than *create* and do you wonder that I lay awake all last night after sketching my first picture. I actually thought my head would have made its final explosion. When once I began to excurse, I could not stop. Three distinct landscapes came forth in full array besides that which I had arranged before I went to bed and it seemed as if I should fly to be up and doing. I have always determined not to force the creative power but wait till it mastered *me* and now I feel as if the time had come and *such freedom and revelry of spirit does it bring!*" (emphasis added)[47] Moreover, the young Sophia was interested in presenting her work to the public, and unlike her husband's Hilda of *The Marble Faun*, she preferred to paint originals rather than copies.[48]

In the early years of her marriage to Nathaniel Hawthorne, she continued to harbor artistic ambitions. According to Louise Hall Tharp, Sophia tried her hand at modeling in clay, taking a bust of Wellington Peabody to be cast in plaster, "almost beside herself with excitement as she watched the cast being completed," frustrated with its imperfections, but taking a penknife to alter the cast, "sharpening the lines with a freedom and confidence that made Clevenger [a sculptor] nod with approval." Sophia attempted a portrait bust of Nathaniel, and she executed a bust of Laura Bridgman, the famous blind and deaf pupil of Samuel Gridley Howe, the husband of Julia Ward Howe. When Sophia and Nathaniel Hawthorne moved into the Old Manse, Sophia outfitted for herself a room of her own behind the parlor, a room that seemed to her a "happier world" she knew "for her own—her studio."[49] Anticipating Mrs. James in the Elizabeth Stuart Phelps story "The Angel over the Right Shoulder," Sophia writes in September of 1849 about a family vacation in the Berkshires: "I intend to paint at least three hours a day, while my husband takes cognizance of the children; as he will not write more than nine hours out of the twelve, and his study can be my studio as well." [50] In a letter to her mother in January 1844, she reports that she does not question Nathaniel about what he is writing "because I always disliked to speak of what I was *painting*," the parallelism placing her work on a level with his. [51]

Again like Mrs. James in the Phelps story, Sophia's life as an artist was destined to end. Two months before her first child was born, she finished the painting *Endymion*. She was enormously pleased with it. "The price must be an hundred dollars independently of the frame; if it be worth one cent, it is worth that. I dearly desire that some one I know should possess it. I shall be glad some day to redeem it, for it has come out of my soul," she wrote her mother. Hawthorne, however, "would not let her sell the picture, after all," their daughter Rose Lathrop Hawthorne reports, and "the artist Sophia now sank into sleep like the mystic shepherd of Mount Latmos." [52]

Imagine, then, what the galleries of Europe awakened in her. Whereas in Paris, according to the biographer James Mellow, Nathaniel Hawthorne felt the burden of the past, Sophia Peabody Hawthorne "had an inexhaustible enthusiasm for visiting the Louvre." [53] The dominant subject of Sophia's *Notes* is gallery visits and impressions of art. In Rome in particular, Sophia was in steady contact not only with art masterpieces but with contemporaries, several women among them, who lived for their art: the English art historian Anna Jameson, the sculptor Harriet Hosmer, and a sculptor from Hawthorne's hometown of Salem, Maria Louisa Lander, among others. As T. Walter Herbert observes, "Living in Italy, [Sophia] got a taste of the public admiration Italians were prepared to bestow on women of artistic gifts." [54]

The impact of galleries, the exposure to art, the presence of women who had followed extradomestic avenues—all of these stood to propose alternative selves, including the artistic self of Sophia Peabody, rising again like the Phoenix in the process first of traveling and then of writing about it, transforming twice over the experience of Europe into prose, once in her journals and again in preparing them for publication. According to Louise Hall Tharp, Sophia "was an artist of more than average ability." [55] So substantial was her promise that, in Patricia D. Valenti's assessment of the evidence, she "should be considered among the earliest serious female painters in America because the only other recognized contemporary women painters acquired their mentors, initially at least, because they were related to them." [56]

Why did a woman with such potential choose to suppress it? She was mightily assisted, of course, by the culture's ideals of womanhood. Her husband, too, assisted her self-destruction in each phase of their relationship. Writing to Sophia during their courtship, he expressed his pleasure in her paintings. He predicts they will "paint pictures together" and her hand shall "give external existence" to their unity of heart and mind. "I have often felt that I could be a painter," Nathaniel Hawthorne writes, "only I am sure that I could never handle a brush; now you will show me the images of my inward life, beautified and etherealized by the mixture of your own spirit." [57] Hawthorne would colonize Sophia's talents, allowing her to hold the brush in order to paint *his* inner life rather than her own, a circumstance hardly conducive to the development and publicity of either a woman's life or her talents. Later, traveling in Europe and praising Sophia's travel letters to his friend, Francis Bennock, Nathaniel writes, "I don't know whether I can tolerate a literary rival at bed and board; there would probably be a new chapter in the 'Quarrels of Authors.'" [58] After returning from Europe, and apparently insecure in the face of women's talents, he labeled as "vainglorious boasts" the attempts of his daughter Rose "to bring the stimulus of great events into the Concord life by writing stories," Rose writes. According to Rose, he hung over her "dark as a prophetic flight of birds" and "with as near an approach to anger as I had ever seen in him, 'Never let me hear of your writing stories!' he exclaimed, 'I forbid you to write them!'" [59]

Sophia was complicit in her husband's attitudes. She subscribed to her wifely and motherly role. Her daughter, Rose, observed "a sharp contrast" between her mother's "earlier life of intercourse with trooping, charming friends, and devotion to art and literature" and "the toils of motherhood in poverty which now absorbed her days." Rose documents her mother's seeming contentment, registered in a letter Sophia wrote to her mother in September 1848, in which Sophia claims, "I am so happy that I require nothing more. No art nor beauty can excel my daily life, with such a husband and such children, the exponents of all art and beauty. I really have not even the temptation to go out of my house to find anything better." [60] Only the dire financial straits that pertained in 1869 when she gathered together her *Notes* could drive Sophia Hawthorne to publish. Laboring to overcome financial difficulties by copying parts of her husband's notebooks, Sophia removed to Dresden, where her son Julian "could attend engineering school; the girls could study art and music; and the cost of living . . . would be less than in postwar America."[61] Preparing her travel writing for publication as part of her financial campaign, she could at least have the consolation of presenting her self to the public as the picture of Woman.

Little evidence of Sophia's earlier, expansive, energetic, and artistic voice has survived. Of the work she accomplished in the arts, there remain a few pencil sketches and ink drawings, two bas-relief heads, five oil paintings, two portrait drawings, and her illustrations for Nathaniel Hawthorne's story "The Gentle Boy," four copies of which are extant.[62] Yet there is an additional testimony to the existence of Sophia Peabody, aspirant to art: her account of travel. *Notes in England and Italy*, even as it exhibits Woman in its pages, preserves the impact of European travel on an American woman and the complexity of a version of self Sophia Hawthorne sought to hide from public view, the energetic and responsive artist.

III

The connection between autobiography and travel writing is explicit in the title chosen by Martha J. Coston for her 1886 book, *A Signal Success: The Work and Travels of Mrs. Martha J. Coston: An Autobiography*. Unlike Abby Morrell and Sophia Hawthorne, who traveled to accompany their husbands in their work, Martha Coston traveled to do her own work: to sell an invention, naval signals. She decorously credits her husband with this invention despite her partnership in the project. Widowed and in financial difficulties, she traveled abroad "to introduce the signals into the navies of the European countries," she writes, "and thus win a proper recognition of my husband's talent and my own labors, as well as the wherewithal to educate my children."[63] The record of her travels is a rosary whose beads add up to her major achievement, the promotion of her husband's invention, undertaken to honor his memory and to assist sailors. Her travel account is also, however, her autobiographical testimony to a rather different achievement, the successful exercise of a considerable business prowess.

In the guise of traveler and widow, Martha Coston writes autobiography as self-revelation. To constitute, in prose, a woman who succeeds in a man's world, she dons the mask of Woman. Unlike Sophia Hawthorne, who sought to hide her unconventional self behind the mask of Woman, Martha Coston uses the mask to make visible, in contrast to her assertive self and Woman, a self who escapes from the margins of the culture's template. Coston inserts the culture's template into her text to underscore through contrast, rather than to obliterate, an unconventional self.

Her accomplishments were in fact considerable. Born in 1828 into a financially comfortable family, she married Benjamin Franklin Coston in 1844 and was widowed four years later at the age of twenty. Transforming herself into an inventor, she took up the work of her husband, experimenting with and perfecting the night signals she then sold to the government of the United States and to foreign governments. *A Signal Success* is the account of the challenges this entailed and the obstacles Martha Coston overcame, from procuring patents to negotiating with congressmen as she made her way in the world. She accomplished enough to be included as an inventor in *The Twentieth Century Biographical Dictionary of Notable Americans.*

Wanting to make her success public, a desire that was itself a challenge to Woman, Martha Coston made *A Signal Success* her vehicle. Her clever title invites plural readings of both "signal" and "success." The title may mean that despite obstacles, she succeeded at marketing her deceased husband's invention, the night signals; that the signals were a success; and that the difficulties of marketing them made the achievement a signal success. The title declares, as well, that Martha Coston has made not merely a success but a signal success of her life, remarkable and conspicuous among women's lives.

Although, or perhaps because, Martha Coston published her account in 1886, when the culture was beginning to spy what later came to be called the New Woman, she includes a conventional preface that situates her as a conventional woman despite her unconventional activities. She dresses autobiography as a biography of Woman and, like writers of woman's fiction, invokes necessity to justify her writing project. Coston claims, "In this attempt to recount my life and some of the varied experiences attendant upon my efforts to perpetuate the name of my beloved husband and to support my children and myself, *I am actuated by no idle vanity, nor yet the wish to pose as a writer, but by the honest desire to encourage those of my own sex* who, stranded upon the world with little ones looking to them for bread, may feel, not despair but courage rise in their hearts; confident that with integrity, energy, and perseverance they need no extraordinary talents to gain success and a place among the world's breadwinners" (SS, 3, emphasis added).

Together with its protestations of humility, this passage is a woman's version of the Horatio Alger story. A woman, too, can be self-made, but she must rise in the world for womanly rather than worldly motives. Yet in her book, Coston makes one more thing needful for the virtuous Woman, "a still higher aspiration than that of supplying daily needs, or even the perpetuation of an honored name." Coston claims "the intense and heartfelt desire to accomplish something for the good of humanity; in some way to lighten the load of watching and responsibility that rests on the shoulders of the brave mariner; and to place in his hands the means of saving not only property but precious human life; to prevent perhaps other women from becoming widows like myself; other children from growing into manhood with no other Father than the wise and all-merciful One above us" (SS, 3).

Even while operating in a man's world of business, however, Martha Coston expects privileges by right and rite of gender. She finds the dishonesty of the French government, for example, to be doubly reprehensible because in its dealings with her it stooped not only to "swindle a stranger" but "that stranger a woman" (SS, 154). As in the instance of Abby Morrell a half century earlier, for whom travel either created or reinforced nationalistic sentiments, Coston operates out of a notion of the superior privilege of the American woman among women: "It has been said truly enough that in America every woman is queen; and while at home we are inclined to smile at the saying as a pretty exaggeration, abroad it strikes us as a plain statement of fact; so different, even among the highly-educated classes of Europe, is the position accorded woman" (SS, 196). She finds in Sweden a painful "degradation of woman." In Stockholm, she observes, in a passage characteristic of the reaction of American women to European women in the lower classes, that woman "practically supplants the beasts of burden, being exclusively employed as hod-carrier and bricklayer's assistant. She carries bricks, mixes mortar, and, in short, does all the heavy work about the building." She continues, "Women sweep the streets, haul the rubbish, drag hand-carts up the hills and over the cobble-stones, unload bricks at the quays, attend to the parks, do the gardening, and row the numerous ferries which abound in Stockholm. The entire dairy business of this city is in their hands," she continues, "and here they take the places of horses and dogs, carrying on their shoulders the heavy cans of milk from door to door, to say nothing of acting as barbers to men. . . . *May we never see American women thus abased by being brought into competition with the pauper labor of Europe is my prayer!*" (SS, 269–70).

Continuing to frame her observations in the class and gender schemata of Victorian America, Coston observes that "while women thus slave in Stockholm, man parades" in various modes of dress, "swaggering about beer-gardens, loafing in the barrack yards, or fishing on the outskirts of the town." Quoting "a recent traveller," Coston continues, "'It is a pity that some of the scatterings of soldiers of these little European powers could not be crystallized into expert hod-carriers or skillful mortar-mixers, instead of weighing woman down under the yoke of a double burden,—viz., the hardest toil and motherhood'" (SS, 269–70).

Exercising her womanly and American privileges when she writes her travels, and donning the mask of Woman, Martha Coston claims she does business to perpetuate her husband's name and to support her children; and writes about it to benefit other single mothers and to advance the safety of seamen. Apparently aware that her work enters a cultural context in which she may be misperceived as a radical woman, she seeks to deflect any such imputation. Yet her text shows that she is bold, and that the "femininity" she parades is a rhetorical strategy. Unlike the text of Sophia Hawthorne, Martha Coston's text *is* an instance of feminist irony—of overt compliance in the code of Woman and covert activity to establish a self that differs from the code. The Martha Coston who emerges from the text of *A Signal Success* is as concerned to show herself and her achievements as she is concerned for the remembrance of her husband and the welfare of children, business, other single mothers, and seamen. The autobiographical self revealed in this account of travel is a woman of "manly" accomplishments. Subjected to scrutiny, each of her claims to conventional womanly motives proves to be a pose.

Is the perpetuation of her beloved husband's name her chief reason for writing? Like Mary Elizabeth Wieting who, as we recall, published an account of *her* life and travels that she nonetheless calls *Prominent Incidents in the Life of Dr. John M. Wieting*, giving all of fifteen pages to Dr. John, Martha Coston generously devotes fifty pages to her youth and her early married life. The rest of the narrative details the development and merchandising of the night signals that became her life and work. Her husband proves to be incidental.

Is the desire to encourage other single mothers her reason for writing? Is this a cautionary narrative that, like woman's fiction of the time, would instruct a female audience in the strength and independence that is theirs if they will but develop and exercise it?[64] Martha Coston was too uncommonly talented and too highly placed in the class hierarchy to serve as a model for ordinary women. In addition to being an inventor and an exceptionally shrewd businesswoman, she was born into a privileged, extraordinary background. Her father, a graduate of Edinburgh college, tutored her; she was sent to the best schools in Philadelphia; and her husband's contacts provided her with a network through which to market the night signals. She is a rugged individualist using her advantages to get ahead in the world, and she understands that womanly protestations of writing for the good of others can be turned to her advantage in a culture in which woman's place, although hotly contested, continues to be primarily in the home and its public extensions that are in need of women's good offices. Does she, like Abby Morrell, write in order to promote the safety of sailors? This was in fact a by-product of her activity. Living in a society labeled by William Dean Howells in his *Suburban Sketches* (1893) as a "hospital for invalid women" who lack purpose or point, Coston's pursuit of business, like Edith Wharton's later pursuit of a writing career, distinguishes her from others of her class.[65] Her wish to dress her desire to write in the cloak of altruism, a version of cross-dressing, like her evocation of a deceased spouse and the wish to perpetuate his name, seems largely formulaic in the light of textual evidence: the voice of another woman, beckoning from behind the formulas and manipulating the persona of Woman, after the first fifty pages of the text, in order to make herself visible.

The persona of the conventional Woman who inhabits the first fifty pages of Coston's book faithfully attends to Martha Coston's marriage and to the accomplishments of her husband, and includes letters from Navy commandants to her husband and a letter from Charles Stewart of the U.S. Navy "which will show the esteem in which that gentleman held my husband" (SS, 28). This persona governs the chapter entitled "Washington Society 'Befo' De Wah," where Coston outlines her symbiotic relationship with her husband. His inventions were "of absorbing interest" to her, she writes. In an echo of the charming "strophe and antistrophe" attributed to his parents by Julian Hawthorne, Martha and her husband passed "the silent hours" of "many nights in his study, he pursuing his investigations, and I at his side to cheer, encourage, and look after his personal comfort" (SS, 33). When the Costons moved from Washington to Boston, Martha became absorbed in her children and gave birth to a fourth son, "welcomed as another source of joy and occupation" (SS, 35)—after what may have been her boredom in what she calls "stiff and dull" Washington with its "society stiff and cold." Shortly thereafter, her husband died, leaving her without her "anchor" and her "pilot." Set adrift, Coston assumes the voice of the self to whom she is in fact devoted, the woman who, prophetic of the New Woman, achieves success in a man's world and relishes it. Martha Coston elevates her success story into a "signal" success by casting her story as a narrative of business adventure complete with serial ordeals that demand intelligence, faith, and patience to procure the grail, success in marketing her naval signals. While the life of a woman who simply and successfully marketed naval signals would have been a success and an achievement in itself, Martha Coston's life was a signal success because of challenges met and overcome.

Coston encounters a series of ordeals. Having had the wit to secure patents in England, France, Holland, Austria, Denmark, Italy, and Sweden before leaving the United States, upon arrival in Britain she immediately "bent all [her] energies to achieve success in the enterprise which had brought [her] over" (SS, 60). Throwing roadblocks in her way, governments attempt to steal the patents and, even when the transaction is above board, to cheat her. Yet she manages not simply to prevail, but to play hardball. When the Chief of the Bureau of Ordnance, for example, refuses to pay for her signals, he levels an accusation at her. "'Mrs. Coston, you are making altogether too much money on those signals,' he charges. 'I have nothing but my pay, and my wife is obliged to make her own dresses and bonnets.'" Unintimidated and undeterred, Martha Coston retorts, "'I can hardly see the connection between the Coston Signals and your wife's millinery; but if you wish to discuss the matter on so personal a basis . . . you receive at least four thousand dollars per annum, and with such an income, were I in your place, I should consider myself rich,—rich enough at least to insist upon my wife having her bonnets and dresses made for her'" (SS, 95). Having quick and incisive responses among the weapons in her arsenal, Martha Coston always got her price by whatever means, even introducing bills into Congress, she proudly reports, in order to secure her rights and the sale of her signals.

When her narrative includes, then, a passage on the temptation to remarry at a time when she felt a failure, the line between convention and sincerity wavers. "I am trenching on a delicate subject in mentioning the only other method of escape from my difficulties open to me, and which was urged upon me by my friends: that is, through the door of matrimony," she writes. "But the marriage estate," she continues, "was to me too tender, too holy a relation to enter into with the sordid motive of gaining a home; and in consequence, opportunities that came, as they do come to all women, unless unnaturally repulsive, were no temptation to me, no matter in how glittering a disguise; and my children were saved from the pain of seeing a stranger put in the place of their dear father, whose memory to them was sainted" (SS, 142).

In her list of discouragements, Coston places her own financial failure first, her husband's recognition second, and her children last. Rationalizing her choice to remain single, she characterizes herself as a loyal, noble, faithful wife and mother, a predictable characterization in the ideological ambiance of her time. Yet her later claim that her serial ordeal "did me no harm, but added zest to my triumphs" (SS, 245) modifies her previous remarks. Quoting in her text an Italian Minister of the Marine who introduced her as "a woman not only of business capacity, but a lady of high social position in her own country" (SS, 175), she reveals that, unlike Sophia Hawthorne, she is happy to publicize polyphonic selves, a lady and variations on her, made particularly visible by the ladylike women in the text.

Martha Coston's writing of travel-as-autobiography, then, is self-advertising. It presents an ingenious woman in a book allegedly designed as a womanly tribute to an ingenious husband. Martha Coston seizes the inventiveness of her husband not simply as an occasion to make her life a success, but to transform her life into a *succès d'estime*. Writing travel-as-autobiography, she makes what Sidonie Smith describes as a characteristic move of the female autobiographer: she "embraces . . . the ideology of individualism" and "grounds the authority to write about herself in the fit of her life to stories of the representative man." In this way she achieves full "human-beingness" and shows herself to be Adam in the dress of Eve.[66] More than simply convenient for her purposes, the travel genre enlarges them. By casting her adventures in marketing in a genre histori-cally associated with male adventures, trials, and conquests, Martha Cos-ton confers on herself the mantle of heroism. She textualizes and memo-rializes a self who is not simply a clever woman but a female veteran of foreign wars.

IV

The autobiographical dimension of women's travel writing in nineteenth-century America is significant for our understanding of women's autobiog-raphy, both as a historical record of women's lives and as a writing practice. If Georg Misch is correct that autobiographies "are bound always to be representative of their period," revealing a "contemporary intellectual out-look,"[67] then the tension between the culture's script of Woman and women travelers writing travel-as-autobiography defines women travelers and perhaps other Victorian women. Furthermore, if Georges Gusdorf is correct when he defines the autobiographical motive, cited earlier, as the idea that "I count, my existence is significant to the world," then the fe-male travel writer rests her importance in, even as she wrests her impor-tance from, the culture's concept of Woman. She turns the concept of Woman to literary and cultural work. In a publishing economy character-ized by a worn tradition of telling travels, women travelers enlist the script of Woman as a tool to create a narrative subtext, a psychological journey running parallel with the traveler's geographical adventures. Depending on the performance the traveler wishes to mount, the scenario differs. The protagonist traveler may encounter the antagonist Woman, or the protag-onist Woman may encounter the antagonist female traveler. The one throws up roadblocks for the other—solo travel, modes of dress and trans-portation, living conditions, encounters with strangers, and other chal-lenges to the "rule of decency." The plot of the narrative subtext reaches its climax when either Woman or the female traveler declares a truce or emerges victorious from the serial ordeals of the journey.

The autobiographical dimension of women's travel writing is an agent of cultural formation. Working a variation on the wording of Jane Tomp-kins's thesis about the work of literature, however, travel-as-autobiography is both cultural and countercultural.[68] It works sometimes in support of the dominant culture and sometimes against it. Much as women's travels, as we recall from chapter 1, may have served to reinforce domesticity in the act of departing from it, so women's writing of travel-as-autobiography may have served to reinforce patriarchal ideas of Woman. On occasion, it does the work Sophia Hawthorne desired to do: it pulls essentialist Woman from the margins into the center of an autobiographical text, emphasizing and perpetuating androcentric views. On occasion, as in the narratives of Abby Morrell and Martha Coston, each in its own way, the culture's essen-tialist understandings of women are problematized and rewritten in travels. Polyphonic selves move on stage, casting the culture's image of Woman in a new light, exposing it as but one of many possibilities available to women. As significant numbers of women traveled abroad and were trans-formed by contact with the world at large, writing travel-as-autobiography transformed notions of women's potential. Travel writing is itself the lib-erating cultural work of revising, complicating, and expanding the culture's idea of Woman, which in turn revises, complicates, and expands the cul-ture's writing of "home," the domain assigned to women. Women's travel writing takes on the cultural work of writing "home" and its politics from a global perspective, the subject of the next chapter.

Chapter Four

Political Occasions

The Public Voices of Margaret Fuller,
Mary Hannah Krout, Kate Field, Nellie Bly,
and Lilian Leland

I am developing a high opinion of myself as a traveler.
I consider that I excel most masculine travelers, for I
travel in all countries without arms to protect me, without Baedecker [sic] and Bradshaw to inform me, and
without boon companion or tobacco to console me.

—Lilian Leland, *Traveling Alone: A Woman's Journey*
around the World

In 1881, Madeleine Vinton Dahlgren published *South Sea Sketches: A Nar-*
rative, an account of life in Peru and Chile. Reminiscent of Abby Morrell
forty years earlier, Dahlgren traveled to South America in 1868 with her
husband, a naval admiral in charge of the South Pacific squadron. Thirteen years later, in 1881, war had "devastated unhappy Peru," she writes,
bringing it "to the verge of annihilation" and prompting Dahlgren to publish "a true picture of Peru before her disintegration." In keeping with
travel writing practice, the "true picture" contains many asides, including a twelve-page disquisition on the deceptively innocent sewing machine. The disquisition is unleashed by three sentences describing a seam-

stress, Beatrice, who sewed "neatly, diligently, and uninterruptedly, from 7 A.M. till 6 P.M." although the Dahlgrens encouraged her to "vary the daily routine,—with a little housework, for instance." [1] The sewing machine is, surprisingly, held responsible for such complex and extensive ills that Dahlgren's remarks warrant quoting at length. She is opposed to the sewing machine because, in addition to being "utterly destructive to the nervous organization of women,"

> it fosters a love of ornate and complex dress, and we have already a partial result in this direction, in the prevailing modes, which are elaborate beyond all previous fashions, involving millions of fine stitches, which could scarcely be attempted except by machinery, so that the employment of this mechanical aid vitiates good taste and stimulates luxury. . . . luxury is necessary in a despotism, not incompatible for an oligarchy, but destructive to a republic. We therefore, for reasons physiological, moral, aesthetic, and political, disapprove of the sewing-machine. Let us rather seek a return to the habits of elegant simplicity of our grandmothers, and not deprive our women of the patient, graceful, pliant needle, type of the feminine, for in its place we have set up an iron Moloch which will in time prostrate soul and body. (SSS, 145–46)

Dahlgren's sewing machine and seamstress are entangled in at least six political issues: the impact of technology, the rise of wealth, the state of the republic, American imperialism, the condition of the laboring and elite classes, and the role of women.

The heteroglossia of Dahlgren's text is typical of travel writing. For women travelers as for men, the travel book was a political occasion, an opportunity to merge literature and politics. This was not an uncommon practice for many nineteenth-century writers in various genres. Mary A. Dodge (Gail Hamilton) argued that suffrage was a "fine, delicate, [and] precise [instrument] as compared with the old-time method of the sword; but coarse, blundering, and insufficient when compared with the pen, the fireside, and the thousand subtile social influences, penetrating, pervasive, purifying." [2] As Joan D. Hedrick puts it, "the pen and the ballot were but different modes of enfranchising women's voices." [3] The travel genre and travel itself were particularly suited to such enfranchisement. The genre's hospitality to a variety of voices traditionally made it what Henry Adams called a sort of ragbag, full of scenery, psychology, history, literature, poetry, art, and anything else worth throwing in.[4] Travel writing worked for women as it worked for Mark Twain, who found in it a license to say what he pleased, without worry over consistency or transitions, and be paid for it.[5] Whether accounts are structured as chronicles of journeys or as memoirs, their looseness invites all comers; and the comers are legion because travel itself is a provocateur. It jostles the traveler out of her habitual round, confronts her with new data and visions of life, confirms or violates the expectations created by predecessor travelers and their accounts, and persuades her that she has something to say and an audience to say it to.

Consequently, travel writing is heuristic and paradoxical. It is preoccupied with topics provoked by, but other than, travel itself (such as sewing machines); and it is preoccupied with the home country under the stimulus of the difference of other lands and cultures that sets home in relief. "Home" and "abroad" are the polarities from which travelers construct meaning. Books of geographical and physical travel in foreign lands, therefore, are equally books of intellectual travel in the traveler's native land, confirming Margaret Fuller's observation that "the American in Europe, if a thinking mind, can only become more American."[6] The becoming "more American," in turn, means writing "home" from the vantage point of "abroad." Travel writing is about home in three of its dimensions: home as ideally imagined prior to travel, home as found to be in contrast with other lands, and home as it might be if women were allowed to implement the lessons of travel. Women's travel accounts write the nation, the United States, in the image of domestic and womanly interests.

The conventions of travel writing—attention to ethnographic and historical matters such as customs and manners, modes of transportation and dress, social class strata and artistic expression, all of them registers of difference and measures of stasis or progress—are lightning rods for ideology and politics. Missionary accounts are predictably ideological and political; they are exercises in colonizing and "othering," authorized by belief in the absolute truth of Christianity and the superiority of the United States, understood as the apex of civilization, Protestant and Anglo-Saxon. In her autobiographical narrative of her call to missionary work, *A Lone Woman in Africa* (1896), for example, Agnes McAllister, a Methodist missionary in charge of the Garaway Mission Station on the Kroo Coast of West Africa, laments "the darkness of the heathen mind . . . so incapable of comprehending the things of God at first" (LW, 217). She writes to encourage others to join the cultural work of the missions until the millennial light of Christianity is brought to the heathen. She places Liberia outside of civilization and conflates Christianity and civilization, observing that women may be more difficult to convert to Christianity than men because "they have been more confined to their homes and have not seen so much of the world, and do not realize the benefits of civilization" (LW, 232). Travel writing was a political enterprise for many travelers other than missionaries, however. Its political dimensions stood to thrive in a century marked by politically charged events (revolutions in Italy and France, the Franco-Prussian War, World War I); by evolutionary theory and millennialism; by didacticism and ideas of women as custodians of culture and morals; and by the movement of women into professions.

The profession that most affected women's writing of travel-as-politics was journalism. During the course of the century, the doors of professional journalism increasingly opened to women. While amateur women travelers wrote letters to friends at home and then gathered them for publication as books of travel, professional women journalists, the prototypes for Henry James's satirical portrait of Henrietta Stackpole in *The Portrait of a Lady* (1881), traveled and wrote letters to the world to be published in periodicals, and then gathered into books. Professional journalism increasingly became a mighty encouragement to travel writing, as we saw in chapter 1, and especially to the political commentary that both journalism and the travel genre invited. Ishbel Ross, historian of women in journalism, says that female journalists "could discuss anything from a bassinet to an audience with the Pope. They reported wars and changing social systems as well as Paris fashions or having tea with the Brownings."[7]

Journalism constituted a scene of writing that offered women alternative definitions of writing and writer. Journalism created space in which women could imagine themselves in a variety of writing roles: as reporters on topical matters, as muckrakers, as political analysts, and eventually as advice columnists. Or if a woman chose to seek entrée to genteel publications addressed to an elite or highbrow audience, she could adopt the persona of art critic. Whatever a woman's preferences might be, journalism offered her an unprecedented range of writing choices. Particularly after the Civil War, journalism set free a chorus of women's voices, giving them an arena in which to be heard. Women often paid dearly for a seat in that arena. As a newspaper woman put it in 1892, "Young ladies who dared to lift their heads in the sea of journalism immediately became the targets for the envenomed shafts of small men. Their abilities were questioned, their intentions suspected, their reputations bandied from sneering lip to careless tongue, and on every hand they were met with discouragements, until the waves of disappointment and all the billows of despair rolled over them."[8] Yet writers come to writing from somewhere, and the world of journalism, fraught with difficulties for women, was frequently the somewhere from which women's writing of travel-as-politics came.

The journalistic texts in which women transformed travel into politics did cultural work. Women travelers wrote from ideology, by which I mean "those unspoken collective understandings, conventions, stories, and cultural practices that uphold systems of social power."[9] Women travelers sought to shape the thinking of their compatriots, to bring it either into conformity with or deviation from collective understandings. Articulating political positions consonant with their systems of values, they sought to influence action on public issues, to write travel as an agent of nation building. At a time when women's public visibility and political activism were on the rise, women working in the travel genre became players in an important phenomenon: the swelling sound of women's voices in national and international politics. As print media multiplied and women made advances into the world of journalism, women pursued ever more vigorously an old branch of women's work, influencing public opinion—but now on a broader scale.

This chapter examines women's writing of travel-as-politics in the hands of travelers who, with one exception, were journalists who wrote articles for newspapers and then gathered them into books, as other travelers who were amateur writers gathered their letters home into books. All travel writing is to some extent political, as all of it is to some extent autobiographical, but I am interested here in travel writing that is designedly, self-consciously political. I call this deliberately political writing the act of writing travel-as-politics, and I have found that four forms of it predominate. In the first form, national politics is given pride of place. The rationale for this form of writing is millennialism and republicanism, the traveler exhorting her compatriots to political positions and acts. In the second form, the politics of gender joins that of statecraft. The culture's conversation about "the woman problem" is incorporated into a text aiming to influence domestic and foreign policy. In the third form of writing travel-as-politics, gender politics occupies center stage. The text aims to shape the culture's attitudes toward the sexes and, in this way, to expand the boundaries of domesticity. In the fourth form, a cousin to the third, the culture's attitudes toward the sexes circulate around a single issue: the politics of the independent woman traveling alone, a politics that incorporates several gender issues. The works of Margaret Fuller, Mary Hannah Krout, Kate Field, Elizabeth Cochrane Seaman (Nellie Bly), and Lilian Leland exemplify these emphases in women's writing of travel-as-politics.

I

Margaret Fuller's dispatches from Europe are representative instances of writing travel-as-politics, urging others toward public positions and acts. Fuller's travels in America were her entrée into European travel and travel writing. Impressed with Fuller's *Summer on the Lakes, in 1843* (1844), an account of her travels in the midwestern United States, Horace Greeley of the *New York Tribune* hired Fuller as his literary critic. Later, in August of 1846, he dispatched her to England and the Continent as his foreign correspondent. Between 23 August 1846 and 6 January 1850, Fuller sent thirty-seven articles to the *Tribune*. Omitting two of her letters to the *Tribune* (perhaps for fear their socialist content would incriminate Margaret), A. B. Fuller, Margaret's brother, published them as *At Home and Abroad; or, Things and Thoughts in America and Europe* (1856), after Margaret's death on 19 July 1850, in a shipwreck off Fire Island on her return from Italy.[10]

Fuller's letters record obligatory visits to obligatory sites in England, Scotland, France, and Italy as well as reports on revolutionary activity in Italy. Travel abroad offers Fuller the occasion to pursue her fundamental interest, cultural critique. Her travel letters are the public space in which she conducts it. Her first letter begins, conventionally, with the ocean passage to England, and her subsequent letters continue, conventionally, with talk about charitable institutions, industry and commerce, museums, encounters with famous people, and topical political and military events of the Italian Risorgimento, Fuller's primary interest. Politically engaged and mindful of her role as journalist for the *Tribune*, Fuller includes, in her travel letters, transcriptions of documents such as the address of "The Provisional Government of Milan to the German Nation" because such documents "may not in other form reach America" (SG, 198–99).

Fuller also uses ritual occasions of travel to expound on issues of her time. For example, she seizes a visit to one of "the stock lions" (Dr. Andrew Combe), a man she believes to have been treated shabbily by American publishers, to address the publisher of the *Tribune* (Horace Greeley) didactically, directly, and lengthily on a pressisng subject of the day: publishers as men of honor (SG, 66). Fuller can be accused of undisciplined writing, as the Transcendentalists often were; Thomas Carlyle, for example, had characterized Emerson's paragraphs as "canvas bags full of duckshot."[11] Yet the eclectic nature of Fuller's letters, like that of her American travels registered in *Summer on the Lakes*, is consistent with generic practice, and much of the "duckshot" in her "canvas bags" is political.

Fuller's letters spill over with subtexts, with the hum and buzz of the home culture that makes texts of travel interesting, the same hum and buzz that Fuller wishes to shape. She opens her account, a letter from "Ambleside, Westmoreland, 23d August, 1846," conventionally, rendering her passage on the steamer *Cambria* and simultaneously enlisting the culture's conversation about one of the most momentous technological innovations of the day, the steamship. Driven by an unspoken subtext, the suspicion that steamships promise more than they deliver, Fuller observes, "As many contradictory counsels were given us with regard to going in one of the steamers in preference to a sailing vessel, I will mention here, for the benefit of those who have not yet tried one, that he must be fastidious indeed who could complain of the *Cambria*. The advantage of a quick passage and certainty as to the time of arrival, would, with us, have outweighed many ills; but, apart from this, we found more space than we expected and as much as we needed for a very tolerable degree of convenience in our sleeping-rooms, better ventilation than Americans in general can be persuaded to accept, general cleanliness, and good attendance" (SG, 39). Later, en route to Lancaster by railroad, Fuller joins the culture's conversation about another technological marvel, the railroad. Having already labeled it a "convenient but most unprofitable and stupid way of travelling" (SG, 50), she launches yet another assault. Because she happily visits England "before the reign of the stage-coach is quite over," she rides "on the top of the coach, even one day of drenching rain, and enjoy[s] it highly." "Travelling by railroad is, in my opinion," she writes, "the most stupid process on earth; it is sleep without the refreshment of sleep, for the noise of the train makes it impossible either to read, talk, or sleep to advantage" (SG, 69).[12]

Although talk about the technology of travel is a staple of travel writing, modes of transportation and the paraphernalia that accompanies them, from station houses to timetables, are also iconic, consequently leading into political waters. Modes of transportation announce cultural similarities and differences at once threatening and exciting; and they mark progress and changing times. Predictably, then, they are magnets that attract the steel filings of ideology, as the tropes of Fuller's further observations about the railway reveal. "Among other signs of the times we bought Bradshaw's Railway Guide, and, opening it," Fuller writes, "found extracts from the writings of our countrymen, Elihu Burritt and Charles Sumner [reformers and abolitionists], on the subject of Peace, occupying a leading place in the 'Collect,' for the month, of this little hand-book, more likely, in an era like ours, to influence the conduct of the day than would an illuminated breviary" (SG, 43). The Bradshaw guide, a tool of travel already politicized by the extracts from Burritt and Sumner, is further charged politically by a metaphor delivering Fuller's judgment on her world. In Fuller's remarks, Bradshaw displaces prayer as the pilgrims' guide on the road to material salvation. In this, the third page of her first letter home, Fuller insinuates the critique in which she persists until the end.

Two other conventional travel topics, the vicissitudes of travel and anti-tourism, offer Fuller further occasions for public analysis of her world. Like other travelers, Fuller sees tourism as an evil. Upon first visiting Rome in May 1847, she laments, "The traveller passing along the beaten track, vetturinoed from inn to inn, ciceroned from gallery to gallery, thrown, through indolence, want of tact, or ignorance of the language, too much into the society of his compatriots, sees the least possible of the country; fortunately, it is impossible to avoid seeing a great deal" (SG, 131–32). Six months later, in December 1847, she compares her second visit to Rome with her first, when she "went through the painful process of sight-seeing, so unnatural everywhere, so counter to the healthful methods and true life of the mind. You rise in the morning," Fuller writes, "knowing there are a great number of objects worth knowing, which you may never have a chance to see again. You go every day, in all moods, under all circumstances; feeling, probably, in seeing them, the inadequacy of your preparation for understanding or duly receiving them. . . . you have no time; you are always wearied, body and mind, confused, dissipated, sad" (SG, 167–68).

The drawbacks of tourism provoke a peroration on the subject of tourists. Having commented that knowledge of Italy requires "long residence, and residence in the districts untouched by the scorch and dust of foreign invasion (the invasion of the *dilettanti* [tourists] I mean)," she mounts an attack on American and British travelers. She claims that Americans are unable to abandon themselves "to the spirit of the place" because "they retain too much of their English blood; and the travelling English, as a class, seem to [her] the most unseeing of all possible animals." While she "admired the English at home in their island," she writes, "they do not look well in Italy; they are not the figures for this landscape. I am indignant at the contempt they have presumed to express for the faults of our semi-barbarous state." "What is the vulgarity expressed in our tobacco-chewing, and way of eating eggs, compared to that which elbows the Greek marbles, guide-book in hand,—chatters and sneers through the Miserere of the Sistine Chapel, beneath the very glance of Michel Angelo's Sibyls,— praises St. Peter's as '*nice*,'—talks of '*managing*' the Colosseum by moonlight,—and snatches '*bits*' for a '*sketch*' from the sublime silence of the Campagna (SG, 132).

Joining the vigorous battle of the books in defense of the United States against attacks by British tourists (see chapter 2), Fuller reserves for Frances Trollope the most vitriolic statement in her dispatches: "Can any thing be more sadly expressive of times out of joint than the fact that Mrs. Trollope is a resident in Italy? Yes! She is fixed permanently in Florence, as I am told, pensioned at the rate of two thousand pounds a year to trail her slime over the fruit of Italy. She is here in Rome this winter, and after having violated the virgin beauty of America, will have for many a year her chance to sully the imperial matron of the civilized world" (SG, 171–72). Yet Fuller's antitourism is complex, both a defense of and a reprimand to her compatriots. Mrs. Trollope may be horrible, but Americans who "run about Rome for nine days, and then go away" are shallow. "No; Rome is not a nine-days wonder; and those who try to make it such lose the ideal Rome (if they ever had it), without gaining any notion of the real," says Fuller. "To those who travel, as they do everything else, only because others do, I do not speak; they are nothing. Nobody counts in the estimate of the human race who has not a character" (SG, 168).

Embedded in Fuller's conventional antitourism is, of course, a preoccupation with the homeland. She finds Americans wanting on many sides. She accuses them of being "exceedingly obtuse in organization,—a defect not uncommon among Americans" (SG, 148). Overhearing a remark by an American in Rome, she labels it "a specimen of the ignorance in which Americans usually remain during their flighty visits to these scenes, where they associate only with one another." She asserts that "the American, on many points, becomes more ignorant for coming abroad, because he attaches some value to his crude impressions and frequent blunders. It is not thus that any seed-corn can be gathered from foreign gardens." "Without modest scrutiny, patient study, and observation," she continues, "he spends his money and goes home, with a new coat perhaps, but a mind befooled rather than instructed" (SG, 258). The convention of antitourism seduces Fuller into more and more talk about America and Americans in letters presumably about Europe.

As the force of Fuller's prose suggests, these attacks are more than casual, more than conventional. Records of a family quarrel, they are energized by the ideology that constructs the meaning and importance of her observations: republicanism, nationalism, and ideas of America's nature and destiny. "With others in the Emersonian age," Margaret V. Allen writes, Fuller "was convinced that the nation had a particular destiny in history among all other nations of the world," and she infused her letters with a Protestant republican vision to such an extent that, as Nina Baym points out, "Horace Greeley received many complaints about her ultra-Protestantism."[13] Fuller brings into the nineteenth century the concept of America as the City on the Hill, the New Jerusalem, assigned the responsibility to lead humankind into a free, independent, republican future. A lengthy passage in a travel letter written at the end of 1847 carries the substance and spirit of Fuller's sense of American destiny.

Yet, O Eagle [America]! whose early flight showed this clear sight of the sun [the American revolution and the Declaration of Independence], how often dost thou near the ground, how show the vulture in these later days! Thou wert to be the advance-guard of humanity, the herald of all progress; how often hast thou betrayed this high commission! Fain would the tongue in clear, triumphant accents draw example from thy story, to encourage the hearts of those who almost faint and die beneath the old oppressions. But we must stammer and blush when we speak of many things. I take pride here, that I can really say the liberty of the press works well, and that checks and balances are found naturally which suffice to its government. I can say that the minds of our people are alert, and that talent has a free chance to rise. This is much. But dare I further say that political ambition is not as darkly sullied as in other countries? Dare I say that men of most influence in political life are those who represent most virtue, or even intellectual power? Is it easy to find names in that career of which I can speak with enthusiasm? Must I not confess to a boundless lust of gain in my country? Must I not concede the weakest vanity, which bristles and blusters at each foolish taunt of the foreign press, and admit that the men who make these undignified rejoinders seek and find popularity so? . . . Can I say our social laws are generally better, or show a nobler insight into the wants of man and woman? I do, indeed, say what I believe, that voluntary association for improvement in these particulars will be the grand means for my nation to grow, and give a nobler harmony to the coming age. But it is only of a small minority that I can say they as yet seriously take to heart these things; that they earnestly meditate on what is wanted for their country, for mankind,— for our cause is indeed the cause of all mankind at present. (SG, 164–65)

Ideologies of republicanism, nationalism, and millennialism ground her conviction that the American cause "is indeed the cause of all mankind." America's destiny makes the meaning and importance of conditions in Europe. In Fuller's prose as in that of many other travelers, America, former colony of Britain, is now the center around which Europe and the whole of humankind revolve. Amerocentrism governs.

Sounding the trumpet and assuming a prophetic role, she wraps events in Italy in republican sympathies. "From the people themselves the help must come, and not from princes; in the new state of things, there will be none but natural princes, great men," Fuller asserts (SG, 156). Tied to Italy ideologically, she stays on despite the urging of friends[14] who "talk of our country as the land of the future." Yet according to Fuller, the spirit that made it so is more alive in Italy than in America.[15]

> My country is at present spoiled by prosperity, stupid with the lust of gain, soiled by crime in its willing perpetuation of slavery, shamed by an unjust war, noble sentiment much forgotten even by individuals, the aims of politicians selfish or petty, the literature frivolous and venal. In Europe, amid the teaching of adversity, a nobler spirit is struggling,—a spirit which cheers and animates mine. I hear earnest words of pure faith and love. I see deeds of brotherhood. This is what makes *my* America. I do not deeply distrust my country. She is not dead, but in my time she sleepeth, and the spirit of our fathers flames no more, but lies hid beneath the ashes. It will not be so long; bodies cannot live when the soul gets too overgrown with gluttony and falsehood. But it is not the making a President out of the Mexican war that would make me wish to come back. Here things are before my eyes worth recording, and, if I cannot help this work, I would gladly be its historian. (SG, 230)

Exhorting America to return to her high calling, to take her place once again as the City on the Hill, she calls for action: "Send, dear America! to thy ambassadors a talisman precious beyond all that boasted gold of California. Let it loose his tongue to cry, 'Long live the Republic, and may God bless the cause of the people, the brotherhood of nations and of men,— the equality of rights for all.' *Viva America!*" (SG, 283–84). Furthermore, she nominates as ambassador "one that has experience of foreign life," a man with "knowledge and views which extend beyond the cause of party politics in the United States . . . a man of unity in principles, but capable of understanding variety in forms . . . a man capable to prize the luxury of living in, or knowing Rome" (SG, 245). Margaret Fuller is herself the person who could prize Rome and should be named ambassador. But the gender politics of her era forbids it. She poignantly writes that "another century, and I might ask to be made Ambassador myself ('tis true, like other Ambassadors, I would employ clerks to do the most of the duty), but woman's day has not come yet" (SG, 245).

Observations made while abroad, grounded in republican, nationalist, and millennialist ideology, occasion political talk, the fundamental interest of the text. The text of foreign travel is transformed into a vehicle for American interests. The conventions of the travel genre create the space into which Fuller steps, seeking to shape the mind of America. She recognized the political nature of her dispatches; she names her writing a "political letter" (SG, 186). Nor was a political undertaking new to her. On the contrary, the feminism that inspired Fuller's *Woman in the Nineteenth Century* taught Fuller the process of political analysis and action that eventually carried her into other struggles. Feminism was, Belle Gale Chevigny explains, "an early exercise in social criticism which led her to live out a much more comprehensive critique of American values." [16] That critique found its ultimate home in Margaret Fuller's dispatches from Italy.

II

One of the first American foreign correspondents of either sex, Margaret Fuller stands at the head of what was to become a line of American female journalists who, having traveled to various parts of the world on assignment, published their findings in articles and books. Nancy Johnson, for example, toured Europe in 1857 and sent her impressions to the *New York Times*; and Anna Benjamin served as a professional war correspondent for *Leslie's Illustrated* during the Spanish-American War of 1898. The work of Mary Hannah Krout (1857–1927) makes common cause with such journalists as these. Having begun her career in 1872 as a school teacher, Krout later became a journalist. She started in 1881 as associate editor of the Crawfordsville, Indiana, *Journal*, and a year later became the editor of the Terre Haute *Express*. From there she became a staff correspondent for the Chicago *Inter Ocean*, reporting from New Zealand and Australia in 1884; Hawaii in 1893 and 1894; and London from 1895 to 1898. Between 1899 and 1900, she wrote letters to the *New York Tribune* from China. In 1898, she published *Hawaii and a Revolution: The Personal Experiences of a Correspondent in the Sandwich Islands during the Crisis of 1893 and Subsequently*. The book was the product of two visits to Hawaii, one in 1892 and one in 1894. Political events dictated Krout's "thousands of miles of travel by land and sea, hours and days and weeks of arduous and responsible toil, conferences with personages in exalted places, interviews with heads of governments." [17] Drawn to Hawaii by an impending "revolution, with a demand for annexation to the United States," she wants "to witness the actual making of history, the evolution of a people from a semi-barbarous monarchy to a state of intelligent and rational self-government" (HR, 33–34).

As her title promises, *Hawaii and a Revolution* delivers, in the mode of Margaret Fuller, a combination of travel and politics. But whereas gender was incidental and references to it occasional in Fuller's dispatches, Krout's use of gender is crucial. Gender supplies both narrative interest and one of the book's major subjects, gender politics. Narratives of adventure are rendered more adventurous by dint of the traveler's gender, enlivening her entanglements in international politics. The adventure, in turn, and the feats of the female traveler serve to discredit a [dominant] male politics of gender that infects the marketplace: the assignment of journalism's most challenging tasks to men because of women's presumed cowardliness and timidity. Disproving this presumption, Krout's undertaking and her account of it do cultural work. They prove what a female journalist can accomplish.

In the hoary tradition of the quest, Krout must face obstacles and a serial ordeal as she seeks the grail, an assignment in Hawaii. She sprained her ankle, an event that threatened to turn "bon voyage" into "non voyage" (HR, 48). Next, she misplaced her tickets (HR, 60). Finally she sets out: "The steam rushed into the air-brakes with a hiss, the wheels revolved, and we moved slowly out of the great North-Western station. I sat up in my berth, drew back the blind, and looked out as the blue and green signal lights went by. I then said, as solemnly and as feelingly as if I were saying a prayer: '*I—am—really—off—at—last!*'" (HR, 63). Even then, she must compensate for her injured ankle while in Hawaii, and she must tolerate intense heat, flies, worrisome natives, and nasty odors. Yet she proves herself the consummate traveler: "All these were the sort of ills that the experienced traveller learns to accept as a matter of course, a part of the price one must pay for seeing the Kingdoms of this world and the glory of them" (HR, 280).

Two agendas inform Krout's journey and render it important, dramatic, and different. The first is the matter of the annexation of Hawaii, a political initiative sanctioned by an ideology not unlike the millennialism and republicanism of Margaret Fuller. Like Fuller, Krout assumes that history is evolutionary. Journalistic-ethnographic observation and reports on the government of Hawaii, the actions of the United States, the makeup of the population, and the manners, mores, and ancient customs of the people bespeak the need for, indeed the inevitability of, progress. Krout's itinerary from Honolulu to Hilo, from Molokai to Kileauea, from the home of

Kaiulani to King Kalakaua's palace provides the structure on which she hangs facts that point to imperialist conclusions. She labels "the cry of theorists, 'Hawaii for Hawaiians,'" as "sentimentality." Either the Islands will be left "in that state of nature when the most cruel rites of paganism prevailed," or "the civilisation ordained and perpetuated by the so-called missionary element" will be accepted (HR, 318).

> This is the sum and the substance of the whole situation; and if America is not ready and willing to assume the responsibility, England may be induced to accept it, and, before her, Japan, who has already upon Hawaiian soil a representation of over twenty-five thousand souls. No matter what the outcome may be, the Hawaiian is a fading race, with remnants of heathen customs still hampering it, confronted by the stronger and the newer, trained in government and refined, or at any rate strengthened, by civilisation . . . events move on irresistibly through that transition which evolves, at last, higher and better conditions. It is the apparent triumph of the strong over the weak; it is, in reality, the natural dissolution of that which has served its time. It seems a hard and pitiless doctrine, but it is the unvarying law of nature and of history. (HR, 321)

The United States, of course, should be "ready and willing to assume the responsibility" and cooperate in the work of "the unvarying law of nature and of history."

Krout's second agenda item is gender. In addition to observing history in the making, Krout wishes to show her stuff as a female journalist. "With the natural instinct of a 'newspaper woman,'" Krout writes, she sought "the professional opportunity to be the one special correspondent in the field": "special" because singled out from others for the assignment; and "special" because she is a *female* correspondent (HR, 33). Krout peppers her text with asides that insistently foreground the matter of gender. Asked satirically if anyone is interested in Hawaiian politics, and replying that "it is a matter of international politics," she continues: "And as I write these words, a woman's spiteful sense of triumph comes over me when I think how time obligingly verified that rash assertion" (HR, 37). Visiting the queen, she reports that "being women, we also very naturally talked of dress" (HR, 193). Comparing home with abroad, she speaks out on gendered matters. Riding side-saddle, for example, "is considered the fit and proper thing for women," she comments, enlisting the vehicle convention of travel writing. But "on seeing the security and ease with which these Hawaiian women sit in their saddles," she writes, "one wonders that there ever could have been any prejudice against women riding in a manner that, like most other comfortable and sensible fashions, has been monopolised by men" (HR, 258).

It is professional issues, however, that give Krout's gender agenda its particular importance. The (male) politics of gender would disqualify women from the profession of journalism at its most exciting. Recounting her difficulties as she angles for the assignment to report on imminent revolution in Hawaii, Krout says, "There dwells in the soul of every man living—and from this category not one is exempted—a fixed belief, confessed or unacknowledged, that political problems are wholly beyond the comprehension of the feminine intelligence. It is not in the least worth one's while to combat this inherent and inherited prejudice. All that the feminine intelligence can do," she continues, "is to show itself capable of grappling with political questions and situations, and it will then be rewarded with a special verdict that one exceptional success simply proves the rule of unalterable incapacity" (HR, 36).

Furthermore, Krout incorporates in her text the (male) politics of gender that denies womanliness to the professional woman, the "New Woman" sweeping over the land in the 1890s. Krout maintains that women are able to be both professional and womanly. Having overcome serious obstacles and about to depart for Hawaii, "I settled down," she explains, "to enjoy that ancient sedative to overstrung feminine nerves, a good cry, and felt immensely relieved. A prospective war correspondent in tears is not a spectacle to be seen every day; but it must be edifying, not to say improving, when it does come within the range of ordinary vision. It simply proves that, even though the war correspondent be a woman, she does not cease therefore to be feminine and human" (HR, 49).[18] In the 1890s, Krout finds herself in the same bind as women between 1820 and 1870, for whom the stress of the times, according to Nina Baym, was "on the preservation of gender identity in spite of the forces on women making for individuation." Women's greatest challenge was not success in becoming "individuals," Baym finds, but, rather, success "in remaining 'women'" as they became "individuals."[19] Krout insists on what many in her culture took to be oxymoronic: a womanly professionalism.

In her quest for light on international politics, the territory she would explore, Krout becomes the hero of her text in two ways. She shows her ability to withstand the discomforts and ordeals that the "travail" of travel visits on all travelers; and she withstands the "travail" of a gender ideology that would restrict her movements, count her incompetent and cowardly, and deny her femininity if she violates its norms. Krout departs twice over from the beaten track, once as a woman and again as a woman journalist. She writes a doubled travel-as-politics.

III

Margaret Fuller used the dispensations of the travel genre to influence national politics, and Mary Krout expanded the agenda to include the politics of gender. Kate Field (Mary Katherine Keemle Field, 1838–1896) concentrated on gender issues in her accounts of travel. A woman who was torn between professional ambitions and the culture's definitions of the womanly, as I have outlined in chapter 1, Field nevertheless arranged with the Boston *Courier* to write about her Florentine days when she traveled to Europe in 1859 to study music and drama. All of her subsequent travels were publishing expeditions, either on the lecture circuit or in newspapers or books. In 1871 she traveled to England and the Continent for the *New York Tribune*; in 1873 she traveled again in England; and in the 1880s she passed two summers in Europe (in addition to travels in the United States and Alaska). A widely known journalist, Field published two books of travel to Europe: *Hap-Hazard* (1873) and *Ten Days in Spain* (1875). She died in Hawaii in 1896, on yet another writing expedition.[20]

Hap-Hazard is a two-part collection of articles "reproduced (with revisions)" from *Every Saturday*, the *New York Tribune*, and the *American Register of Paris*. Part I, "Leaves from a Lecturer's Notebook," is a record of Field's ruminations as she traveled in the United States on a lecture tour, traveling by train and overnighting in boarding houses. "Leaves from a Lecturer's Notebook" shows that, like Margaret Fuller's earlier *Summer on the Lakes*, writing one's travels in the United States, like writing one's travels abroad, was a political act. Part II, "Americans Abroad," is occasioned by Field's travels to London, Ems, and Paris. Field ritualistically proclaims in her preface that "the contents of this volume lay no claim to profundity.

If their perusal entertains the American at home, and leads the American abroad to commit one folly the less, my highest ambition will be realized." In a book devoted to cultural critique, satirically delivered in chapters such as "Republicanism in England" and "The Divine Right of Kings, and Kingsley," Field's recurring issue is gender and its politics. Gender serves as a heuristic that produces and energizes *Hap-Hazard*. Opening, closing, and punctuating Field's text, "the woman question" binds it together and transforms it from a book of travels into a reflection on gender and the superior position of women in the United States.

Hap-Hazard is a casebook of the discourses of gender and difference that circulated in Kate Field's America, from women's work to woman suffrage. In a chapter called "Travelling Companions," Field transcribes the voices of travelers expounding on "the woman problem," particularly woman's work and sphere. Field is accosted by a "severe woman in spectacles" who thinks women should not be lecturers, and another who dislikes women who write theater reviews and travel out of curiosity rather than necessity.[21] Driving fast horses and being "quite likely to smoke" are equated with frivolous writing and travel, and the lot is counted as "very unfeminine" (HH, 41). Field is approached, as well, by a man who thinks women are too often idle. His solution is to allow them to live wherever there is work, even if far from home. Rather than staying in Massachusetts to "live and die old maids," he asserts, "they ought to leave home. . . . There's no more reason why women should stick in one place than men." His reasons, however, are pragmatic rather than theoretical; economics, not equal rights, is his issue. "I believe in work for everybody," he says. "These dolls of girls that do nothing, what do they amount to? They ain't worth their feed. They're just about as much use in the world as poodles, and I'd enough sight rather board a poodle, for he costs less." As if to moderate his statement, he then introduces patriotism into his argument. "I tell you society is all wrong," he sermonizes, "and we've got to have a revolution if we want republican institutions to last. We've got rid of slavery, and now we must get rid of all these confounded notions about what makes ladies and gentlemen. I want to see full-length men and women, *I* do" (HH, 61–62). Putatively transcribing this dialogue, Field inserts into her text a call for a second American revolution to fulfill the promise of the republic, a break for women's liberation from their colonial status.

Field juxtaposes these remarks with those of another man, big-hearted, "great, strong," and "externally rough," who asserts that women are already "worked to death"—and therefore should not be granted suffrage. "The Lord never intended they should have so much put upon them," he declares, because "men are stronger, and ought to take care of them." His companion replies that voting won't increase women's cares, and, moreover, it will make women "think more," an activity that is "good for them." Taking up arguments against suffrage in order to discredit them, he points out that "women are not obliged to hold office if they don't want to"; that voting requires less time than "making a call and serving up a dish of gossip." "This woman's suffrage has got to come," he proclaims, "and it's going to give women the same rights we have, and it isn't going to make them less women either. That's what you're all afraid of." Encoding the incivility that characterized debates about "the woman problem" in her time, Field adds that "nobody called anybody 'unwomanly,' or 'scoundrel,' or 'fool,' or 'shrieking sisterhood,' which last is the most recent pet name of derision" (HH, 58–59).

Reminiscent of Mary Krout's insights, the operative clause in this dialogue on suffrage is "it isn't going to make them less women either," a response to the here unspoken but common notion that a widened sphere of activity unsexes women. In the minds of many Americans, the likes of female lecturers, journalists, travelers, and others who have moved furthest into the public domain, blurring the line between male and female spheres, are at greatest risk of losing their womanliness. Kate Field argues for the expansion of woman's sphere on grounds that reach back to the first half of the century. She sees woman as the transcendent measure and ultimate guarantor of American superiority and human progress. "The greatest proof of our [American] superiority," she writes, "is that the roughest man will not be lacking in the greatest essential of civilization,—respect for women" (HH, 177). In an arresting extension of Tocqueville's reading of the American woman, and incorporating a subtext of millennialism and nineteenth-century belief in progress, Field replaces the patriarchs and Brother Jonathan, precursor to Uncle Sam, with women in the march of civilization. Field declares, "I have been persuaded that 'the coming woman,' like Brother Jonathan, will 'lick all creation'" (HH, 76). This is why women's roles, woman suffrage, and their relationship to womanliness are urgent issues. Whereas Mary Krout insisted on the compatibility of womanliness and professions, Kate Field ties this compatibility to woman's salvific role. If the American woman stands at the apex of Western civilization, then certainly the "woman" must be left in American women.

Field joins Margaret Fuller and the collective voice of various women's associations in urging women to take their safety into their own hands, even if it requires the use of force. Carroll Smith-Rosenberg explains that, in attacking the double standard and male sexual license, women's reform societies in Victorian America characterized men as "destroyers of female innocence and happiness." Men were beasts, and "no man was above suspicion." Women were encouraged to take their sexual integrity into their own hands rather than relying on males for protection.[22] In 1849, Margaret Fuller had raged in a travel letter against the brutality of the drunken male. "Enough! if I felt these things in privileged America, the cries of mothers and wives beaten at night by sons and husbands for their diversion after drinking, as I have repeatedly heard them these past months," she writes, "the excuse for falsehood, 'I *dare not* tell my husband, he would be ready to kill me,' have sharpened my perception as to the ills of Woman's condition and remedies that must be applied" (SG, 246). Field joins Fuller, associating "that good time," marked by women's "licking of creation" with women's self-defense. She writes that

> woman will have her rights because she will have her muscle. Then, if there are murders and playful beatings between husbands and wives, the wives will enjoy all the glory of crime. What an outlook! And what a sublime consolation to the present enfeebled race of wives that are having their throats cut and their eyes carved out merely because their biceps have not gone into training! Barnum's female gymnast is an example to her sex. What woman has done woman may do again. Mothers, train up your daughters in the way they should fight, and when they are married they will not depart this life. God is on the side of the stoutest muscle as well as of the heaviest battalions. It is perfectly useless to talk about the equality of the sexes as long as a man can strangle his own mother-in-law. (HH, 76–77)

Hap-Hazard does the cultural work of addressing the anxieties attendant to "the woman question," undermining their logic, allaying the public's fears, and promulgating strategies to bring about a new order, to write "home" in new ways.

Observations gathered while traveling in Europe drive home to Field— and to those to whom she playfully (and with historical accuracy) dedicates her book, "young women in search of careers or titled husbands"—the superiority of the American woman and her salvific role. Leaving American shores in *Hap-Hazard*, Field travels to England and makes the ritual visit to the House of Commons, using this as yet another occasion to seize the conventions of travel writing in the interests of gender politics. When a genial M.P. invites her "to take the Speaker's chair, which, though rather hard to sit on, is very becoming," traveler Field observes that "dignity and authority steal o'er me" (HH, 125). As the chair makes the Speaker, so it could make a Speaker of a woman as well. In the coming race, she writes, "Dame Britannia will preside with far more grace" and, moreover, "will not spoil her good looks by donning a black gown and a dreadful big wig, whereby hangs a tail" (HH, 125). Dame Britannia will be much more sensible about both governance and attire than men.

Envisioning an arena far larger than the House of Commons, Field would also correct the misrepresentation and supplement the lack of women in the written record that is called History.[23] If women are allowed at all into the realms of government and History, Field notes, it is only in the margins of the text. She proceeds to the Ladies' Gallery of the House of Commons, the observation post allocated to women and dreadfully inadequate even by the most patriarchal standards. Having stood outside a locked door for no less than a half hour, the women then face "exasperation . . . added to fatigue." The Ladies' Gallery "is nothing more nor less than a box," a "coop" fronted by "a heavy iron grille, so that I soon feel as if I were shut up in prison for some unknown crime. I can flatten my nose against the bars and see without being seen,—by which arrangement the intellect of mighty man is not distracted by the presence of lovely women." Yet the gallery of the House of Lords is open. This "puzzles the understanding," she writes. "Are strangers to conclude that the Lords can bear the feminine ordeal, because they have no brains to be distracted?" (HH, 126).

Social as well as political rituals come under Field's scrutiny. The male rituals of the toast to "the ladies" and the after-dinner speech draw her fire. Twenty years before Field traveled to England, Harriet Beecher Stowe had traveled there at the invitation of abolitionist societies. Toasts and after-dinner speeches in her honor were delivered by the score and responded to by her husband because women were not allowed to speak in public. Harriet Beecher Stowe sat by while Calvin Stowe addressed the crowds gathered explicitly to celebrate Harriet's accomplishments.[24] Twenty years later, Field seizes an after-dinner speech and the conventions of travel writing to do political work on an especially opportune occasion, the festival of the London Hospital for throat diseases, a celebration of the gift of speech, held in the Willis's Rooms in London in May 1872.

Field heaps up ironies in her disquisition upon this occasion. She declares that, although she had at first declined to return thanks for a toast because she had never done such a thing and thought she never could, she reconsidered and concluded that "as this is the age of revolution, as humanity is stronger than caste or sex, as Royalty shakes hands with Democracy by acknowledging allegiance to the republic of letters, I asked myself why, after all, women should not be heard as well as seen at public dinners" (HH, 166). Next, this dextrous rhetorician satirically anticipates objections, historical and otherwise, in a passage that warrants quoting at length.

> It is true that an august body of men—of course I can mean none other than the House of Commons—quotes St. Paul as though saints were their perennial guides, philosophers, and friends; and declares that women should keep silence, conveniently forgetting that St. Paul is addressing the women of Corinth, according to the law of A.D. 59; that elsewhere he contradicts himself; and that the proper reading is "Let your women keep silence in the churches." If honorable M.P.'s persist in proving their intimate acquaintance with Scripture by misquoting it when they desire to keep lovely woman in her proper sphere, they should first descry strangers in the ladies' gallery, and order their summary ejection. But now, although at this post-prandial hour we are all supposed to be incapable of reasoning, let us try to be logical. Women sing in public, act in public, read in public; why, then, should they not speak? Why should it be considered feminine for a woman to interpret Shakespeare's ideas, and unfeminine to interpret her own,—provided she has any? It seems to me that if public speaking be tolerated at all,—which is doubtful, especially at dinners,—it should be from the lips of women, and for this reason. Ever since chaos, men have been talking. For six thousand years, at least, they have, to use an Americanism, "stumped" creation, and impressed the world with their views on all subjects, but as there is as much sex in mind as there is in matter, we have seen everything in profile. (HH, 167–68)

In a characteristically clever deconstruction of the logic of arguments against woman's participation in various activities, Field next enlists the idea of difference, the rationale usually invoked to exclude women from public speaking, and turns it on its head, proving the unconventional proposition that women should speak in public precisely *because* of their difference from men. "Women are born more graceful; they have the great gift of beauty and the great privilege of dress" that makes them gratifying "to the eye, and the majority of people hear with their eyes," Field claims. More impulsive, sympathetic, and persuasive, "they are more likely to touch the heart; and when you have made an audience feel, half the battle is won." Constructing a long, satirical disquisition about why she would "hail public speaking as a blessing in disguise" if she were a man, she enlists Eve, "the original orator"; Miriam, "among the first to prophesy"; Deborah, "elevated to the dignity of judge of Israel"; Greek oracles that "proceeded from the lips of women"; Socrates, who "learned rhetoric from Aspasia"; and the Gracchi, who "owed their eloquence" to their mother, Cornelia. As modern examples, Field cites "six Englishwomen—the majority of them young, and two of them very pretty," who "speak at Hanover Square Rooms in a manner that might be imitated with advantage by the gentlemen in the House of Commons, who recently referred to them as creatures of sentiment" (HH, 168–69). Field wraps up this epic catalog of weapons that equip women for public speaking by returning to her starting point, the occasion of the festival of the London Hospital for throat diseases. "It is useless to talk of the equality of the sexes," she concludes, "so long as men sit down to turtle soup in one room, and women stand up to tea and sandwiches in another, waiting with becoming humility for admission to the Barmecide [illusory] feast of reason and flow of soul." Women, after all, "are as effective in opening the purses as they are in touching the hearts of their lay brothers" (HH, 170).[25]

Having astutely opened her book with material on the situation of the woman in America, creating an egalitarian and republican predisposition that throws Europe in the shade, Field concludes her book of reflections occasioned by travel with a chapter entitled "European *versus* American Women." She reports that in Germany, where women are held to be inferior, they carry the heaviest loads or are "yoked with dogs or cows"; in France, "though women are the more industrious half of the population

[and] as a rule, are cleverer than the men [and] show the greater aptitude in managing business, men speak of them lightly, and see in them probable or possible *filles de joie.*" The regeneration of France, Field maintains, will be accompanied by "a proper appreciation of women," with the political result that "when women are strong enough to dictate terms, Americans will readily sympathize with this same abused France" (HH, 247–48). Operating as a one-woman Chamber of Commerce, Field draws from her observations the conclusion that "Europe is the place to visit" and "America is the place to live and work." The United States is "the widest field for activity and intelligence" because "there you breathe the purest air, there you are least trammelled by conventionalities, there you have the fairest chance of being a whole man, and, yet more, a whole woman." This thought sends Field off, heuristically, into reflections on her foremothers to whom she "cannot be too grateful," those "stern Puritans" who were remarkably courageous and had a profound effect on civilization. The duchess and its equivalent, "an American woman of wealth and position," seem to have everything, Field writes. But in Europe, "woman as woman is not respected." If one is a *grande dame*, she is "courted, admired, treated with deference." Yet on the Continent, woman is "an object of insulting interest, a creature whom no man is bound to respect" (HH, 246–47).

Because the superiority of the United States is in her women, and because the future of women is the world's best chance, Kate Field colonizes the terrain of Europe and of the travel book to speak for women's issues. In a class-ridden statement that, masking class in gender, renders women of the working class invisible, Field asserts, "The great comfort of America is that a woman is not always made to feel her sex. She really is allowed to exist as a human being, not, unfortunately, with the liberty of a man, but still with so much more than elsewhere as by comparison to be free" (HH, 248). Kate Field is a stellar instance of travel's ability to recuperate for the domestic status quo the restlessness of the Victorian woman. Having complained, as we have seen in chapter 1, of women's lot—indoor life, sewing, and babies—Field nevertheless judges, upon traveling abroad, that the half loaf of latitude granted U. S. women is better than none.[26] Travel moderates her critique of "home" as written.

A systematic excursion into the discourses of difference, *Hap-Hazard* is anything but haphazard. Travel occasions the text, but gender issues are its subject. Europe and America are merely excuses to make the real journey of the book, travels into the politics of gender as they operate on the homefront.

IV

As the travel accounts of both Kate Field and Mary Krout pursue gender politics and international politics, they touch lightly on the politics of the lone woman traveler. Kate Field insists that "women, old and young, ugly and handsome, can travel alone from one end of this great country to the other, receiving only such attention as is acceptable. Having journeyed up and down the land to the extent of twenty thousand miles, I am persuaded that a woman can be anywhere and do anything, provided she conducts herself properly" (HH, 11). Mary Krout insists that "if the generality of [women] only knew how safe are the high roads and even the uninhabited places of the world, and how purely imaginary are the dangers that seem to threaten when one leaves the beaten track, there would be a hundred explorers like Mrs. Bishop and Miss Kingsley where there is one to-day" (HR, 38–39). In asides such as these, Field and Krout extend and gender the meaning of "the beaten track." Ordinarily understood as the province of the guidebook from which travelers seek to escape, "the beaten track" is made to signify the domestic track from which the solo female traveler departs, putting herself, her reputation, and her sexual integrity at risk. The lone female traveler sometimes signifies marital status (unmarried), sometimes traveling status (either by herself or with other women, which amounts to the same thing), or both. A major player in the game of gender politics, the figure of the "woman alone" in whatever incarnation became more than a passing point of reference, as in the work of Krout and Field. She became a point around which women travelers organized entire accounts of travel; and she became a point around which entrepreneurs marketed accounts of travel. The politics of gender, that is, was a two-way street. Women travelers used the figure of the solo female traveler in the interests of a woman's agenda, while business used the same figure in the interests of profits, creating the fourth variety of writing travel-as-politics: the politics of the lone woman traveler.

The culture's conversation about the lone woman traveler did not, of course, come from nowhere. Interest in lone female travelers was fueled by the exploits of British women travelers such as Isabella Bird, Marianne North, Mary Kingsley, Gertrude Bell, Mary Gaunt, and Ella Christie.[27] Changes in American life fed it as well. Following the Civil War, there were greater numbers of single women in the United States than ever before.[28] Moreover, the lone woman traveler and all women travelers emerged simultaneously with issues of women and public space. As the historian Glenna Matthews has found, the advent of the department store in antebellum America, bringing female shoppers into public streets, and the incursions of women into the workplace, bringing women into new contact with males in the Gilded Age, fueled the discourses of femininity and provoked charges of female impropriety. They also challenged male possession of public space.[29] If a woman alone on a shopping expedition was subject to comment, small wonder that the lone female traveler was a subject of interest, prurient and otherwise. Moreover, more women were traveling solo, prompting Mary Cadwalader Jones, in her book of travel conduct entitled *European Travel for Women* (1900), to point to the real problem: women often travel "in parties which do not include a man."

Perhaps the largest and most threatening specter evoked by the lone female traveler, however, is female virtue and its vulnerability, riddled with class and status implications. We recall from chapter 1 that "endangered" women of the middle classes and above—the traveling classes—were conventionally accompanied and protected in public by men, while "dangerous" women of the lower classes menacingly moved about independently. Absent the male, how is one to read and classify a woman in public? The lone woman traveler stood to be misread, to be declassified and reclassified before the eyes of the world. She risked her class status when she assumed the "unprotected" position of women of the lower classes. The class status ascribed to travel is destabilized by the figure of the solitary female traveler. Her chastity, her possession by one man alone, is also cast into doubt. Social class and sexual conduct echo one another.

The lone female traveler is rendered even more problematic by the mores peculiar to the American girl, with her "frank, level gaze with which . . . not thinking any evil, [she] meets the eyes of men who are strangers to her," as Mary Cadwalader Jones puts it.[30] Echoing James's *Daisy Miller*, expressions of concern for the unchaperoned woman refer to the vulnerability of her reputation (and that of the husband or father or brother responsible for her) and the vulnerability of her body. When a woman is alone, conduct is her only protection, as is clear in Jones's remarks: "Of late years manners have everywhere become so much more democratic that it is not now so unusual as it used to be to see young girls going about alone or together, and, as a general rule, if a woman will dress quietly, walk quickly, and look ahead of her, she will not be molested; but if one who is strikingly pretty and showily dressed saunters slowly along," Jones continues, "looking into shop windows and also staring at the passers-by, she will very likely be followed by some man who is willing to take the chance of possible amusement; nor is he altogether to blame, because the nice women whom he has known have not laid themselves open to such misunderstanding."[31] Better to enlist the services of Thomas Cook.

Mary Cadwalader Jones addressed an audience of privileged women, many of whom traveled abroad while their husbands traveled to Wall Street to clip coupons. Her text assumes class status, whereas other texts sometimes announce and glory in class status and link it to chastity. In his preface to Mary E. Hitchcock's *Two Women in the Klondike*, for example, Elisha Dyer finds the exploits recounted in the book remarkable because "the two travellers were born and reared in luxury and refinement." Their daily life in Alaska, therefore, is "not only a tribute to their own perseverance and determination," according to Dyer, "but to the character of intelligent and fearless Anglo-Saxon women, who, among all sorts and conditions of men, never fail to secure protection and respect."[32]

When the matter of the lone woman and her vulnerability joins the economics of travel, the unprotected female takes on considerable interest for ideological and other reasons. The vulnerable female was a boon, as we have seen, to the ubiquitous Thomas Cook and the touring industry, ensconced in unlikely places all over the globe, including Jaffa. Mary Thorn Carpenter found him near the Jerusalem Hotel, where "the sun strikes a more familiar sign in clear and distinct letters, 'Cook and Son,'" she writes, finding the sign as absurd as the transplanted New England cottages nearby.[33] Joining the touring industry, the publishing industry stood ready to capitalize on interest in the lone woman. Such novels as William Dean Howells's *Dr. Breen's Practice* (1881), Elizabeth Stuart Phelps's

The Silent Partner (1871) and *Dr. Zay* (1882), and Henry James's *The Bostonians* (1886) emerged in a market interested in the single woman (by definition a problem). The market was prepared long since by a literature of seduction that began, on the American side, with captivity narratives and Susanna Rowson's *Charlotte Temple* (1791) and, on the British side as it invaded the United States, with such novels as Samuel Richardson's *Clarissa Harlowe* (1747–48). Predictably, the travel account of a solitary woman traveler made an attractive commodity. Wittingly or not, and virtually always corseted by discursive restraints, such an account tapped into interest, perhaps prurient or perhaps merely curious, in female sexual integrity. The defense of woman's sexual integrity calls, in turn, for chivalry: male action presumably undertaken on woman's behalf but in fact undertaken on man's behalf, to prove his masculinity. Thus the masculine role is propped up at the moment it is seriously called into question by independent female travel.

The last quarter of the nineteenth century saw several women's books of travel that were organized around solo travel, the most famous of which was *Nellie Bly's Book: Around the World in 72 Days* (1890). We recall from chapter 1 that Nellie Bly, the pseudonym of the journalist Elizabeth Cochrane Seaman, was sent, late in 1889, by Joseph Pulitzer to travel around the globe in order to exceed, in the real world, the record set by Phileas Fogg in the fictional world created by Jules Verne. Thinking to capitalize on the market created by women travelers such as Isabella Bird, Pulitzer gave front-page space in the New York *World* to Bly's travels. Bly became a sensation. Upon her return to the United States, crowds greeted her at railway stations from San Francisco to New York, journalists from across the country interviewed her, dinners and parades were held in her honor, songs and dances were dedicated to her to celebrate her feat, and toys were named for her. Bly proceeded to publish *Nellie Bly's Book* (complete with wrappers advertising dresses and soaps), a revision of Verne's *Around the World in Eighty Days*, but now with a female hero who has conquered the globe in a mere seventy-two days.

The sheer fact of Bly's travels, we recall, does not account for their notoriety. Rather, gender constraints created the resonance of Bly's undertaking, making it a sensation. Bly's grit was lauded as "more than masculine" and a tribute to "American womanhood and American perseverance."[34]

Seeing a writerly opportunity in her gender, Bly herself constructed her account around gender and gendered issues such as luggage and womanly conduct. In *Nellie Bly's Book*, in fact, gender and the matter of traveling alone launch the text. According to Bly, her proposal to circumnavigate the globe received this reply from her editor: "In the first place you are a woman and would need a protector, and even if it were possible for you to travel alone you would need to carry so much baggage that it would detain you in making rapid changes . . . no one but a man can do this."[35] Notions of female vulnerability and female vanity (requiring mounds of clothing and luggage)—or in other words, gender—stand between Bly and travel. She takes up the challenge in fact and in prose. On the matter of a protector, she makes an issue many times over of *not* having one. She reports, for example, that "someone suggested that a revolver would be a good companion piece for the passport, but I had such a strong belief in the world's greeting me as I greeted it, that I refused to arm myself. I knew if my conduct was proper I should always find men ready to protect me, let them be Americans, English, French, German or anything else" (NBB 10–11). Like Joseph Pulitzer, Nellie Bly shows an entrepreneur's grasp of the usefulness of gender politics and the allure of female vulnerability—an allure sanitized as chivalry. As for her luggage: Bly takes up where Caroline Kirkland left off forty years earlier when she made an ado about luggage. Kirkland had called "a small carpet bag" her "best friend" and recommended that "every petticoated voyager" provide herself "with one of these unpretending conveniences." She went so far as to provide dimensions: "eighteen inches long, by about a foot in height." Kirkland would "give the price of a courier for a carpet-bag" because it serves as "pillow, cushion and footstool," even a handbag upon occasion. "I shall always love mine and keep it as a relic," Kirkland writes, and "perhaps leave it by will to some dear friend" (HA, 1:167–68). Kirkland, however, canonized a hand bag that supplemented her trunks. Bly takes the gendered question of luggage further. She travels trunkless and with only one bag. She makes an ado over packing but a single dress that could "stand constant wear for three months" and one silk bodice (NBB 7–9). Nellie Bly is the hero of an adventure off the beaten track women are thought, stereotypically, to follow.

Bly's account of travel was the most publicized, but the travel account that perhaps best exemplifies the cooperation among travel writing, the lone woman traveler, and the politics of gender is *Traveling Alone: A Woman's Journey around the World* (1890), the source of the epigraph of this chapter. On 21 February 1884, Lilian Leland set sail from Sandy Hook, New Jersey, on a new steamer, the *Santa Rosa*, to take a trip around the world, making the circuit by way of Cape Horn to California and Yosemite, to the Sandwich Islands and Japan, China and Ceylon and India, the Holy Land and Greece, Holland and England, and homeward by land by way of Yosemite again and Yellowstone Park and finally New York. She was twenty-five years old at the time, and she traveled for two years, covering a total of 60,000 miles. She then published *Traveling Alone*, an account that undertakes at least two cultural works within the politics of gender. First, *Traveling Alone* redefines three concepts crucial to the politics of gender: Woman, Woman alone, and Woman traveling alone. Second, it seeks to encourage women to undertake travel and adventure.

As the title of her account proclaims, Leland writes to publicize her ability to travel alone. Her anonymous editor seconds her proclamation and associates her feats with famous British women travelers, piggybacking her success on the well-publicized exploits of British female adventurers. "She traveled without escort or protection except chance acquaintances met on the way," the editor writes. "No woman has ever traveled so far alone, with the single exception of Ida Pfeiffer who went twice around the world. Next to Lilian Leland is Isabella Bird, whose admirable books have earned for her a well-deserved fame." Moreover, the editor continues, "she possessed an amount of nervous energy and a power of endurance seldom found in a woman."[36] The book concludes with Leland's tribute to Ida Pfeiffer, of whom Leland writes, "Certainly no woman has approached her as a far and wide wanderer on the face of the earth." Like Leland, Pfeiffer proves that "all the advantages [are] in favor of the woman who travels alone" (TA, 356, 358).

Remarks about solo travel punctuate Leland's account, making it unmistakable that, although travel gives Leland a reason to write, *Traveling Alone* is a book about "woman" and being "alone." Traveling "without escort or protection except chance acquaintances," Leland found that as she "grappled with each new country [she] found no actual danger in it whatever; any woman could do it that chose" (TA, 93). "Really it does amuse me," she claims, "to see myself loafing around depots at all hours, changing cars at midnight, always calm and comfortable and safe. . . . No one ever molests me; people look at me curiously as I go about alone, but no one disturbs me. I have never had occasion to feel uneasy" (TA, 294). People were astonished that she traveled by herself. At the Birmingham train station, for example, the guard looked at her ticket "and in a surprised voice asked if [she] was alone, and showed considerable anxiety on the subject" (TA, 287). She revels in "the glory and fame of an unusual undertaking"—unusual for a woman (TA, 212). She finds that, far from getting along better "for being taken charge of [by a man]," she is "guilty of a private opinion that I could manage better by myself" (TA, 108). Linking her lone ventures to her nationality, casting herself as Brother Jonathan licking all creation, she exclaims, "Hurrah! American independence once more rampant and victorious! . . . Here I am, at Darjeeling, and here I have come alone, to climb the Himalayas absolutely alone" (TA, 121).

Leland's anecdotes and asides, contributing to the cultural work of *Traveling Alone*, unmask and redefine four concepts: the idea of "alone"; the idea of "woman" when coupled with "alone"; the trinity of "woman," "alone," and "travel"; and the real motivation behind chivalry and courtliness. The work begins early in Leland's account. Enumerating fellow passengers as she gets "a jolly start" in her "life at sea," Leland writes that "there are also two other ladies, traveling alone together . . . and two more ladies with their husbands" (TA, 46). The oxymoron of "alone together" unmasks the operative meaning of the word "alone." Rendering invisible any companion who is female, "alone" means to be without a man. Moreover, "Everybody is surprised, amused at, and interested in my voyage," Leland observes. "They tell me that they never saw or heard of such a thing before as a young woman of my quiet inoffensive type starting out on such an enterprise" (TA, 47). The subtext here is that a "woman" who is "alone" is likely to be an offensive person; she is likely to be of the lower orders. Exclaiming "at my daring in traveling alone," Leland notes, "they observe that I act very quietly and independently, but they conclude that I am a desirable acquaintance, and make up to me accordingly" (TA, 109). The "but" clause is the key: her independence makes it surprising that she is a "desirable acquaintance." In the public mind, "woman" plus "alone" plus "travel" ordinarily spells "pariah." Leland and her activities redefine these terms.

Traveling Alone unmasks courtliness as well. In Germany, Leland encounters "a couple of wild Western cowboys." They insist on helping her with her luggage because she is a woman, "and the great American heart, whether it throbs genteelly under the broadcloth of a fine gentleman or beats in a sturdy chest of the rough Western cowboy, can't reconcile its ideas of manliness to permitting women to carry heavy burdens if they can help them" (TA, 233). "Ideas of manliness" rather than womanly needs are the issue in Leland's sentence. On another occasion, a clerk in a Singapore hotel is thrown into "a pitiable state" by the lone Leland. Thinking that she "ought to feel strange and frightened at being alone in a hotel," he escorts her upstairs and down. Leland comments, "What a shockingly sinful thing a woman is, to be whisked away and tucked into a back room, out of sight. I ought evidently to blush for my womanhood. But I don't. On the contrary, I glory in it" (TA, 93). Concerned for the reputation of his hotel rather than the reputation of the woman, the innkeeper musters chivalry for his sake, not hers. Solo travel is not a problem for women travelers, though it is for the men they encounter. Chivalry has been undone.

The second task undertaken by *Traveling Alone* is to encourage women, through example, to venture out into the world. To accomplish the task, Leland underscores the advantages of solo travel. First, it is an ego trip: everyone everywhere pays attention to the lone woman, from the Paymaster who "had it on his conscience to look after a certain lone feminine creature" (TA, 52) to the head of the bank who "called on [Leland], loaded [her] up with advice, and ended by sending [her] pillows and linen for [her] trip" (TA, 57). Second, solo travel permits the traveler to move at her own pace. As Leland puts it, "I enjoy loneliness immensely; roaming streets, wandering through galleries, sitting silent and self-absorbed at table, with no one to interrupt my train of thought and pleasant fancy. . . . no one to detain me or to hurry me here or there" (TA, 205). Third, traveling alone offers freedom from whiners. Staying in a wretched hotel in Singapore, Leland reverses the idea of the female traveler as an ornery nag[37] and claims, "I am glad I have no husband or brother, or masculine companion of any sort, along with me to make it more uncomfortable by grumbling" (TA, 94).

Does it take an unusual person to do what Lilian Leland has done? Leland thinks not. "I don't feel as if [my travels] were a very great thing to have done; it is the novelty of it that I enjoy, and I do look back with a great deal of gratification and happy remembrances on my vanquished countries" (TA, 212). Among the countries Leland's account sought to vanquish was the land of gender difference that fences women in. *Traveling Alone* is an act of writing travel-as-politics, the politics of gender.

There is, however, a possibility that Leland's book is a pseudoaccount, a parody of other travel accounts by lone female travelers, American or British. The name of Lilian Leland, all but vanished, remains only on the title page of *Traveling Alone* and on a card in the Library of Congress catalog (without dates of birth and death). The given name of Lilian does not appear in the lists of Lelands in biographical dictionaries. Given the invisibility of Victorian women in the annals of history, this is perhaps insignificant. Yet the appearance of Leland's travel account coincides with the touted exploits of Nellie Bly and Elizabeth Bisland, and with the feats of Fanny Bullock Workman, Ida Pfeiffer, and a host of women. Reinserted in its historical context, certain features of *Traveling Alone* suggest parody. One such feature is its hyperbole. After exclaiming over "American independence once more rampant and victorious," for example, Leland writes, "Now I just adore myself. Now I am happy. Custom, prediction, advice to the contrary. . . . This is the biggest feather in my cap yet" (TA, 121–22). Basking in glory and fame, she enumerates a suspiciously large number of people simultaneously paying attention to her: "from half a dozen to twenty" (TA, 212). Another curious aspect of the text is its echo of Mark Twain, its irreverent attitudes at shrines and art galleries and its "Twainesque" diction, from "a raid" (TA, 188) on churches, a "losing flesh" (TA, 214) in Venice, and a guide who "shovel[s] out information" (TA, 215). Finally, there is the matter of repetitions: "alone" and "woman alone" punctuate the text at virtually every turn, rendering them suspect.

Yet *Traveling Alone* as parody stands to confirm the lone woman traveler's visibility and the prominence enjoyed by her accounts of travel. If "Leland's" book is a spoof, its success as a spoof depends on readers' acquaintance with the material being parodied. The phenomenon of the solitary female traveler must be known if "Leland" is to be enjoyed. *Traveling Alone* as parody testifies to the popularity and power of the figure of the lone female traveler, demonstrating what women can do without men.

V

Women's travel writing was a political practice, and texts of travel were an arena in which women made themselves heard on national and international issues, including concepts of gender and rules of decency that impinged on their daily lives at home and abroad. Women's travel writing was a space in which women cast themselves as the homemakers of the world. Rewriting "home," they undertook to remake the world into a home for women, a place in which women could work, travel, and live freely, independently, and fearlessly. Journalism was a major outlet for this dimension of the cultural work of travel, the writing of travel-as-politics.

There were other cultures of letters and scenes of writing, in addition to journalism, that shaped the contours of travel writing across the century and beyond: the classification of culture as highbrow and lowbrow, of literature as professional work or high art, and of writers as popular or elite. The next chapter examines women's travel writing as a participant in the shifting cultures of literature in the United States, from antebellum America until the end of World War I.

Chapter Five

Cultural Occasions

Form and Genre in the Texts of Harriet Beecher Stowe, Constance Fenimore Woolson, and Edith Wharton

Some irrepressible comments upon works of Art, which may be found here, are offered without the slightest pretense to connoisseurship. I am of those who think that a sincere love of Beauty and an appreciation of its high office, with a reasonable allowance of plain common sense and sincerity, may be allowed to express a certain class of opinions on works of Art, without deserving the charge of assumption; and I hope some of my readers will think so, too.

—Caroline Kirkland, *Holidays Abroad; or Europe from the West*

Writing about her Italian travels in 1902, Elizabeth Robins Pennell confesses at the start that "I have no Latin" and "I know Virgil and Horace only in translation. The scholar may say this is equivalent to not knowing them at all," Pennell continues, but "in the poorest paraphrase the long-horned white oxen drag the plough across the pastures, the vines hang in festoons between the mulberries, the beech-trees and the chestnuts offer their grateful shade. . . . Leagues of Italian country remain exactly as in the time of Virgil and Horace." Pennell observes, "Nor need you be a Latin scholar to feel this charm of association." Pennell sounds the note of earlier travelers like Caroline Kirkland who, in the epigraph to this chapter, eschews the label of connoisseur in order to elevate the virtues of "plain common sense and sincerity." Enjoying the look of Italy and feeling its charm as she rides along on her bicycle with her husband, Joseph, Pennell concludes that "we might have examined the rival sites with an air of archaeological wisdom, but the country of Horace was so beautiful we were quite willing to leave exact archaeology and topography to the plodding pedant and the cultivated tourist." [1]

Pennell seems determined to parse travelers, to distinguish pedants, archaeologists, Latin scholars, and cultivated tourists from herself. It is odd that she dissociates herself from the "cultivated" because she had been educated at convents of the Sacred Heart in France and elsewhere; became a writer and critic; published on the decorative arts, history, and mythology in the *Atlantic Monthly* and *Scribner's Magazine*; collaborated with her husband Joseph on nine books of travel; and earned a reputation in England for her hospitality among a wide circle of friends, including Aubrey Beardsley, George Bernard Shaw, and James McNeill Whistler. If not "cultivated," what sort of traveler was she? What persona does she present to her readers? Pennell styles herself as a "picturesque" traveler and, in a tone reminiscent of local color writing, evokes a charming world of travel, now receding and being replaced by the incursions of specialists.

Pennell's will to classify travelers echoes Margaret Fuller, who divided Americans into three species: the servile, the conceited, and the thinking. The servile is "utterly shallow, thoughtless, worthless," coming to Europe for clothes, cooking, contacts, gossip, and self-importance upon his return home. The conceited is "Jonathan in the sprawling state" who, bristling against art and history, would become "a man of might" if he ever adds "thought and culture to his independence." The thinking American recognizes "the immense advantage of being born to a new world and on a virgin soil, yet does not wish one seed from the Past to be lost." Rather, "He wishes to give them a fair trial in his new world" (SG, 162–63).

Fuller and Pennell's classifications are only a half century apart, yet there is a world of difference between them. Fuller's remarks are moralistic. Fuller uses the occasion of writing about travel to instruct her compatriots in the uses of Europe and the past for the betterment of the republic and, by extension, the world. Her text is continuous with another discourse, that of history and the American mission. Pennell's remarks, on the other hand, are sentient and evocative. Pennell takes travel writing as an occasion to instruct her genteel readers in the art of landscape appreciation and the preparation it does and does not require. Her text takes pains to be *discontinuous* with other discourses, the scholarly and archaeological. Fuller's remarks express concern with the national character; Pennell's express concern with degrees of expertise and cultivation.

What accounts for this difference? Margaret Fuller and Elizabeth Robins Pennell, separated by fifty years, write in and to different cultures, with different definitions of "writer" and "literature." By the time Pennell wrote, affluence and technology had set increasing numbers of the element for which Fuller expressed "unspeakable contempt," the "servile American," en route to Europe and other destinations. The uses of travel and culture had been transformed between the 1840s and the last quarter of the century. Cultural hierarchies had formed and institutions of literature had changed, creating what Lawrence Levine identifies as highbrow and lowbrow cultural divisions and what Richard Brodhead calls new "cultures of letters" and "scenes of writing." [2] By the last third of the nineteenth century, fissures that were hairlines at mid-century had widened, dividing the arts into elite and popular, reiterated in divisions between male and female artists and writers.

In the first two-thirds of the century, "forms of expressive culture," according to Levine, "were part of the general culture and were experienced in the midst of a broad range of other cultural genres by a catholic audience that cut through class and social lines." Museum collections might include waxworks as well as Chinese ornaments, air guns, and guillotines complete with beheaded wax figures; performances of Shakespeare in cities and in river towns were punctuated with gymnastics, farces, magicians, and minstrels. [3] Accommodating a range of literary and other entertainments, evenings at the theater resembled, generically, many travel books before 1880: accounts, such as Lydia Sigourney's *Pleasant Memories of Pleasant Lands* (1842), mixing narrative with poems and chatty information with serious reflections.

By the final third of the century, Shakespeare was classified as highbrow and performances were purged of what had come to be defined as lowbrow elements. Hierarchies became manifest in the worlds of music, opera, drama, the arts of sculpture and painting, museums, libraries, and literature. The lines between amateur and professional, blurred for much of the nineteenth century, became sacralized and institutionalized. The role of the artist changed as well, from that of the teacher actively communicating with the people, in the first half of the century, to that of an enlightener of the already enlightened. Margaret Fuller writes her travels as a teacher, instructing her compatriots, while Elizabeth Pennell writes hers for an already enlighted, cultivated audience, a complacent, self-satisfied assemblage of insiders who reassure themselves of their status as they recognize the "charm of association."

The sea change through which literature and its institutions passed in the last quarter of the nineteenth century was visible in various features of the literary landscape. In the antebellum United States, male writers such as Emerson and Hawthorne had not yet been canonized and institutionalized. "Woman's fiction" flourished between 1820 and 1870 in a culture in which domesticity and domestic values were in the ascendancy. Women writers envisioned themselves working out of what Richard Brodhead calls the "domestic-tutelary" model. Their antebellum work, child-centered, religious, and evangelical, carried the standard of domestic piety and sentimental family nurture; literature was seen as an arm of the discourses of domestic morality and Christian belief; and the writer was expected to be a public guardian,[4] like Margaret Fuller exhorting her fellow Americans to the proper uses of travel, Europe, and the past.

Following the Civil War, new scenes of writing opened and the work of writers and of literature was reconceptualized. High culture came to be distinguished from popular culture and the writer, no longer an amateur, was envisioned as an "artist" who served the religion of "high art," divorced from religion, piety, and nurture. Rather than serving as an arm of other beliefs and institutions, literature was assigned a sphere and value of its own.[5] Belles-lettres, valued for aesthetic rather than informative or didactic work, was in the ascendancy among the genteel and the elite. In short, institutions of literature, in the honorific sense of "literature," came to favor art history rather than world history; the religion of art rather than evangelical religion; and the work of the expert and the connoisseur, often a professional writer of fiction, over the work of the self-identified amateur. Perhaps in reaction to women's inroads into literature before and the professions after the Civil War, a masculine canonical hierarchy in literature, including Emerson and Hawthorne, was constructed. The leading writers, according to the leading magazines, were all male: Walt Whitman, James Russell Lowell, John Greenleaf Whittier, and Oliver Wendell Holmes; and at the top of the list of novelists, Howells, Henry James (despite considerable public exasperation), Twain, and E. P. Roe.[6]

The world of publishing underwent parallel changes. Before the Civil War, the "gentleman publisher" governed the world of publishing.[7] After the Civil War, publishing was a potpourri of subscription publishers, book distributors, and a protean magazine industry, connected in the 1880s and 1890s with the development and power of a mass market and mass culture in which writers had to compete and negotiate. Magazines, too, became increasingly hierarchical. *Harper's New Monthly*, *Atlantic Monthly*, and *Century Magazine* were vehicles of high culture appealing to the upper classes, while newspapers and women's magazines such as *Cosmopolitan*, *Ladies' Home Journal*, *Good Housekeeping*, and *Ladies' World* appealed to the middle class.

This chapter examines the impact of antebellum and postbellum understandings of the writer and of literature on women's work in travel writing, when the definition of the writer changed from "amateur" engaged in an arm of civic, religious, and domestic work to "artist" engaged in belles-lettres. The change was not, of course, abrupt and totalizing. The tutelary model of writer as cultural guardian and of writing as civic and religious service continued into the twentieth century in the political work of women's travel writing, published for a mass audience in newspapers and popular magazines, the subject of the previous chapter. The increasing commodification of literature in mass-audience newspapers and magazines in the Gilded Age and the Progressive Era created space for travel writing as an arm of politics and for the publication of what might be called "stunt" travels, like those of Nellie Bly and Elizabeth Bisland. The writing provoked by "stunt" travels, undertaken in the interests of financial capital for publishers, was used by women travelers to make political capital. As we have seen in chapter 4, writers such as Mary Krout and Kate Field addressed a journalistic audience and conceptualized their role along the lines of the New Woman.

This chapter is concerned with another matter, what I call the writing of travel-as-culture and the accumulation of cultural capital. Writing travel-as-culture proceeds in two phases: writing that conforms to the tutelary-domestic expectations of writers and writing in antebellum America; and writing that conforms to concepts of "high art" in the last quarter of the century.[8] I examine the work of female travelers who imagined writers and the institutions of literature as agents of history and religion before the Civil War, and as agents of high culture afterward. As agents of high culture, they would write, like Elizabeth Robins Pennell, to an audience interested in what Frank Mott calls "curious and picturesque aspects of foreign life in the mood of the carefree observer," producing "leisurely, stylized, well-illustrated articles" for outlets such as *Scribner's* and *Harper's*, those organs of high culture and high class featuring the "pictorial and curious rather than [the] political and sociological."[9] This imagination of self as writer was problematic for women because, by the Progressive Era, high culture was a masculine affair, "artists" were males, and women were offered a place in this world as "idealizing appreciators"— exactly the persona assumed by Elizabeth Robins Pennell—and only reluctantly seen as creators.[10]

The texts of Harriet Beecher Stowe, Constance Fenimore Woolson, and Edith Wharton record the relationship, from the antebellum years until World War I, between institutions of literature, concepts of the self as writer, and women's writing of travel-as-culture. Stowe, Woolson, and Wharton each matured in different phases of American women's history from 1830 to 1920: Stowe during the reign of the True Woman, Woolson during the transitional era of what Cheryl Torsney calls the "twilight" woman, and Wharton during the age of the New Woman.[11] Perhaps as a result of their different situations in women's history, each established a different relationship to Europe. Stowe traveled in Europe with her husband; Woolson lived there in her maturity, unmarried and nomadic, intending to return eventually to the United States; and Wharton, eventually divorced, decided to live permanently in Europe, buying a property outside of Paris, leasing another in southern France, and never again returning to the United States after 1924, when she accepted an honorary Doctor of Letters degree from Yale.

Each of these women was a professional writer, yet each configured herself differently in relation to the profession of letters. At the time that Harriet Beecher Stowe traveled to Europe and wrote her book of travels in the 1850s, she presented herself as a womanly reformer and an amateur writer, wielding the pen as a tool (even as she was in fact rather fiercely professional). Constance Fenimore Woolson and Edith Wharton, on the other hand, constructed themselves primarily as artist-writers when they wrote their travels as well as their fictions. Acting as authorities, both of them published reviews of the work of others and theorized their own in personal letters.[12] Taking herself as artist perhaps even more seriously than Woolson, Wharton published a book of writing theory, *The Writing of Fiction* (1924), and in her autobiography she makes it unmistakably clear that she discovered her vocation, her personality, her soul when she published her first volume of short stories in 1899. She marks herself as a New Woman when she claims in her autobiography that it was success with its "recognition as a writer" that had "transformed" her life.[13] The differences among these women and their writing of travel-as-culture constitute a concise history of the interaction between women's travel writing and the institutions of literature, from women's early initiatives in publishing travels until the close of World War I.

I

Harriet Beecher Stowe first traveled to Europe in 1853, in the company of her husband Calvin and her brother, Charles Beecher, who acted as her travel agent and secretary. In the wake of the immensely popular *Uncle Tom's Cabin*, she was invited to Great Britain by the Glasgow Ladies' Anti-Slavery Society and the Glasgow Female New Association for the Abolition of Slavery. Enlisting Stowe as an ambassador from British to American women, these groups asked her to carry back to America an antislavery petition entitled "An Affectionate and Christian Address from Many Thousands of Women of Great Britain and Ireland to Their Sisters the Women of the United States of America," with over half a million signatories. Stowe arrived in England on 10 April 1852 and returned to the United States in September 1853. She traveled in England and Scotland until June, and then traveled in France, Switzerland, and Germany. Feted and lionized in the British Isles to the point of exhaustion, she wrote to "Dear Aunt E" a few weeks into her travels that she "was so worn out that

[she] could hardly walk through the building [the cathedral in Glasgow]."[14] Enlisting biblical metaphors to describe the crowds that descended on her, she groaned, "As I saw the way to the cathedral [in Glasgow] blocked up by a throng of people, who had come out to see me, I could not help saying, 'What went ye out for to see? a reed shaken with the wind?'" (SM, 1:23). Later, seeking Christ-like to escape the multitudes after feeding them, the "much exhausted" Stowe left Edinburgh, she reports, "with the determination to plunge at once into some hidden and unknown spot, where we might spend two or three days quietly by ourselves" (SM, 1:191). From her experiences abroad came her two-volume *Sunny Memories of Foreign Lands* (1854), a travel guide that, according to her biographer, Joan D. Hedrick, "tourists carried under their arms as they would later carry Baedeker's and Fodor's."[15]

Stowe's "guide" is alive with contemporary political issues, from abolition to cheap labor, but it is also a manifestation in the travel genre of "woman's writing" in the first half of the nineteenth century.[16] *Sunny Memories* is an epistolary, folksy account that translates to travel the characteristics of what Hedrick identifies as parlor literature. Typifying a woman's writing practice that persisted beyond the 1860s but was most common before the Civil War, *Sunny Memories* is crafted in a homely voice at a particularly interesting moment in American cultural history, the moment when the fissure between popular and highbrow work in the arts was becoming visible. According to Hedrick, *Sunny Memories* found itself in "the cultural gulf that was opening in the 1850s between the age of homespun and the Gilded Age that was to emerge full-blown after the Civil War." "In a seemingly artless and effortless style," Hedrick writes, Stowe's account of European travel anticipates the "fall" of the innocent American into high culture. Stowe "both observes the increasing codification of high culture and takes steps to undercut it. In the process she attempts to empower both the unsophisticated traveler and her humble self. . . . She is determined to resist the voice of the 'artist,' the 'expert,' the keeper of culture."[17] What form does her resistance take? Stowe's resistance is formalized in the style, the tropes and diction, of *Sunny Memories*. Its style, in turn, is a vehicle for moralizing and promulgating values in an era in which literature was still understood as continuous with rather than distinct from common life.

Taking advantage of the formal dispensations of the genre, *Sunny Memories* is decidedly eclectic. Its preface heralds the mix of politics and genteel impressions that make up the volume. Characteristic of women's pre–Civil War work in the genre, Stowe speaks of herself in the third person and issues an apology, claiming to publish her letters because her travels had been misrepresented in certain quarters, compelling her to tell the plain truth. Emphasizing that her letters are, oxymoronically, personal although published, she adds that those who do not care to have their "sphere of hopefulness and charity enlarged" should "treat the book as a letter not addressed to them, which, having opened by mistake, they close and pass to the true owner" (SM, 1:iv).

The body of the text includes the work of three writers during and after the journey, and a variety of forms: letters; speeches delivered by Stowe's husband, Calvin; and poems. The preface by Harriet's hand is followed by Calvin Stowe's "Introductory," perhaps the most conspicuous (fifty-four pages) and indisputable intervention of gender in women's travel writing in the course of the century (SM, 1:xi–lxv).[18] The tale of the continental tour that largely makes up volume 2 of *Sunny Memories* alternates between letters written by Harriet and journal entries "from the pen of the Rev. C. Beecher," Harriet's brother. Some are "compiled from what was written at the time and on the spot" and some "entirely written after the author's return" (SM, 1:v).[19] Those written after Harriet's return are substantially essays, logically developed and argued, whereas the tone of the volumes' typical letters is casual, conversational, intimate, and associational—a tone Sophia Hawthorne would likely have envied. They retain the epistolary practice of writing home, using salutations such as "My Dear Children" and "Dear Aunt E," "Dear Father," and "Dear Cousin."

Stowe labors to create the persona of a simple, ordinary woman. This persona is at one and the same time a defense of her egalitarian credentials and a disguise of her fame. She stays at Rose Cottage, Walworth, outside of London and at a distance from the West End "so that my American friends, of the newspapers, who are afraid I shall be corrupted by aristocratic associations," she writes, "will see that I am at safe distance" (SM, 1:268). Masking and deflecting her status as a famous personage, a status that would work against the homespun, she deploys three rhetorical strategies to construct a simple persona of the perfect democrat, common but accomplished.

First, Stowe displays interest in ordinary people even as she visits the rich and famous. When, for example, she "rode through several villages [and] met quite warm welcome," she claims that "what pleased me was, that it was not mainly from the literary, nor the rich, nor the great, but the plain, common people. The butcher came out of his stall, and the baker from his shop, the miller, dusty with his flour, the blooming, comely, young mother, with her baby in her arms, all smiling and bowing with that hearty, intelligent, friendly look, as if they knew we should be glad to see them" (SM, 1:76).

Second, she redirects attention from her reknown to her homely childhood, making herself small and minimizing, even obfuscating, the grand proportions of her reception abroad, as when she recounts an invitation to the lord mayor's dinner on the night of her arrival in London. "'What!' said I, 'the lord mayor of London, that I used to read about in Whittington and his Cat?' And immediately there came to my ears," she writes, "the sound of the old chime, which made so powerful an impression on my childish memory. . . . It is curious what an influence these old rhymes have on our associations" (SM, 1:258).

Third, she modestly claims for others the praise heaped on her in her procession through the British Isles. Meeting with such notables as Archbishop Richard Whateley and Thomas Macauley, Stowe hastens to say, "I am far from appropriating it [the meeting] to myself individually, as a personal honor. I rather regard it as the most public expression possible of the feelings of the women of England on one of the most important questions of our day—that of individual liberty considered in its religious bearings" (SM, 1:298).

Having performed in her prose strategies a womanly humility, Stowe reinforces it, waxing domestic and sentimental at seemingly every turn. Writing her first letter from Scotland, for example, she immediately recalls "the views of Scotland, which lay on my mother's table, even while I was a little child, and in poring over which I spent so many happy, dreamy hours" (SM, 1:41). She interjects charming comments, as when she spends a pleasant hour with the Douglas family. "I enjoy these little glimpses into family circles more than any thing else," she writes; "there is no warmth like fireside warmth" (SM, 1:170). Nor does she admit to erudition. On the contrary, she coyly enlists domestic allusions to wrap knowledge in sentiment and discharge any taint of prideful learning. The "household treasure" of pictures and Scotch ballads and the songs of Robert Burns are referred to hearthside occasions. "Literature which has charmed us in the circle of our friends," she says, "becomes endeared to us from the reflected remembrance of them" (SM, 1:41–42). Finally, Stowe manages to domesticate the world's luminaries, describing "Willie" Shakespeare, as she calls him, "muddying his clothes" as a boy (SM, 1:204). Concluding *Sunny Memories* on a note that domesticates the whole of Britain even as it echoes the usual American concept of Our Old Home, she pictures herself in these words: "And thus, almost sadly as a child might leave its home, I left the shores of kind, strong Old England—the mother of us all" (SM, 2:432).

Stowe's attention to "domesticals," as Charles Beecher called them, includes descriptions of interiors, a commonplace in the parlor literature of the day on which *Sunny Memories* draws. As Hedrick explains, letters that passed from the East Coast of the United States to the West and back, between family members, sought to convey the scenes of daily life to those who were absent. Thus rooms, and where people sat in them, were described in detail.[20] Before Stowe wrote her travels, Emma Willard had adapted this practice to travel. Writing to her sister from Le Havre in 1830, Willard offers a meticulous description of writing "upon a round table, covered with a red and blue cotton cloth" on "a polished oaken floor—an octagon of perhaps eight inches in diameter." Willard renders the scene in scrupulous detail: "Sit down by my round table. . . . Now let us turn to our left. . . . Now let us wheel round, and examine that part of the room opposite the windows. . . . We have now inspected three sides of the room, and the fourth has nothing worthy of note but the door, which leads into a corridor. But before we go out, let us take a look from the window, which you see opens like a double door, and as easily."[21] Stowe follows suit. A letter to "Dear Aunt C," for example, takes her on a slow tour of the house, from passage to hall to drawing room to picture gallery.

Stowe's work in the travel genre, like that of Willard and most other female travelers who published accounts before the Civil War, borrows another feature of parlor literature: chatty material couched in novelistic devices to create a sense of intimacy and fireside chat. Action, characters, and setting invite the reader into a lively scene, taking place across a continent in the instance of parlor literature and across an ocean in the instance of foreign travel. Stowe writes, for example, that at Warwick "we walked on the wall four abreast, and played that we were knights and ladies of the olden time, walking on the ramparts" (SM, 1:237). She interjects phatic devices, such as "well" and "now," to connect with her audience. "Well, now it was all done," she writes; and "Now, I dare say that you have been thinking, all the while, that these stories about the wonderful Guy are a sheer fabrication, or, to use a convenient modern term, a myth" (SM, 1:238, 240). She imitates the erratic continuity of women's letter writing, begun at a stolen moment, then set aside, then taken up at another stolen moment later that day or the next. "Monday, May 9. I should tell you that at the Duchess of Sutherland's an artist, named Burnard," she writes, "presented me with a very fine cameo head of [William] Wilberforce, cut from a statue in Westminster Abbey" (SM, 1:316). An actual letter from Stowe to Mary Beecher Perkins shows the degree to which such passages echo her own letter writing practices. The letter begins: "Evening. . . . I stick in my needle and sit down to be sociable. . . . There! the tea-bell rings. Too bad! I was just going to say something bright. . . . After tea. Well, we have had a fine time."[22] What might be called a "literature of stolen moments" mimics the rhythms of the traveler, snatching moments here and there to keep diaries or write letters home.

Completing its evocation of parlor literature, Stowe's text includes drawings reminiscent of women's practice in letter writing. Women's letters often included an exchange of small items such as recipes, pieces of carpet, items of food, and plant clippings.[23] In *Sunny Memories*, Stowe not only memorializes in prose such items as the holly, the daisy, the primrose, and robin redbreast (SM, 1:21, 29); she memorializes them a second time in drawings that substitute for the tangible items slipped into letters. *Sunny Memories* contains sketches of the bluebell, a yew branch, ivy, velvet moss, starry gentian, and purple witch, to name a few. The subjects of these sketches of course bespeak Stowe's True Womanliness even as they acquaint the reader with the unseen or unknown, and they associate *Sunny Memories* with the domesticity, intimacy, and values of women's common practice in writing. It becomes clear why an early biographer of Stowe, Catherine Gilbertson, says that "*Sunny Memories*, which Mrs. Browning praised for its simplicity and deprecated for its provincialism, is so simple and so provincial, such an American document, in fact, even to the casual spelling of foreign names, that it is worth preserving and dwelling upon for the very reasons that made it unacceptable as literature to the literati of Mrs. Stowe's own generation."[24]

At the same time, an analytical streak runs through the dominant hominess of *Sunny Memories*. Marrying learning to domesticity, Stowe occasionally uses the terminology of the expert, but contrives to make it common. Giving "Dear Aunt E" an architectural tour of Melrose Abbey, for example, Stowe introduces such terms as "corbel" and "gargoyle," but self-consciously (in keeping with the persona of the approachable amateur promoted throughout the text). "Speaking of gargoyles—you are no architect, neither am I, but you may as well get used to this descriptive term," she writes. "It means the water-spouts which conduct the water" (SM, 1:159). She includes, as well, architectural sketches of British lodging houses for the poor (SM, 2:116). In a modest anticipation of Edith Wharton's *The Decoration of Houses* (1897), she articulates principles of interior design, comparing room arrangement with the composition of a picture, "what painters call the ground tone, or harmonizing tint" that "renders a very simple room extremely fascinating" or, when missing, "makes the most splendid combinations of furniture powerless to please" (SM, 1:288).

Why this labor on Stowe's part? These strategies are more than reiterations of womanliness to fend off an imagined criticism of unwomanly departures into fame and the marketplace. Rather, in intermixing expertise and folksiness, the public and the private, Stowe appropriates authority at that moment in antebellum culture when the expert was becoming visible. Stowe's writing practice makes a display of the sufficiency, merits, and power of the amateur. If *Sunny Memories* were merely folksy, its omissions would leave empty a space that the expert might be invited to fill. Stowe seeks to fill all available space. Far from lacking erudition and values, *Sunny Memories* shows that expertise need not be the province of the expert. It shows the domestic and intimate as repositories of knowledge and, in fact, necessary vehicles to deliver learning and values to the populace—in keeping with the aims of an egalitarian republic. Expertise separated hierarchically from the commoner is undemocratic. It works against the diffusion of knowledge and independence crucial to republicanism. Domesticity and its values, on the other hand, are the key to republicanism, egalitarianism, and sound public morality. The writers of "woman's fiction" would project the values of the home into the world, as Nina Baym has found, and Stowe would do the same through *Sunny Memories*.[25]

To this end, *Sunny Memories* engages in moralizing and sermonizing at will, a womanly and hearthside practice. The perception that the encroachments of the expert mark the end of this salutary moralizing was registered by Caroline Kirkland in her *Holidays Abroad*. Impressed by conversions to kindness that travel promotes among travelers, Kirkland comments, "How one might moralize upon such conversions! How enviable are the writers of former days, to whom moralizing was permitted. . . . People are supposed to do their own moralizing now" (HA, 22–23). Moralizing is to be a private affair rather than a public event in the pages of a book. Stowe swims against what Kirkland takes to be the tide and, in harmony with women travelers before her and after, moralizes and emblematizes her observations. The softening action of water on an iceberg "destined to pass away," for example, is made emblematic of "those institutions of pride and cruelty, which are colder than the glacier, and equally vast and hopeless in the apparent magnitude, [but] may yet, like that, be slowly and surely passing away" (SM, 2:238). The decadence of Henry VIII, captured in a portrait by Holbein, foreshadows "the disposition which bows down and worships any thing of any character in our day which is splendid and successful, and excuses all moral delinquencies, if they are only available" (SM, 1:234). It is of vast importance to Stowe to make the moral clear because she, like Margaret Fuller, reads history millennially: America, Stowe asserts, is "leading on a new era in the world's development" (SM, 1:18). The stakes are high in the competition between the amateur and the expert. The grand design of history, moving providentially from tyranny, monarchy, and class hierarchies to freedom, republicanism, and egalitarianism is in the balance.

Using *Sunny Memories* to stump for the virtues of the amateur, Stowe stumps for artistic and aesthetic independence in American artists and travelers. In this she joins the chorus demanding arts commensurate with the political independence of the United States, urging "our American artists" to "remember that God's pictures are nearer than Italy," and urging God to "send us an artist with a heart to reverence his own native mountains and fields" (SM, 2:347). She urges travelers, too, to cultural independence. Visiting Warwick Castle, she makes fun of studiousness, which she seems to translate as tediousness. Finding certain pictures of Salvator Rosa to be "extremely ugly," she remembers being told that if she "would study them two or three months in faith, [she] should perceive something very astonishing. This may be," she declares, but "one can see any thing he chooses." Then, satirizing the skills of the expert and calling on her compatriots to stand on their own feet, she derides the process "by which old black pictures are looked into shape," and declares herself "obstinately determined not to believe in any real presence in art which I cannot perceive by my senses" (SM, 1:235–36). Stowe confesses, further, to "great suspicions of these old masters." "One thing I am determined," she writes, "I will keep some likes and dislikes of my own, and will not get up any raptures that do not arise of themselves" (SM, 1:278–79).

Like travel writers before and after her, Stowe attacks guidebooks and engages in antitourism. She calls it "rather a damper" to have one's raptures prearranged, "set down in the guide book and proclaimed by the guide, even though it should be done with the most artistic accuracy" (SM, 1:62). The "damper" becomes, later, a decided annoyance at Melrose, a site, she writes, "which has been berhymed, bedraggled through infinite guide books, and been gaped at and smoked at by dandies, and been called a 'dear love' by pretty young ladies, and been hawked about as a trade article in all neighboring shops, and you know perfectly well that all your raptures are spoken for and expected at the door, and your going off in an ecstasy is a regular part of the programme" (SM, 1:150).

Ever earnest, Stowe annexes republicanism to her attack on guidebooks, making them not merely agents of generic exhaustion, the "belatedness" problem (discussed in chapter 2) but obstacles to the virtue of self-reliance. Arriving at Windsor Castle, she remarks, "So, you see, like an obstinate republican, as I am, I defend my right to have my own opinion about this monument [to Princess Charlotte in St. George's Chapel], albeit the guide book, with its usual diplomatic caution, says, 'It is in very questionable taste'" (SM, 2:48). By the end of her travels, Stowe registers an incorrigible independence. "I went to Dresden as an art-pilgrim, principally to see Raphael's great picture of the Madonna di San Sisto, supposing that to be the best specimen of his genius out of Italy," she explains. "On my way I diligently studied the guide book of that indefatigable friend of the traveler, Mr. Murray, in which descriptions of the finest pictures are given, with the observations of artists; so that inexperienced persons may know exactly what to think, and where to think it." Jettisoning Murray and the artist experts he quotes, she determines to look with her own eyes for, as she says, "they are the best God has given me" (SM, 2:353).

In the process of traveling and writing about it, Stowe works her way toward independence and away from the controlling aura of Europe and its artistic traditions. She becomes, accordingly, more American, testifying to Emerson's observation, cited earlier, that "we go to Europe to become Americanized" and Fuller's observation that "the American in Europe, if a thinking mind, can only become more American." *Sunny Memories* is Stowe's declaration of independence from the Old World, enabled by travel and the process of writing about it. She thinks it imperative that Americans free themselves culturally and stand on their own two feet because their own two feet are all they have: "We have nothing but our men and women to glory in," Stowe writes, "no court, no nobles, no castles, no cathedrals; except we produce distinguished specimens of humanity, we are nothing" (SM, 1:275). Those "distinguished specimens of humanity" will be produced, not by the mercenary and masculine culture of the expert and the professional, but by the domestic, common virtues of plain speaking, honesty and sincerity, intimacy, and family ties. These are the virtues embedded in the form and rhetorical strategies of *Sunny Memories of Foreign Lands*, the virtues of "parlor literature" and woman's culture translated from the parlor into the wide wide world of travel.

II

By the time Constance Fenimore Woolson ventured into the publication of her foreign travels in 1884, the women's culture Harriet Beecher Stowe sought to validate in *Sunny Memories of Foreign Lands* had receded, giving way to the cultures of professionals, aesthetes, and artists. In "At the Chateau of Corinne," a title redolent of Italy, travel, Madame de Staël, and a woman's power, Constance Fenimore Woolson dramatizes the increasingly deep divide between the private and the public spheres, between the female and the male, entrenching itself in literary culture and expectations. She assigns to a male character, John Ford (the name of a subscription book publisher), the discouragingly familiar, frequently reiterated attitude toward women writers that pertained before, during, and after her time.[26] "We do not expect great poems from women any more than we expect great pictures," Ford asserts. "We do not expect strong logic any more than we expect brawny muscle." Worse still, "what cannot be forgiven," Ford continues, is "a certain sort of daring, an essential, unpardonable sin. . . . A woman should not dare in that way. Thinking to soar, she invariably descends. Her mental realm is not the same as that of man; lower, on the same level, or far above, it is at least different. And to see her leave it, and come out in all her white purity, which must inevitably be soiled, to the garish arena where men are contending, where the dust is rising, and the air is tainted and heavy—this is indeed a painful sight."[27] "Brawny muscle" and "daring," the province of the male writer, were institutionalized as "Art," effectively relegating the work of women writers to the margins, at best, of high culture. This masculinist attitude persisted and perhaps became even more adamant when women were on the move in a double sense: women were attempting to scale the walls thrown up around an increasingly specialized world that sealed women out of newly professionalized territory, such as midwifery, while men moved into territory previously populated by women, at the same time that women were traveling and writing books of travel in ever greater numbers.

Constance Fenimore Woolson was herself destined to defy diminished expectations for women writers and to create the fictional equivalent of "great poems." Nevertheless, her historical and geographical situation obscured her achievements. She first published fiction in the 1870s and died in 1894, so Woolson matured in the transitional years between the True Woman and the New Woman and was classified as a local colorist.[28] Betwixt and between in her personal world, Woolson lacked confidence in her appearance and wondered why literary women were subject to mental breakdowns. Depreciating herself, she wrote to her great friend Henry James, "I do not come in as a literary woman at all, but as a sort of—of admiring aunt," and referred to her work as "my small writings."[29] In the words of Cheryl Torsney, "Woolson's world (and in many ways, Woolson herself) saw literary ambition . . . as a stain on the pretty frills of feminine consciousness."[30] Accordingly, she found herself betwixt and between in the worlds of publishing and literary culture, as well. Unlike Edith Wharton, later, who became a tough negotiator with her publishers, Woolson used the conservative strategies of an earlier generation, relying on powerful intermediaries and friends to wrest contracts and raises from her publishers.[31] She worked between local color and literary realism, the one female-identified and ghettoized though highly marketable, the other male-identified and associated with high culture.

Working in this complicated context and between political, social, and literary watersheds, Woolson expanded the boundaries of women's practice in the travel genre. Abandoning epistolarity altogether, she made extensive use of those novelistic devices deployed only occasionally in parlor literature and in its kin, travel accounts such as those of Emma Willard, Catharine Sedgwick, and Harriet Beecher Stowe. She undertook the fictionalizing of actual travels, an undertaking distinct from what I call the travelizing of fictions. Fictionalizing travels is a travel writing practice whose results are travel accounts; travelizing fictions is a fiction writing practice which, stretched to its limit, makes international novels. Harriet Beecher Stowe had travelized fiction in her *Agnes of Sorrento* (1862), furnished with an Italian setting drawn from her travels. Henry James, of course, routinely travelized his fiction, casting the traits of Americans in relief as they traveled and lived abroad. William Dean Howells, having published two travel accounts, travelized three novels. Though never having set foot outside of the United States, Marietta Holley boldly sent a backwoods character, Samantha Allen, first to Europe and then around the world. Edith Wharton, of course, steadily published travelized fiction across her career.[32]

Working the border between local color and realism, and translating the interests of local color to Italian settings, Woolson herself wrote a number of travelized fictions collected in *The Front Yard and Other Italian Stories* (1895) and *Dorothy and Other Italian Stories* (1896). Her work in the travel genre, however, and particularly in "In Mentone," is distinct from these. A writing of travel rather than fiction, Woolson's work in the genre reinvigorates travel writing. Woolson wrote in a publishing culture in which travel writers were under great pressure to "make it new" because, as a reviewer of Wharton's *Italian Backgrounds* said in 1905, "We have fixed our gaze so long on obvious 'monuments' that we are virtually hypnotised by them, and lose all sense of their meaning and value."[33] Woolson's work revivifies the narrative possibilities of travel through a massive injection of fictional devices. Writing travel-as-culture, and despite the diffidence that marked her conception of herself as both artist and woman, Woolson placed her work in *Harper's*, a leading journal of literary culture.[34] As was the practice of publishers, the house of Harper then collected her travel accounts, with some additional material, in a volume entitled *Mentone, Cairo, and Corfu* (1896).

Woolson's travel writing emerged from her nomadic life. She was educated at the Cleveland Female Seminary, and, after her father's death in 1869, she traveled with her mother in the East and the South, from Mackinac Island to Florida, eventually drawing regional fiction from this experience. Traveling to Europe in 1879 and remaining there in various places for the rest of her life, she first landed in England and then ventured to Mentone, Florence, Venice, Milan, and Switzerland. It became her pattern, with frequent variations, to spend summers in Switzerland and autumn and winter in Florence. From 1883 to 1886 she lived in London and Warwickshire; in 1889 she made a trip to the Greek Isles and Athens; in 1890 she traveled from Athens to Cairo, and from there she repaired to England, staying in Oxford for more than two years. Having returned to Italy in 1893, she died in Florence in January 1894, and was buried in Rome.[35] Her enthusiasm for the Old World influenced and energized her travel writing as well as her international fiction. She wrote to a friend in 1880 that Florence "is all I have dreamed and more . . . here I have attained that old-world feeling I used to dream about, a sort of enthusiasm made up of history, mythology, old churches, pictures, statues, vineyards, the Italian sky, dark-eyed peasants, opera-music, Raphael and Old Michael, 'Childe Harold,' the 'Marble Faun,' 'Romola,' and ever so many more ingredients—the whole having, I think, taken me pretty well off my feet!"[36]

As its title declares, Woolson's *Mentone, Cairo, and Corfu* is divided into three parts. Each is punctuated with picturesque illustrations typical of nineteenth-century accounts of travel: street scenes, statuary, scenic views, and local inhabitants in traditional costume (in contrast with Stowe's drawings of bluebells, yew, and moss). The first of the three parts, "In Mentone," grew from her travel to Mentone in 1879 with Clara Woolson Benedict and Constance's niece, Clare Benedict. Woolson remained there, "perfectly charmed," for three months, working on *For the Major*, a novel set in the South of the United States, and taking notes for the article that became "In Mentone" and appeared in *Harper's*.[37] "In Mentone" is the only travel account that Woolson chose to fictionalize. Why did Woolson eschew the fictionalizing of Cairo and Corfu, the other two-thirds of the travels she published in *Harper's*? Her account of travel to Cairo gives a clue. Even the Middle East, not to mention Europe, had become tediously familiar. Referring to the tourist as the victim of an excess of temples, she writes, "In this case the victim, with his head in his hands, is ready to echo the (extremely true) exclamation of Charles Dudley Warner, 'There is nothing on earth so tiresome as a row of stone gods standing to receive the offerings of a Turveydrop of a king!' This was the mental condition of a lady who last winter, on a Nile boat, suddenly began to sew," Woolson continues. The lady on the Nile boat says, "'I have spent nine long days on this boat, staring from morning till night. One cannot stare at a river forever, even if it *is* the Nile! Give me my thimble.'"[38]

Travel and accounts of it, Woolson knows, can be more tedious than sewing; they can provoke the writer of travels to make a textual ado, as we have seen in chapter 2, over what *does not* happen and what *is not* interesting. Woolson joins the conventions of the meta-travel book and the "belatedness" problem, the lament of generic exhaustion, to report of the Pyramids: "Paintings, drawings, engravings, and photographs" have made them so familiar that "one views them at first more with recognition than surprise. 'There they are! How natural!' And this long familiarity makes one shrink from arranging phrases about them" (MCC, 292). Visiting Cairo and becoming entangled in the "meanwhile" problem created by continuous life in sacralized sites, Woolson finds that the beauties of a Saracenic house have been tragically diluted by "a modern French carpet, chairs and tables of the most ordinary modern designs . . . ornamented with hideous bouquets of artificial flowers under glass . . . the tiles which have fallen from the lower part of the walls have not been replaced by others; a coarse fresco has been substituted. What would not one give to see the sheyk . . . seated in this splendid hall of his fathers as it once was." This is, of course, an impossibility. Why? Because, Woolson observes, "In 1889, 180,594 travellers crossed Egypt by way of the Suez Canal. In this item of statistics we have the reason" (MCC, 201–2). If this is true of the Pyramids, Cairo, and Saracens, then how much more so of the familiar resort of Mentone, another account of which threatens even the interested tourist, not to mention the armchair traveler of her time, with terminal déjà vu.

Perhaps this is why Woolson chooses Mentone as the place in which to spend her remarkable insight into the pliability of the travel genre and its fundamental status as a narrative art. Whereas Harriet Beecher Stowe creates a persona and occasionally interjects a novelistic device such as dialogue into the otherwise epistolary and descriptive *Sunny Memories of Foreign Lands*, Woolson jettisons all pretense to epistolarity in all of her accounts of travel and relies, in "In Mentone," entirely on novelistic devices. Like Mark Twain in *The Innocents Abroad*, she creates characters from fellow travelers and assigns distinct personalities. Woolson understood what another writer of fiction, Catharine Maria Sedgwick, understood forty years earlier: travel narrative often lacks what an engaging narrative requires. According to Sedgwick, "It requires a skilful artist to make his landscape attractive without figures" (LA, 1:234). Woolson uses figures to make her landscape attractive.

Thus it occurs that Woolson creates what she calls an "aggregation," Mrs. Trescott and her daughter Janet, Professor Mackenzie, Miss Graves, the two youths Inness and Baker, and the narrator and her niece. Woolson, the narrator, assigns herself a pseudonym, "Jane Jefferson, aged fifty," and she names her niece "Margaret Severin, aged twenty-eight." "Jane Jefferson" explains that these people had "accumulated" each other and become a party, "formed not by selection, or even by the survival of the fittest (after the ocean and Channel), but simply by chance aggregation" (MCC, 3), the same way Twain's pilgrims in *The Innocents Abroad* came together. The intersection of their foibles makes a fair field for humor. Travel in this accidental group of tourists offers incident and escape from the mundane—not because of *travel* but because of *character*, happily revealed in reactions to the scenes and sufferings of foreign travel.

Pursuing characterization and dramatic presentation, Woolson unites the conventions of literary realism, the masculine "high art" culture of letters of her time, and the travel genre. As William Dean Howells in *The Rise of Silas Lapham* (1885) assigned editorial opinions and background information to the mouths of characters in order to render the narrative more dramatic, so Woolson places the statistical catalogs of the travel tradition in the mouth of a likely character among the aggregation of travelers, the earnest and dry-as-dust Professor Mackenzie. Intent on instructing everyone in sight, he is an object for satire even as he provides the history and statistics endemic to travel writing. In this way Woolson artfully transforms tedious material into humorous characterizations while retaining the didactic dimension of the genre.

The Professor is, in fact, a reworking of the convention of the guide figure. He is Twain's Ferguson, now set loose in Woolson's Mentone. The professorial style of his mini-lectures adds a layer of humor to the history and statistics he relishes. He is given to a royal, ludicrous, and patronizing "we": "The first mountains behind us," he remarked, "are between three and four thousand feet high; the second chain attains a height of eight and nine thousand feet, and, stretching back, mingles with the Swiss Alps. *Our* name is Alpes Maritimes; we run along the coast in this direction (indicating it on the table-cloth with his spoon), and at Genoa we become the Apennines" (MCC, 11). He is always in search of listeners (who flee the minute they smell "the search for a listener beginning" [MCC, 11]). Unwary, trapped souls are as anxious to escape his web of words as is the armchair traveler to escape passages of statistical information.

A figure who unifies the narrative, the Professor is used to work still other effects. The Professor appears at a picnic at Roccabruna. Now reminiscent not only of Twain's guide, Ferguson, but also of Twain's traveling companion, Blucher, the Professor has "come out from Mentone on a donkey. We immediately became historical," says the narrator (MCC, 92). The Professor does, in fact, immediately become historical, delivering a lecture the minute he dismounts his donkey. Further, the donkey and the Professor make a unit; the Professor is associated with an ass as he waxes historical. This makes the picnickers hysterical. Woolson puts characterization in league with the vehicle convention to render hysterical the historical information travel writing threatens to provide.

In this way, Woolson painlessly assaults the reader with information and rescues her travel narrative from the generic disease of tedious statistics and information—a disease that travel writers had long sought to avoid. Caroline Kirkland, for example, would "make a compromise with modesty by seeking to resist all temptation to put anything in my book which could be suspected of an intent to convey information, properly so called" (HA, v–vi). Historical and statistical information is often ferried into travel books by way of numbing blocks of quotation from others, even on occasions when the writer promises otherwise. Caroline Paine pledges, in 1859, that she will not belabor what is already known, such as the pyramids of Ghizeh that have "already given rise to volumes"; but she resorts to quoting Burckhardt for five pages because he "has given so fine a description of this magnificent ruin [Aindoor]," she writes, "that I cannot refrain from copying it for the benefit of those who may not have access to his interesting work." [39] The characterization of Professor Mackenzie (or Ferguson/ Blucher) allows Woolson to render in engaging fashion the dreary facts with which travel writers often tortured readers. She purges conventionally requisite information of tedium by embedding it in character and dialogue.

While Woolson maximizes dialogue, using it to characterize travelers, to forward the narrative, and to create variety in constrasting styles of speech, her most clever use of it constructs a philosophy of history. Various voices "read," polyphonically, the same sights, scenes, and historical/ hysterical events—but differently. Readings of the world become versions rather than transcriptions. The enterprise of history—and of travel writing—is undone. Dialogue orchestrated at the sight of Corsica demonstrates the process through which talk becomes an agent of philosophy.

> "It is almost as beautiful at sunrise," said Mrs. Clary; "and then, too, you can see the Fairy Island."
>
> "What is that?" I asked.
>
> "Never mind what it is in reality," answered Mrs. Clary. "I consider it enchanted—the Fortunate Land, whose shores and mountain-peaks can be seen only between dawn and sunrise, when they loom up distinctly, soon fading away, however, mysteriously into the increasing daylight, and becoming entirely invisible when the sun appears."
>
> "I saw it this morning," said Miss Graves, soberly. "It is only Corsica."
>
> "Brigands and vendetta," said Inness.
>
> "Napoleon," said all the rest of us.
>
> "My idea of it is much the best," said Mrs. Clary; "it is Fairy-land, the lost Isles of the Blest." (MCC, 60–61)

Woolson shows that travelers/characters make the world in their own image and preoccupations. Whatever Corsica may be, constructions of it are versions, responses that grow from temperament, more or less or not at all referential. Woolson brings her travelers/characters to evoke the conventional associations and intertexts of the culture, the Napoleons and brigands and vendettas that overlay and invade their own temperamental constructions of the world. Voice upon voice is built into the discourse. In the process, Woolson satirizes tourists themselves, fancifully parading about the world in search of knowledge that is often merely a reiteration and recitation of what they knew before leaving home.

This approach produces the philosophical stance of a skeptic. History is shown to be a conglomerate of information and misinformation; travelers are shown, in a manifestation of the convention of antitourism, to be pompous and naive; and their accounts, in an incarnation of the convention of intertextuality, are revealed to be unreliable. Woolson achieves multiple effects and accomplishes multiple ends with a single device, witness this dialogue between Janet and the Professor:

> "As recently as 1830, Miss Trescott, when the French took possession of Algiers, they found there thousands of miserable Christian slaves, natives of this northern shore, who had been seized on the coast or taken from their fishing-boats at sea. There are men now living in Mentone who in their youth spent years as slaves in Tunis and Algiers. These pirates, these scourges of the Mediterranean, were Saracens, and——" "Saracens!" said Janet, with an accent of admiration; "what a lovely word it is! What visions of romance and adventure it brings up, especially when spelled with two r's, so as to be Sarrasins! It is even better than Paynim."
>
> I could not see how the Professor took this, because we were now all entirely in the dark, groping our way along a passage which apparently led through cellars. (MCC, 21)

History, indeed! Readings of the world and its past are but projections. The clause "we were all now entirely in the dark," placed hard on the heels of the exchange between the Professor and Janet, transforms their dialogue into a passage as dark as those leading to the cellars. The philosophical stance of "In Mentone" extends our understanding of the roots of a theme that became common thirty years later, the revolt against the search for culture and the desire to distance oneself from what the quest for culture had become.[40] In other words, Modernism is foreshadowed in "In Mentone." Woolson's writing of travel-as-culture leads to a decidedly modern destination that Henry Adams reached a decade later: a world in which no knowledge is certain.

III

Italian Backgrounds and *A Motor-Flight Through France*, two of Edith Wharton's five accounts of travel, were published just after the turn of the century.[41] Reviewers immediately enmeshed them in hierarchies of high-brow and lowbrow, male and female, and placed them at the intersection between the amateur traveler, on the one hand, and the expert on the other. Having praised *Italian Backgrounds* for its "brilliant style, historic research, and a catholicity of taste," a reviewer in the *Nation* claims that only "the serious study of [Italy's] history and art development can prepare one for seeing intelligently and understanding the *raison d'être* of the different epochs which have left their mark on all the great cities with such astonishing predominance." In the *New York Times Saturday Review*, Walter Littlefield disapprovingly associates Wharton's work with "the academic investigator," writers like Arthur Symonds, Maurice Hewlett, and Edward Hutton who "sneer at the tourist and the guidebook," the type of investigators from whom Elizabeth Robins Pennel would dissociate herself, as we saw at the start of this chapter. These academic investigators, according to Littlefield, constitute a "cult" that "has sadly needed a liturgy and a priestess to formulate it. It has now gained both through its latest convert"—Edith Wharton.

G. R. Carpenter of the *Bookman* unloaded his gender cannons on *Italian Backgrounds*. Observing that *The Innocents Abroad* "rudely and sanely . . . shattered, a generation ago, the cheap sentimentalism then current among sophisticated travellers," he complains that "Mrs. Wharton unwittingly has allowed herself to be hypnotised by Italian art. She has denationalised, defeminised herself. Her writing is not that of an American of today, not even of a woman, but merely of the art-antiquarian." "It seems to me," Carpenter continues, that "Mrs. Wharton is merely following, in her polished essays, the familiar method of Symonds and Vernon Lee. Her style is extraordinarily good, but her thought is pedantic and inhuman. There is more freedom of vision in the Baedeker of our grandfathers' [and in]

Vallery's quaint and sage *Voyages historiques, littérarires, et artistiques en Italie*." Wharton's erudition is unappreciated, depreciated, and labeled un-American and unfeminine. Wharton is caught writing the history of art rather than, womanlike, the art of history. A woman's work found on the side of highbrow or academic culture is the work of a woman unsexed.

The organization of *Italian Backgrounds* into chapters named for and devoted to places and topics (such as "What the Hermits Saw" and "March in Italy") announces its erudite leanings, whereas the organization of Wharton's second book of travels, *A Motor-Flight Through France*, into chapters named for movement between geographical points (such as "From Rouen to Fontainebleau") foregrounds the narrative as an adventure in travel. Accordingly, perhaps, *Motor-Flight* was more relaxed. The British *Spectator* delights in the "inexhaustible subject" of *Motor-Flight*, "the beauty and romance of France." As if to italicize a preference for the intelligent amateur, the *Spectator* mentions "the merely technical study of these architectural wonders—which some hold to be the one right and necessary method," an aside that creates a contrast with Wharton's "own way of looking at things." The reviewer uses Wharton's words to define her way of looking: a "'confused atavistic enjoyment'" and "'a blind sense in the blood of its old racial power.'" In the *Review of Reviews*, another critic marshals terms dear to the amateur, claiming that the "charm" and the "literary touch" of *Motor-Flight* make it "stand out from the great mass of books of European travel and description." [42]

Wharton's travel accounts are, as Sarah Bird Wright points out, the work of a connoisseur. [43] Edith Wharton understood that a wave of professionalism had washed over travel writing by the turn of the century. She wrote in her autobiography that in the 1870s and 1880s "there had appeared a series of agreeable volumes of travel and art-criticism of the cultured dilettante type, which had found thousands of eager readers." While the cultivated reader continued to enjoy these, Wharton writes, "Literary 'appreciations' of works of art were being smiled away by experts trained in Bertillon-Morelli methods, and my deep contempt for picturesque books about architecture naturally made me side with those who wished to banish sentiment from the study of painting and sculpture." [44] Thus it came about that as Harriet Beecher Stowe's rhetorical strategies associate her travel writing with traditions in women's writing; and as Constance Fenimore Woolson worried about her womanliness even as she moved in the margins of the world of high art, Wharton sidestepped the strategies of Stowe and moved more deeply than Woolson into regions associated with male writers and scholarly expertise. Amy Kaplan's observation that Wharton sought to dissociate her fiction from "woman's fiction" extends to Wharton's writing of travel-as-culture as well.[45] Making academic byways central to her work, she dissociates it from women's usual, more "picturesque" practice in the travel genre, as her reviewers understood. She did this by writing into her travels unabashed erudition, embedded in skillfully manipulated narrative devices. Wharton's insistence on the right of women to write about such presumably masculine subjects as science, politics, and history shows itself most keenly in the art history written into her travel accounts.[46]

Wharton's intellectual prowess approaches the legendary. She furnished herself with formidable intellectual credentials, including fluency in Italian, French, and German as well as English, and broad reading that began in her father's library and was honed thereafter in conversation with friends such as Egerton Winthrop, Bernard Berenson, and Vernon Lee.[47] When she traveled, she took with her a remarkable stock of books. She did what Shari Benstock calls "exhaustive research" for *The Decoration of Houses* (1897) (an erudite successor to Catharine Beecher's advice on the construction of houses in *A Treatise on Domestic Economy* [1841]).[48] Preparing to write *Italian Villas and Their Gardens* (1904), she acted the "exacting scholar who classified villas by architectural 'school,' region, and historical period." She "verified her findings in old books on gardens and villas and consulted architectural drawings," Benstock continues. "Hers was to be a systematic, comprehensive study of a subject that heretofore had been treated in the most amateurish fashion."[49] When she wrote in 1920 of her travels in Morocco at the invitation of General Lyautey, Wharton rejoices in the romance of going to "a country without a guide-book," where "the vast unknown is just beyond," where, if one loses one's way, "civilization vanishes as though it were a magic carpet rolled up by a djinn." Yet always rejoicing in the intellect as well, she concludes *In Morocco* with a chapter on Moroccan history, another on Moroccan architecture, and a list of books consulted.

Wharton's erudition figures heavily in her travels. A lifelong, inveterate, and insatiable traveler descended from a family of travelers, she used her boundless energy from the start to the finish of her life to explore the unknown, to visit places the standard guidebooks ignored. As Millicent Bell puts it, "The taste for travel became a ruling passion in [her] life." [50] Wharton sailed through the Aegean islands in 1888; she motored through Italy, Sicily, England, Spain, and Germany at various times; she traveled in Algeria and Tunisia in 1914 and Morocco in 1917; she toured in Holland and Scotland in 1934; and she paid a final visit to England in 1936, one year before her death. "The delight of the road" that, in the words of her traveling companion, Percy Lubbock, "never failed her" measures her decline into illness and her approaching death. [51] Her love of motoring (in autos named "Alfred de Musset" and "George" [Sand]) consistently punctuates her correspondence with Bernard Berenson (a correspondence urgent with yearning to travel with so learned a companion as Berenson) from 1912 until 1936. Her consistency in registering her delight in the road becomes a record of her physical decline. On 30 April 1936, she wrote to Berenson: "I find motoring, which does me lots of good in small doses, rather too fatiguing if kept up beyond three or four hours, and therefore hesitate to go too far from my base until I make another step forward—as I suppose I shall." On 21 July 1936, she writes Berenson from England that she had to give up Scotland, the place she most wanted to visit, for she found after two or three days of motoring nearer London that it would tire her too much. She ends on this poignant note: "I love so to hear from you when you are on your travels. Yes, I've known the Dalmatian enchantments— how I wish I could know them again! Nobody ever felt more acutely than I the pang of: 'Il faut donc quitter tout cela?'—but beyond the 'tout cela' there are other realms of gold where I still prowl." [52] Edith Wharton died a year later, on 11 August 1937, and was buried at Versailles.

Wharton was well aware of the challenge faced by anyone who would succeed and excel in the art of travel narrative in her time. She observes that amateurs were encouraged in her day "to dash off impressionistic sketches of travel," having been led to "obscure corners" and "unnoticed landscapes" by "charming little amateur books." [53] In 1901, she wrote that "the author who comes forward with a book on the great land-marks— who boldly heads his chapters with immortal names . . . who has anything to say about Rome, Florence, or Siena must justify himself by saying it extraordinarily well." [54] The manner of the telling, the craft, may have been all, but Wharton wanted as well to make the substance new, to assist in what she calls a "redistribution of values." In *Italian Backgrounds*, she reveals her agenda: she would revise John Ruskin. According to Wharton, "Ruskin taught a submissive generation of art critics to regard as the typical expression of the Italian spirit" what Wharton calls "the pseudo-Gothicisms, the trans-Alpine points and pinnacles" (IB, 155) that ignore the rich, indigenous beauty of Italy. [55] The guidebooks have kept the Ruskin tradition alive, but of late, she writes,

> a new school of writers, among whom Mr. J. W. Anderson, and the German authors, Messrs. Ebe and Gurlitt, deserve the first mention, have broken through this conspiracy of silence, and called attention to the intrinsically Italian art of the post-Renaissance period; the period which, from Michael Angelo to [Filippo] Juvara, has been marked in sculpture and architecture (though more rarely in painting) by a series of memorable names. Signor [Gaetano?] Franchetti's admirable monograph on Bernini, and the recent volume on Tiepolo in the Knackfuss series of Kunstler-Monographien have done their part in this redistribution of values; and it is now possible for the traveller to survey the course of Italian art with the impartiality needful for its due enjoyment, and to admire, for instance, the tower of the Mangia without scorning the palace of the Consulta. (IB, 156)

Understanding that "picturesqueness is, after all, what the Italian pilgrim chiefly seeks," she maintains that picturesqueness is compatible with the Latin ideal that "demanded space, order, and nobility of composition" (IB, 157), the traits she will pursue. Ruskin's work is pentimento, and Wharton seeks to strip his canvas of Italy in order to lay bare the original he painted over, the post-Renaissance period. Ruskin has dominated the "foreground . . . the property of the guide-book and of its product, the mechanical sight-seer," whereas Wharton undertakes to "deconventionalize" the view of Italy, to let in "the open air of an observation detached from tradition," to replace the foreground with Italy's "background, that of the dawdler, the dreamer and the serious student of Italy" (IB, 177–78). Wharton's prose plants a thicket through which Wharton must pass to revise previous authorities. Where Constance Fenimore Woolson came in as "an admiring aunt," Wharton constitutes herself an authority.

Having analyzed elsewhere Wharton's consummate exploitation of the conventions of travel writing,[56] I will concentrate here on how Wharton conducts her writing of travel-as-culture as the expression of both a cultivated traveler and a scholar-adventurer as well—but cleansed of pedantry. As travelers such as Sarah Maria Aloisa (Britton) Spottiswood Mackin, in *A Society Woman on Two Continents* (1896), set out to discover society; and as others such as Fanny Bullock Workman, in *Algerian Memories; A Bicycle Tour over the Atlas of the Sahara* (1895), set out to explore a strange land by the innovative means of bicycling (a mode of transportation that Wharton used in doing research for *The Decoration of Houses*[57]), so Edith Wharton set out, from her first travels to her last, on an intellectual adventure to discover the wonders of art and architecture—a rather bold and confident act for a woman writing in a world in which men were the scholars and arbiters of arts and letters.[58]

Her first narrative of travel, a diary of her Aegean cruise in 1888 that remained unpublished until 1992, reveals a scholarly intelligence in references to Goethe and Homer, *Eothen* as well as the untrustworthy *Mediterranean Hand Book*. Many pages of *Italian Backgrounds*, as well, are devoted to theories of art, its appreciation and its history, as Wharton comments on "the average spectator" (IB, 112) and on "the sentiment that Correggio embodied" (IB, 113), on "Piranesi's etchings—those strange compositions" (IB, 157) and on the difficulty of tolerating "that peculiar form of intolerance which refuses to recognize in art the general law of growth and transformation, or, while recognizing it, considers it a subject for futile reproach and lamentation" (IB, 182–3). In *A Motor-Flight Through France* she delivers lectures on the art and architecture of Rheims and the "two ways of feeling" the arts.[59] In her last book of travels, *In Morocco* (1920), she expatiates on subjects such as town planning and the architecture of private homes, concluding, as mentioned earlier, with chapters on history and architecture, and a full-blown bibliography.

Wharton's canon of travel writing looks forward to modern publishing history when, as Paul Fussell observes in his analysis of British travelers between the wars, "the essay as a salable commodity" virtually disappeared and the travel book became "a way of presenting learned essays."[60] Yet she manages to avoid pedantry, to make her essays "a salable commodity," by embedding her learning in narrative devices such as Mark Twain and Con-

stance Fenimore Woolson had used to fictionalize travels. Wharton transforms acts of the mind into dramatic action. She frames her erudition in a
quest narrative that, incorporating the picturesque so desired by the traveler in Italy, infuses scholarship with vitality. She accomplishes in her travel
prose what Amy Kaplan attributes to her fiction. Kaplan explains that "a
definition of the professional author as an expert with the authority to
represent social reality depends on drawing a sharp contrast with [the sentimental and domestic woman artist], who must be devalued as merely
amateur and popular. For Wharton," Kaplan continues, "this demarcation
provides an important strategy for keeping her own writing from being
consumed by the same tradition of women's fiction that her aunts and
grandmother devoured." [61]

In Wharton's writing of travel-as-culture, much the same demarcation
pertains. She does not "devalue" the picturesque travel writing of her predecessors but, rather, she incorporates it into her texts, making it the avenue into erudition. [62] A picturesque quest narrative inoculates her learning
even as it displays it. The contrast makes particularly visible Wharton's
difference from her predecessors. The chapter of *Italian Backgrounds* entitled "A Tuscan Shrine," the story of Wharton's journey to view the terra-
cottas of San Vivaldo, shows Wharton's typical writing practice, putting
the scholar in league with the narrative artist to create two adventures: one
of geographical and another of intellectual discovery.

In "A Tuscan Shrine," Wharton launches her adventure and sets the
stage for geographical and intellectual discovery with an adventure in travel
writing: carving to her own needs a convention of the genre, the "belatedness" problem examined in chapter 2. Circumventing the compiler of
the guidebook, she observes, is one of the most difficult even as it is one of
the most rare and delicate pleasures of the continental tourist. The only
solution to the problem seems to lie "in approaching the places he [the
compiler of the guidebook] describes by a route which he has not taken"
(IB, 85). Wharton then adds the element of expectation to "the brief exhilaration" of discovery, the "escapes from the expected" (IB, 86). Adopting such evocative terms as "vague" and "obscure" and "somewhere," she
writes that "for some months we had been vaguely aware that, somewhere
among the hills between Volterra and the Arno, there lay an obscure monastery containing a series of terra-cotta groups which were said to represent

the scenes of the Passion." Next, expectation is flavored by mystery both intellectual and geographical: "No one in Florence seemed to know much about them; and many of the people whom we questioned had never even heard of San Vivaldo." So unknown are these terra-cottas that even such experts as Professor Enrico Ridolfi, we learn, know them only by hearsay and attribute them to "an obscure artist of the seventeenth century, much praised by contemporary authors, but since fallen into merited oblivion" (IB, 86). Wharton's narrative and rhetorical strategies associate her adventure with the quest for the grail, the cup of salvation that is hidden away so that, as Robert Frost was later to write in "Directive," "the wrong ones can't find it." As Frost's speaker, in the footsteps of hundreds of questers, is made to travel an abandoned and eerie road to find the grail, so Wharton has constructed a dark and intriguing passage whose atmospherics then hover over the erudition immediately following.

The reader learns that Giovanni Gonnelli was the blind modeler of Gambassi, working during a "debased period of taste"; that Italian sculpture maintained a spark of its old life "here and there in the improvisations of the *plasticore*, or stucco modeller." Wharton and her companions hope to find, therefore, "something of the coarse naiveté and brutal energy which animate their more famous rivals of Varallo." To conclude her introduction to the narrative of adventure that follows, Wharton returns to the "belatedness" problem with which she began: "We started in search of San Vivaldo; and as the guide-books told us that it could be reached only by way of Castel Fiorentino, we promptly determined to attack it from San Gimignano" (IB, 87). The stage for geographical and intellectual adventure has been set.

In the first leg of adventure, the train leaves the explorers at Certaldo, where they "found an archaic little carriage" with a coachman, a guide figure who "knew a road which led in about four hours across the mountains from San Gimignano to San Vivaldo" (IB, 87). Departing from San Gimignano the next morning "before sunrise," the travelers "felt the thrill of explorers sighting a new continent. It seemed, in fact, an unknown world which lay beneath us in the early light" (IB, 88). Wharton and her companions "seemed to be driving through the landscape of a missal," where at first they had "this magical world" to themselves (IB, 88). The Tuscan hills unroll ahead of them, the "fantastic towers of San Gimignano" rise up behind them, and the "picturesque" tourist passes through "slopes trellised with vine and mulberry" with "here and there a farmhouse," and tall cypresses outlined "against the neutral-tinted breadth of the landscape" and "distributed with the sparing hand with which a practised writer uses his exclamation-points" (IB, 89–90). The road "winds continuously upward" beyond agriculture to regions with "a scant growth of oaks and ilexes" (IB, 90). The explorers skirt the edge of a basin of hills for "nearly an hour," then turn "into a gentler country, through woods starred with primroses, with the flash of streams in the hollows; and presently a murmur of church bells reached us through the woodland silence." Finally they turn into a twisting lane with an abrupt descent "between mossy banks," where the end of their quest begins: "a grass-plot before a rectangular monastic building adjoining the church of which the bells had welcomed us. Here was San Vivaldo," and here were "the terra-cottas of which we were in search" (IB, 91).

At long last, after this lengthy journey along back roads, bathed in the atmosphere and the contrasts that constitute the picturesque, Wharton approaches the holy of holies, the chapels housing the terra-cottas. Wharton has made the picturesque do her bidding: to create a relaxed and receptive audience and to make an intellectual exploit exciting rather than pedantic. She now begins the adventure central to this segment of her travels, the adventure of the scholar. Tracing the steps of a learned researcher, Wharton closely studies the terra-cottas until she forms a hypothesis: "They were the work of an artist trained in an earlier tradition," that of Giovanni della Robbia or his school. Her evidence follows: the "modelling of the hands, the quiet grouping . . . the simple draperies, the devotional expression of the faces, all seemed to point to the lingering influences of the fifteenth century; not indeed to the fresh charm of its noon, but to the refinement, the severity, of its close" (IB, 100). Evidence leads her to expand her hypothesis to include a Presepio at the Bargello Museum in Florence, a Presepio that was removed, she now speculates, from San Vivaldo. Without recording her return trip from San Vivaldo to Florence (for now the adventure lies in intellectual rather than geographical travel), Wharton now turns to the Bargello and the adventure of testing her hypothesis.

The rest of the chapter narrates the intellectual travels of the scholar-adventurer, excavating the final problem the terra-cottas pose: how it came to be that the "Via Crucis of San Vivaldo should not long since have been studied and classified" (IB, 103). After delivering a lecture in miniature, a series of erudite speculations to situate the details of the terra-cottas in the history of art, Wharton writes, "My first care was to seek expert confirmation of my theory." She sends photographs of the terra-cotta groups at San Vivaldo to Professor Ridolfi, whose reply "shows that [Wharton] had not overestimated the importance of the discovery" (IB, 105). The chapter concludes with quotations from Ridolfi's letter to Wharton, the climax of the chapter and of the scholarly adventure: "I therefore declare with absolute certainty that it is a mistake to attribute these beautiful works to Giovanni Gonnelli, and that they are undoubtedly a century earlier in date" (IB, 106).

Wharton succeeds in transforming her travels into texts brimming with the knowledge of the expert. Like Woolson enlisting the device of the fictional Professor Mackenzie, Wharton saves her travel accounts from tedium by enlisting the picturesque and the quest narrative that informs the history of travel writing. Moreover, Wharton's writing of travel-as-culture does cultural work. It appropriates what was perceived as male discourse, the discourse of the expert; embeds it in the picturesque that belonged to both genders; and plants women's travel writing in the territory of highbrow culture.

The differences between Wharton and Stowe are instructive. Stowe did not serialize her travel account. She launched herself as a publisher in outlets like *Godey's Lady's Book*, associating herself with women's literature. Only later, well after *Sunny Memories*, did she publish in *Atlantic Monthly*. Wharton did as Woolson had done: she published her travels immediately in leading journals, *Scribner's* and *Atlantic Monthly*. Only later, in the 1920s, was she sufficiently confident in her position as a professional writer to take the risk of publishing in outlets associated with women's writing and issues (and more lucrative, as well), such as *The Red Book Magazine* and *Ladies' Home Journal*. Unlike Woolson, Wharton worked directly with her publishers, negotiating contracts and demanding higher fees. Unlike Stowe, who incorporated homely drawings reminiscent of parlor literature into *Sunny Memories*, and unlike Woolson, whose accounts include typical picturesque travel sketches, Wharton did battle with her publishers to secure expert and architectural drawings and prints rather than mistily picturesque perspectives on the world.[63] As if determined to diminish rather than enlarge the role of the picturesque, she resorted to photographs to illustrate her texts, associating her work with the era of Modernism. What she said of her beloved Geoffrey Scott can be said of her as well: she "was happy with that best happiness, the sense of mastery over one's work."[64] Her travel writing was part of the work that transformed her, as she said of her fiction writing, from "a drifting amateur into a professional," shaped by conceptions of high art, belles-lettres, and artist-writers that governed her historical moment.[65]

IV

In their travel writing, Stowe, Woolson, and Wharton each achieved the status of a master of genre, defined by Robert Scholes as the writer who "makes a new contribution to [her] tradition, by realizing possibilities in it which had gone unperceived, or by finding new ways to combine older traditions—or new ways to adapt a tradition to changing situations in the world around [her]."[66] These female practitioners of the art of travel writing in America are "honey-mad" women, to echo Patricia Yaeger, gatherers intent on meeting the challenges of the blank page and intent on constructing various sorts of adventures from the fruits of their travel.[67] They contribute to a women's tradition in travel writing that is a honeycomb of women's self-knowledge, their knowledge of the world, and their desire to shape home and the world in the image of their own American, domestic, intellectual, and aesthetic values.

Edith Wharton lived through World War I, the event that marked the end of an era and demanded sweeping adaptations to unprecedented situations. Another of Wharton's books of travel, *Fighting France: From Dunkerque to Belfort*, grew out of the situation of war. *Fighting France* marshals virtually all of the nineteenth-century conventions of travel writing, the ideological characteristics of Victorian American travel writing, and the expectations of travelers before 1920, making it an icon of a twilight era in travel and travel writing and an appropriate conclusion for this study.

Coda

The war was over, and we thought we were returning to the world we had so abruptly passed out of four years earlier. Perhaps it was as well that, at first, we were sustained by that illusion.

—Edith Wharton, *A Backward Glance*

An era of travel that had begun in the 1820s effectively ended in the trenches of World War I. Between the 1820s and 1920, the people of the United States had crossed the oceans in steam-powered ships and eventually in luxury liners and learned of an amazing new mode of transportation, the aeroplane, destined to shrink the globe. They had traveled on land in diligences and donkeys and jinrickshaws, later on railroads and bicycles, and eventually in motor-cars that, in Edith Wharton's judgment, "restored the romance of travel" stolen earlier by the railroad. They had witnessed the birth of what was to become a massive tourist industry, with "Cookies," as the patrons of Thomas Cook were called, covering the face of the earth and paying their way with travelers' checks in place of letters of credit. Between 1820 and 1920, travel had been transformed. The world of American women, too, had been transformed, as the passage of woman suffrage in 1920 made manifest. Meanwhile, the historic practice of transforming travels into narratives of adventure and essays about foreign lands had incorporated the transformations of travel into the conventional practices of the genre, building rhetorical displays from the itineraries and accouterments of travel, monuments and landscapes, tourists and indigenes, talk about travel talk, and comparative reflections on the homeland. Travel writers male and female had recorded, debated, and shaped into travel accounts the major and minor discourses constituting the culture of the United States as it came of age and entered maturity. As the epigraph to this coda suggests, the end of World War I marked the end of an era in culture and travel, an era during which women travelers had (re)written home from abroad.

Edith Wharton's *Fighting France: From Dunkerque to Belfort* (1915) stands as the beneficiary, repository, and culmination of this epoch in travel and travel writing. *Fighting France* is an autobiographical and political, professional and highbrow narrative. It incorporates virtually all of the conventions we have seen in texts prior to Wharton's: attention to vehicles, visits to sacralized sites, "othering," and disclaimers, all of these built into a narrative of adventure. And as we shall see, *Fighting France* undertakes a specific cultural work. Yet what is remarkable about *Fighting France* and makes it an apt conclusion for this study is the nature of its reliance on the history and traditions of travel writing. *Fighting France* uses the conventions of the genre to evoke the world of travel before World War I, the world whose end is marked by the war. Inserting the grotesqueries of war into a narrative frame, and inverting a tradition historically associated with the opposite of war, a world of peace and leisurely travel, *Fighting France* is a journey into a nightmare. It is travel writing in the grotesque. Edith Wharton was later to write two war novels, *The Marne* (1918) and *A Son at the Front* (begun in 1918, published in 1923). But at the moment of the greatest urgency to enlist financial and ideological support for the cause of France and French culture, Wharton chose the vehicle of the travel adventure to accomplish her ends. She marshals the conventions of the travel genre for one of their traditional purposes: political work. Even as *Fighting France* testifies to Wharton's awareness of the accumulated, evocative power of travel writing, it registers her sharp insight into the political dimension of the genre.

Fighting France is part of the seemingly tireless Wharton's effort on behalf of the French during World War I. With Elisina Tyler, she formed the Children of Flanders Rescue Committee and American Hostels for Refugees. She organized an "ouvoir" where refugees worked to support themselves, while Wharton supported the "ouvoir" on funds solicited by various means, including the sale of *The Book of the Homeless* (1916), a

collection of works by artists sought out by Wharton herself. As Shari
Benstock puts it, Wharton "cleverly joined philanthropy to propagandism,
using all her social, diplomatic, and political connections to further the
war relief effort."[1] The French recognized Wharton's work on behalf of
France by making her a Chevalier of the Legion of Honor in 1916, and the
Belgian government recognized her work with refugees with the Médaille
Reine Elisabeth in 1918.[2]

Like Margaret Fuller, Edith Wharton became a war correspondent. She
continued the war work, the political work, of foreign travel and writing
about it begun by Fuller when she sent dispatches from revolutionary Italy
to the *New York Tribune* from 1846 through 1849. Again like Fuller in Italy,
Wharton took remarkable risks, immersing herself in a world at war, skirt-
ing the front lines within sight of the Germans, parking her motor and
proceeding by foot to reduce the danger of being shot. She echoed Margaret Fuller again, identifying with the French as Fuller had identified
with the Italians. The French were not "other" to her; their cause was her
cause.[3] As Margaret Fuller sought to shape the attitudes of her compatriots
toward an Italy in the throes of conflict, so Wharton undertook to publish her impressions of France at war so that "the description of what I
saw might bring home to American readers some of the dreadful realities
of war."[4] Her adventure exceeded Annie Smith Peck's ascent of Mount
Huascaran and Fanny Bullock Workman's triumph in the Himalayas.
More than simply adventuresome, Wharton's undertaking was extraordinarily dangerous. Immersed in war work, Wharton made four trips to the
front in 1915: to Verdun, Lorraine and the Vosges, western Belgium, and
the Alsace front. She agreed to write a series of articles for *Scribner's Magazine* that were subsequently collected in *Fighting France*, a "little book," as
she called it in the hoary tradition of the disclaimer. "Wishing to lose no
time in publishing my impressions," Wharton explains, "I managed to
scribble the articles between my other tasks."[5]

Writing the essays for *Scribner's* that were then gathered in *Fighting
France*, she became, as Sarah Bird Wright observes, "an anguished beggar."[6] She was writing about the war for a recalcitrant America unwilling
to bring France and the Allies in under what she called, in a poem sent to
the *New York Times* in August 1915, "the great blue tent of rest" offered by
the American flag. Faced with a daunting task in persuasion, how was she

to accomplish her ends? By now an established professional writer, she choose as her vehicle a genre in which she was long since expert, travel writing and its conventions. The very idea of travel and travel writing "sets free," as Edith Wharton wrote about Vezelay in *A Motor-Flight Through France*, a "rush of associations," and she knew that her target audience was susceptible to such a "rush."[7] Wharton wished to tap those "rich and generous compatriots" of hers who might be persuaded to come to the aid of France.[8]

She could rely on this audience to associate travel with journeys into civilization, with echoes of leisure, adventure, and aesthetic satisfaction. Transatlantic travel was common among her class and armchair travel, enabled by innumerable books of travel, were staples of that class. She knew this audience harbored generic expectations that, rendered in the grotesque, would provoke shock and horror that might, in turn, prompt action. Turning the conventions of travel writing on end, she could emphasize and deliver in bold face, as it were, the destruction of the very civilization into which Wharton's contemporaries and their parents and grandparents had journeyed before the war in an effort to appropriate the past for American use. Two of her own travel books in particular, *Italian Backgrounds* (1905) and *A Motor-Flight Through France* (1908), had been immersed in the ambiance that war transgressed. Dressing this war and its horrific new machinery in the old, familiar cloak of the conventions of travel writing, she could amplify the monstrosities of war, making them resonate against a backdrop that, having everything to do with the evolution of civilization, makes thunderous the twisted devolution of civilization that was World War I.

Having selected the travel genre as her vehicle, Wharton proceeded to amplify her purpose. In *A Motor-Flight*, she had transformed several "flights" in a Panhard to various places in France, including the northeast, with her husband Teddy. Wharton's travel to the front lines in 1915, this time accompanied by Walter Berry, Mildred Bliss, and Victor Bérard, with the faithful Charles Cook at the wheel of Edith's Mercedes, repeated this earlier journey. Likewise, *Fighting France* repeats and revises *Motor-Flight*, whose original appearance was also in the pages of *Scribner's Magazine*.

Motor-Flight had evoked safe passage, an enlarged liberty, leisure, prosperity, pilgrimage, discovery, enchantment, and the preservation of historical and artistic treasures for the traveler's perusal. Wharton the traveler had been led to the grail, to knowledge of the past and the accumulated art and wisdom of the ages. She had made an excursion into civilization, an enabling immersion in history and culture. Like other travelers, she had come to see herself in perspective, to arrive at self-understanding, and at the end of the journey, to reflect in tranquillity on what she has seen in order to, in the words of Robert Frost's "Directive," "drink and be whole again beyond confusion." [9]

Fighting France, on the other hand, records a dangerous and frightening, rather than safe, passage to the war lines; the fatiguing work of war rather than the relaxation of leisure; hunger, cold, and poverty rather than satiation, warmth, and prosperity; the devastation, rather than preservation, of buildings, the countryside, and, in Wharton's view, Western culture. While travel ordinarily serves to renew the traveler, in this case horror creates a species of perverse exhilaration. Tourist sites are here the sights/sites of war, and the culture in which the traveler is immersed is jerry-bilt, made up of odd, impermanent architecture to house a temporary population. This is a nightmare journey. The travel frame enables the "unnatural" juxtapositions that place *Fighting France* as a book of travels in the tradition of the grotesque.

The dream of travel inscribed in *A Motor-Flight Through France* is immediately invoked and reversed in *Fighting France*, to be contorted into the nightmare of war. Whereas one of Wharton's "flights" in *Motor-Flight* takes Wharton and her companions from Paris to Poitiers, *Fighting France* opens on the road, going in the opposite direction, from Poitiers to Paris. *Motor-Flight* begins with the memorable opening line, "The motor-car has restored the romance of travel." *Fighting France*, too, begins with motoring, this time "north from Poitiers" on 30 July 1914. On this "flight," Wharton and her companions have picnicked "by the roadside" (FF, 3) as Wharton and her companions had done in the travels of *Motor-Flight*. Despite ominous thunderclouds, they are en route to a sacralized tourist site, as they invariably were in *Motor-Flight* as well. They are about to visit a hoary object of the ritual and liturgy of travel, Chartres Cathedral, whose incomparable windows, "steeped in a blaze of mid-summer sun," on this occasion prophetically "glittered and menaced like the shields of fighting angels" (FF, 4–5). As if to create a contrast with what is to come upon arrival in Paris, Wharton includes in *Fighting France* her stop at Chartres, excluded from *Motor-Flight*. Establishing the magnificence of the history and civilization threatened with destruction in the Great War, Wharton writes this poetic and affecting sentence: "All that a great cathedral can be, all the meanings it can express, all the tranquillizing power it can breathe upon the soul, all the richness of detail it can fuse into a large utterance of strength and beauty, the cathedral of Chartres gave us in that perfect hour" (FF, 5)—perhaps the final "perfect hour" Wharton knew until the end of the war. Leaving Chartres, the travelers approach Paris at sunset, to see "The Look of Paris," as the chapter is called, evoking again the history of travel and the traveler as observer.

What they come to see, however, is a crazy-mirror image of the world of travel. War has replaced "travel" as ordinarily understood. Travel is now dictated and circumscribed by a war that has effectively destroyed the larger liberty associated with travel. Whereas the thrill of "travel" requires leisure and the abandonment of routine,[10] it is now war, rather than travel, that disrupts routine, that brings about "the abeyance of every small and mean preoccupation" (FF, 15). Ordinarily, architecture and the Old Masters are the art works the traveler "reads," as in *Motor-Flight* Wharton reads "the poetry of the descent to Rouen" (MF, 18) and "the great hymn inter-rupted" (MF, 17), as she calls the cathedral at Beauvais. Now, in Paris, it is "a great poem on War" (FF, 15) that is read. The "army of midsummer travel" has been "immobilized" and replaced by "the other army" of sol-diers who must now be mobilized. Refugees, "dazed and slowly moving—men and women," carrying "sordid bundles on their backs" (FF, 33), the baggage of refugees rather than of sightseers, are now the travelers Wharton sees in the streets of Paris. Rather than carrying tourists, "rare taxi-cabs [are] impressed to carry conscripts to the stations" (FF, 15). The ritual of writing travel letters to friends and family at home has ceased because now correspondence is forbidden (FF, 19). In short, the energy the "casual sight-seer" of *Motor-Flight* had given over to the study of civilization is redirected and absorbed in *Fighting France* into the study of war.

In *Fighting France*, that is, Wharton reverses the characteristics and ritu-als that resonate in the history of travel writing and in her own previous texts of travel. The "sights" that Wharton, leaving Paris en route to the front, goes out to see in the rest of *Fighting France* are the sites of war, "sights that the pacific stranger could forever gape at" (FF, 50–51) as she used to "gape" at art and architecture. She travels through a "chartless wilderness" (FF, 83) that, in the absence of map and guidebook, would have thrilled her on other journeys but is now frightening. Wharton piles up details that, to the devotee of travel and travel accounts, jostle against the conventions of ordinary and peaceful travel and travel writing to create the grotesque.

Whereas in *Motor-Flight*, for example, Wharton is the romantic traveler enchanted by ruins, ruing the importunities of Viollet le Duc at Carcassonne and cherishing the "gashed walls and ivy-draped dungeons of the rival ruins" alongside the "curious church of Saint Pierre" in Chauvigny (MF, 93), she now visits the ruins of the town of Thann, a "tormented region" where the "lamentable remains of the industrial quarter along the river" had been "the special target of the German guns" (FF, 190–91). Describing the towns of Lorraine, "blown up, burnt down, deliberately erased from the earth," she uses the name of an iconic tourist site to suggest the dimensions of the destruction: "At worst they [the towns of Lorraine] are like stone-yards, at best like Pompeii" (FF, 152). The traveler to Belgium traditionally shops for lace. But on an afternoon in Poperinghe, "bound on a quest for lace-cushions of a special kind required by our Flemish refugees," Wharton "roams from quarter to quarter" and finally comes upon an "orderly arrest of life": "rows and rows of lace-cushions" emblematic of "the senseless paralysis of a whole nation's activities" (FF, 156–57). Whereas an earlier Wharton, energized by the automobile, would have thrilled (as she later did) to the thought of air travel, in *Fighting France* she hears "a whirr overhead, followed by a volley of mitrailleuse": "High up in the blue . . . flew a German aeroplane" (FF, 154), the symbol of a new era of travel, but harnessed in this instance to the destruction of the old.

On a larger scale, the movements of the traveler as she progresses through once-peaceful landscapes toward historic monuments, previously staged in *Motor-Flight* as exhilarating, breathtaking, and highly adventurous become an exercise in horror in *Fighting France*. A comparison of Wharton's ascent to Vezelay in *Motor-Flight*, her *Paradiso*, and her ascent to the German frontier in *Fighting France*, her *Inferno*, shows the deftness of Wharton's generic work not simply in the details but in the broad strokes of her travel prose, exercised in the interests of bringing home to her compatriots the monstrosity of war. The ascent to Vezelay in *Motor-Flight* is developed along the lines of a suspense narrative, heightening the adventure of travel by repeatedly and tantalizingly naming the object of desire, Vezelay, in order to magnify the delay of desire's gratification and the serial ordeal required of those who prove worthy of the grail. The "hungry travellers" in "the final stage of their pilgrimage to Vezelay" must sacrifice the full enjoyment of a luncheon filet and "fragrant coffee" to get on the road in timely fashion. "Old villages perched high on ledges or lodged in narrow defiles" must be sacrificed on the altar of the greater glory of Vezelay because of "the strain of our time-limit" (MF, 158). Wharton imposes obstacles to prolong the agony of desire, observing, for example, that Avallon brings them nearly to "defer Vezelay," but "the longing to see the great Benedictine abbey against such a sunset as the afternoon promised was even stronger" (MF, 159). Suspense is made to mount: "All day," Wharton writes, "the vision of the Benedictine church had hung before us beyond each bend of the road" until "at length we saw its mighty buttresses and towers clenched in the rock, above the roofs and walls of the abbatial town." (MF, 159–60). Having created a sizable ado and a serial ordeal from the ascent to Vezelay, Wharton finally allows herself to arrive. Wharton's narrative dexterity refreshes and renews a ritual performance of travel to a sacralized site.

The pilgrimage to Vezelay is, to echo Yeats, utterly transformed in *Fighting France*. The adventure and suspense of arriving at Vezelay and the salvation promised to pilgrims to the cathedral church are inverted. The renewal offered by travel, leisure, and a religious pilgrimage becomes the paradoxical renewal of war: "War is the greatest of paradoxes: the most senseless and disheartening of human retrogressions," Wharton writes, "and yet the stimulant of qualities of soul which, in every race, can seemingly find no other means of renewal" (FF, 53–54). The religious exercises to secure the salvation of the individual soul, at Vezelay, are now war exercises to secure the salvation of civilization, or the soul of Western culture.

Wharton builds a suspenseful narrative to create and delay the fulfillment of desire, the gratification of seeing war at work, as she had delayed the gratification of seeing faith at work in the architectural splendor of Vezelay. This time, the front lines of the Germans are the traveler's destination, and the landscape leading there is "furrowed by a deep trench—a 'bowel,' rather—winding invisibly from one subterranean observation post to another" (FF, 117). The pilgrims en route to the front lines lurch from a "vigilant height" and "down the hillside to a village out of range of the guns" (FF, 118). "Below the village the road wound down to a forest that had formed a dark blue in our bird's-eye view of the plain" (FF, 119). The quaint town of Avallon that had threatened to detain the pilgrims on the way to Vezelay, in *Motor-Flight*, is replaced by the "'villages negres' of the second line of trenches, the jolly little settlements to which the troops retire after doing their shift under fire" (FF, 119). The next day, "an intenser sense of adventure" comes about, not from the unknown of history and land-scape but from the security precautions of war. "Hitherto we had always been told beforehand where we were going and how much we were to be allowed to see," Wharton writes, "but now we were being launched into the unknown" (FF, 122). "Up and up into the hills" they go, and "higher still," until finally "we were within a hundred yards or so of the German lines," the "other" at the root of war. This is the end of the quest, and this is what Wharton finds: "I looked out and saw a strip of intensely green meadow just under me. . . . The wooded cliff swarmed with 'them,' . . . and here . . . one saw at last . . . a grey uniform huddled in a dead heap." (FF, 133–34). The sacralized site of the Vezelay of *Motor-Flight* has been replaced by a dead German soldier. The hallmarks of travel and pilgrimage, danger and suspense, desire and adventure, devolve into a dead body on the front lines.

Creating sympathy for war-racked France, *Fighting France* is the cultural work and another form of war work to which Wharton turned her deft hand in the dark days of the Great War. Evoking the shades of a long tradition of travel and travel writing that lingered in the minds of travelers and readers, *Fighting France* transforms what were the dreams of a century into the nightmare of war. *Fighting France* drew down the curtain on a period in Western history and on an epoch in women's practice in travel writing.

Notes

INTRODUCTION

1. Figures compiled from Harold Smith, *American Travellers Abroad: A Bibliography of Accounts Published Before 1900* (Carbondale: Southern Illinois Univ. Press, 1969). Magazine and newspaper accounts are not included in Smith's bibliography. Smith notes that many fugitive items may have escaped his count.

2. African-American women, as well, traveled abroad between 1830 and 1920 and wrote about it. Their work in its historical and cultural context remains to be studied. See my introduction to *Telling Travels: Selected Writings by Nineteenth-Century American Women Abroad* (DeKalb: Northern Illinois Univ. Press, 1995), xix–xxi, for a discussion of African-American women travelers. A selection from perhaps the best-known account, *A Narrative of the Life and Travels of Mrs. Nancy Prince* (1850), is included, 113–29.

Although I am aware that the term "American" is fraught with difficulties, I have nevertheless chosen to use it rather than "United States" in the title and text of this study. I have done so because nineteenth-century travelers referred to themselves as Americans; travelers to the United States referred to us as Americans; and in our time, the people designated by the word "American," as distinct from Canadian and Mexican, for example, is clear in common parlance. (The Mexican situation indicates the difficulty of using the proper names of nations; Mexico's proper name is "The United States of Mexico." "United States" may be as appropriative as "American.") "American" and its connotations are apt for the historical period of this study.

3. Although Caroline Elizabeth Cushing's two-volume *Letters, Descriptive of Public Monuments, Scenery, and Manners in France and Spain* (1832) appeared the year before Morrell's account, death interrupted Cushing's preparation of her travel letters for publication. Her husband completed the work and published it posthumously (see Nina Baym, *American Women Writers and the Work of History, 1790–1860* [New Brunswick: Rutgers Univ. Press, 1995], 133). Morrell's book is the first brought to press by the woman traveler herself.

4. See Jane Tompkins, *Sensational Designs: The Cultural Work of American Fiction, 1790–1860* (New York: Oxford Univ. Press, 1985), x–xix.

5. Estimates compiled from Smith, *American Travellers Abroad*.

6. The travel writing of British women has increasingly been the subject of studies by such students of the genre as Dorothy Middleton, Mary Russell, Dea Birkett, Catherine Barnes Stevenson, Sara Mills, and Karen R. Lawrence. Their inquiries have provided important frameworks and perspectives for my own and are cited in the course of my study.

7. Dudley Warner, "Editor's Drawer," *Harper's New Monthly Magazine* 78 (January 1889): 324.

8. Baym, *American Women Writers*, 1–2.

9. Marguerite Duras and Xavière Gauthier, *Les Parleuses*, quoted by Domna Stanton in "Language and Revolution: The Franco-American Dis-Connection," in *The Future of Difference*, ed. Hester Eisenstein and Alice Jardine (Boston: G. K. Hall, 1980), 76.

CHAPTER ONE · MAPPING THE TERRITORY

1. Lydia Maria Child, *The American Frugal Housewife* (1832), 99. In answer to this question, Child tells of a farmer and his wife who concluded to "go to Quebec, just to show they had a *right* to put themselves to inconvenience, if they pleased. They went; spent all their money; had a watch stolen from them in a steamboat; were dreadfully seasick off Point Judith; came home tired, and dusty. And what do you get in return for all this? Some pleasant scenes, which will soon seem to you like a dream; some pleasant faces, which you will never see again" (101). I am indebted to Suzanne Matson for drawing my attention to Child's remarks on travel.

2. Russell Baker, *The Fortunate Pilgrims: Americans in Italy, 1800–1860* (Cambridge: Harvard Univ. Press, 1964), 20; Foster Rhea Dulles, *Americans Abroad: Two Centuries of European Travel* (Ann Arbor: Univ. of Michigan Press, 1964), 44. The first two steamships to cross the Atlantic were the *Sirus* and the *Great Western*, arriving in New York harbor 23 April 1838. See Julia Edwards, *Women of the World: The Great Foreign Correspondents* (Boston: Houghton Mifflin, 1988), 11.

3. Allison Lockwood, *Passionate Pilgrims: The American Traveler in Great Britain, 1800–1914* (Rutherford NJ: Fairleigh Dickinson Univ. Press, 1981), 283; and Mrs. John Sherwood, "American Girls in Europe," *North American Review* 150 (1890): 681.

4. Henry James, *The Art of the Novel: Critical Prefaces* (New York: Scribner's, 1962), 48, 56.

5. Figures compiled from Smith, *American Travellers Abroad*. The itineraries of those women who published book-length accounts of their journeys (far fewer than the numbers that traveled) show the proportions of women's journeys to the Middle East and the Far East as well as Europe and the Continent. The 195 books of travel published by American women before 1900, many of these books including extensive itineraries to several lands on a single journey, record 19 visits to China; 17 to Palestine; 11 to India; 22 to Egypt; 2 to the East Indies; 22 to Greece; 3 to Arabia; 6 to Algeria; and 4 to what is specified as Africa, in addition to 538 accounts of travel in Britain and continental Europe. Comparative figures from the books of male travelers who, like the women, often visited several lands on one tour, are as follows: 2,606 visits to Britain and the Continent; 92 to China; 145 to Palestine; 99 to India; 190 to Egypt; 22 to the East Indies; 118 to Greece; 30 to Arabia; 27 to Algeria; 56 to what is specified as Africa.

Figures for women's accounts of European countries most frequently visited by Americans are as follows (with figures for male travelers in parentheses): Austria, 27 (132); Belgium, 36 (160); England, 95 (556); France, 90 (470); Ireland, 28 (143); Italy, 66 (369); Scotland, 40 (170); Spain, 14 (108); Switzerland, 64 (212).

6. Paul Fussell offers the following taxonomy of voyagers: explorers (who seek the undiscovered); tourists (whose way is thoroughly paved by entrepreneurs and mass publicity); travelers (who retain "the excitement of the unpredictable attaching to exploration," fusing it "with the pleasure of 'knowing where one is' belonging to tourism") (*Abroad: British Literary Traveling between the Wars* [New York: Oxford Univ. Press, 1980], 39). Sometimes explorers, sometimes thoroughgoing tourists, sometimes travelers as Fussell defines these terms, Victorian American women travelers call for a fourth category required by gender: explorer-traveler. Women were "travelers" because the way had been prepared for them by (primarily) male predecessors, but they were also "explorers" because they sought that which had not yet been "discovered" by women.

7. See Geoffrey Trease, *The Grand Tour* (London: Heinemann, 1967), 3–4. Trease points out that men of all economic brackets and types made the Grand Tour, "poor men as well as rich . . . the middle class as well as the aristocracy, the eccentric individualist and the conforming trend-follower, the scholar, the satyr and the snob. To some it was a serious preparation for a career, to others a pleasure jaunt, to others again a boring but obligatory finish to a gentleman's upbringing." Some Americans, as well as Europeans, made the Grand Tour and, in fact, continued the tradition into the nineteenth century, when it was on the wane for the British. Neither financial status nor nationality, that is, excluded women from the ranks of "grand tourists" before the nineteenth century. Their gender made them ineligible. See, also, Nona Wilson, "The Decline of the Grand Tour," in *Grand*

Tour: A Journey in the Tracks of the Age of Aristocracy (New York: Dutton, 1937), 155.

8. Leo Hamalian, introduction to *Ladies on the Loose: Women Travellers of the 18th and 19th Centuries*, ed. Leo Hamalian (New York: Dodd, Mead, 1981), x. In the seventeenth century, female members of dissident religious sects, in addition to preaching, prophesying, writing, and publishing, traveled extensively "to testify to their faith . . . often coming into conflict with the law as a result of these activities. Constrained by the law and by social expectation within their marriages, many chose to travel with women friends . . . or alone . . . and to do so with defiance rather than compliance. . . . Far from being unquestioningly deferent, passive, and silent creatures praised in the conduct books, women consistently challenged many elements of the status quo" (*Her Own Life: Autobiographical Writings by Seventeenth-Century Englishwomen*, ed. Elspeth Graham, Hilary Hinds, Elaine Hobby, and Helen Wilcox [London: Routledge, 1989], 10).

9. See Annette Kolodny, *The Land before Her: Fantasy and Experience of the American Frontiers, 1630–1860* (Chapel Hill: Univ. of North Carolina Press, 1984), 10.

10. Sarah Orne Jewett, *The Country of the Pointed Firs and Other Stories* (Garden City: Doubleday, 1956), 58. Her mother having accidentally left her daughter's clothing at home, Susan Fosdick remembers wearing her brother's britches, allowing her "'quite a spell o' freedom'" until they came into a port and her mother bought material to make a skirt. After this, Susan felt "'the hem at [her] heels every minute.'" Mrs. Fosdick remembers that she "'like[d] the trousers best; I used to climb the riggin' with 'em and frighten mother till she said an' vowed she'd never take me to sea again.'"

11. I am indebted to my colleague, Gail White, for bringing Annie Smith Peck to my attention.

12. Miss L. L. Rees, *We Four. Where We Went and What We Saw in Europe* (1880), 7.

13. Edith Wharton, *The Custom of the Country* (New York: Scribner's, 1913), 360, 380.

14. William W. Stowe, *Going Abroad: European Travel in Nineteenth-Century American Culture* (Princeton: Princeton Univ. Press, 1993), 16–28. Dean Mac-Cannell explains sightseeing as a modern ritual in *The Tourist: A New Theory of the Leisure Class* (New York: Schocken Books, 1989), 42–43.

15. Dr. George Beard's *A Practical Treatise on Sea-Sickness* (1880). Titles of others are George Putnam's *The Tourist in Europe* (1838), John Henry Sherburne's *The Tourist's Guide* (1847), Roswell Park's *Handbook for American Travellers in Europe* (1853), Professor James Hoppin's *Old England* (thirteen editions between 1867 and

1893), and numbers of nineteenth-century equivalents to our *Europe on $50 a Day* such as William Helmstreet's *The Economical European Tourist* (1875) and the Thomas Knox series of six travel guides launched with a basic *How to Travel* (1881).

16. Travelers east had available to them John Lloyd Stephens's *Incidents of Travel in Egypt, Arabia and the Holy Land* (1837), Alexander Kinglake's classic *Eothen* (1844) and Bartholomew Warburton's *The Crescent and the Cross* (1844), Edward Robinson's *Biblical Researches* (1841), William H. Bartlett's detailed *Walks about the City and Environs of Jerusalem* (1844), and the enormously popular *The Land and the Book* (1859) by William M. Thomson of the American Mission in Beirut. These guides were joined by the Murray guide to Syria and Palestine (1858) and by a Baedeker in German (1875). By the middle of the nineteenth century "the conditions of the roads, the virtues and faults of dragomen, the hospitality of convents and the filth of khans were all fairly well-known to travelers coming to the Holy Land" (Franklin Walker, *Irreverent Pilgrims: Melville, Browne, and Mark Twain in the Holy Land* [Seattle: Univ. of Washington Press, 1974], 23–24). For the influence of the East on American writers, see Dorothee Metlitsky Finkelstein, *Melville's Orienda* (New Haven: Yale Univ. Press, 1961), and Luther S. Luedtke's *Nathaniel Hawthorne and the Romance of the Orient* (Bloomington: Indiana Univ. Press, 1989), xxi. Luedtke points out that "*The Arabian Nights' Entertainment* was one of four 'best sellers' published in the United States in 1794" and that "Thomas Moore's elaborately annotated *Lalla Rookh: An Eastern Romance* (1817) was the best-selling title in America between Walter Scott's *Waverley* (1815) and *Rob Roy* (1818)."

17. Stowe, *Going Abroad*, 29.

18. Jewett, *Pointed Firs*, 50.

19. Caroline Kirkland, *Holidays Abroad; or, Europe from the West* (1849), 69.

20. Edith Wharton, *A Backward Glance: The Autobiography of Edith Wharton* (1934; rpt. New York: Scribner's, 1964), 102; letter to Bernard Berenson, in *The Letters of Edith Wharton*, ed. R. W. B. Lewis and Nancy Lewis (New York: Scribner's, 1988), 272–73. On women and the Oregon Trail, see *Women's Diaries of the Westward Journey*, ed. Lillian Schlissel (New York: Schocken Books, 1992).

21. David Finnie, *Pioneers East: The Early American Experience in the Middle East* (Cambridge: Harvard Univ. Press, 1967), 204, 160–61.

22. Harrison Gray Otis Dwight, *Memoir of Mrs. Elizabeth B. Dwight, including an account of the plague of 1837* (1840); Caroline Paine, *Tent and Harem: Notes of an Oriental Trip* (1859).

23. Fanny Bullock Workman, *Algerian Memories; A Bicycle Tour over the Atlas of the Sahara* (1895), 32–33.

24. Information from Fussell, *Abroad*, 39.

25. Pregnancy was of course a serious obstacle to and difficulty in travel. The mid-nineteenth-century diary of a Georgia woman records the impact of pregnancy on women's ability to travel even within the United States: "happily planning a trip to the North because 'I have no infant and cannot tell whether next summer I will be so free from care,' in four days her dreams of travel vanished abruptly" when she found herself again pregnant. Travel was sometimes used to prevent pregnancy: the niece of James L. Petigru of South Carolina, for instance, having borne six children in nine years, spent sojourns of three months with her mother "to prolong the time between babies" (Anne Firor Scott, *Making the Invisible Woman Visible* [Urbana: Univ. of Illinois Press, 1984], 178–79). Julia Ward Howe gave birth in Rome to a daughter, Julia Romana, while on her wedding journey in 1844. As the last quarter of the nineteenth century approached, increased educational opportunities for women, together with delayed marriages, contributed to a reduction in the birth rate that further unfettered women. See Yasukichi Yasuba, *Birth Rates of the White Population in the United States, 1800–1860* (Baltimore: Johns Hopkins Univ. Press, 1962), and Carroll Smith-Rosenberg, *Disorderly Conduct: Visions of Gender in Victorian America* (New York: Knopf, 1985), 245–96. The numbers of female travelers increased as birth rates decreased.

26. Anna Dickinson, *A Ragged Register (of People, Places and Opinions)* (1879), 8.

27. For an illuminating discussion of the relationship between hydropathy, women's diseases, and women's relationship to their bodies between 1840 and 1890, see Kathryn Kish Sklar, *Catharine Beecher: A Study in American Domesticity* (New Haven: Yale Univ. Press, 1973), 204–9. See also Dulles, *Americans Abroad*, 3–4.

28. See Pierre Bourdieu, *Distinction: A Social Critique of the Judgement of Taste*, trans. Richard Nice (Cambridge: Harvard Univ. Press, 1984).

29. See Stowe, *Going Abroad*, 37–40.

30. Thorstein Veblen, *The Theory of the Leisure Class: An Economic Study of Institutions* (New York: Viking Press, 1945), 45. See David Leverenz, *Manhood and the American Renaissance* (Ithaca: Cornell Univ. Press, 1989), 72–90, on social class.

31. See Lawrence W. Levine's discussion of high culture and immigrants in *Highbrow/Lowbrow: The Emergence of Cultural Hierarchy in America* (Cambridge: Harvard Univ. Press, 1988), 206–8.

32. See, for example, Baker, *The Fortunate Pilgrims*; William C. Spengemann, *The Adventurous Muse: The Poetics of American Fiction, 1789–1900* (New Haven: Yale Univ. Press, 1977); Neil Harris, *The Artist in American Society: The Formative Years, 1790–1860* (New York: George Braziller, 1966); Cushing Strout, *The American Image of the Old World* (New York: Harper, 1963); Dulles, *Americans Abroad*; Christopher Mulvey, *Anglo-American Landscapes: A Study of Nineteenth-Century*

Anglo-American Travel Literature (Cambridge: Cambridge Univ. Press, 1990); Christopher Mulvey, *Transatlantic Manners: Social patterns in Nineteenth-Century Anglo-American Travel Literature* (Cambridge: Cambridge Univ. Press, 1990).

33. See Anne Firor Scott, "What, Then, Is the American: This New Woman?" *Journal of American History* 65 (December 1978): 679.

34. Ralph Waldo Emerson (24? August, 1847, rpt. in *Selections from Ralph Waldo Emerson: An Organic Anthology*, ed. Stephen E. Whicher (Boston: Houghton Mifflin, 1960), 311.

35. In millennialist thinking, Myra Jehlen explains, history is "an affliction brought on by a poor Constitution and America's growth is seen instead as the unfolding realization of its inherent form and meaning. Paradoxically, the middle class's faith in a progressive history had thus achieved an annihilating apotheosis in the conviction that all progress led to America." American writers felt privileged "to be in at the second coming of Western Civilization" (Myra Jehlen, "The Novel and the Middle Class in America," *Ideology and Classic American Literature*, ed. Sacvan Bercovitch and Myra Jehlen [Cambridge: Cambridge Univ. Press, 1986], 127–28, 133).

36. From *The Polish-American System of Chronology*, quoted in Nina Baym, "The Ann Sisters: Elizabeth Peabody's Millennial Historicism," *American Literary History* 3 (spring 1991): 30. See also Ruth H. Bloch, *Visionary Republic: Millennial Themes in American Thought, 1756–1800* (New York: Cambridge Univ. Press, 1985).

37. Catharine Beecher, *A Treatise on Domestic Economy for the Use of Young Ladies at Home and at School* (1841), 12.

38. See Daniel Walker Howe, "American Victorianism as a Culture," *American Quarterly* 27 (December 1975): 507–32.

39. Lockwood, *Passionate Pilgrims*, 297. Those who traveled in steerage, however—blacks and immigrants—suffered abominable conditions: cramped quarters, inadequate bathroom facilities, poor food, and filth. See Frank C. Bowen, *A Century of Atlantic Travel, 1830–1930* (Boston: Little, Brown, 1930).

40. There were always those who recognized the role of ideology in the circumscription of travel for women. Commenting on the heavy labor of "the Indian squaw" and "the washerwoman [who] stands at the tub and carries home her work at all seasons and in all states of health," Margaret Fuller unmasks as arbitrary the foundation of arguments against travel for women by observing that "the favorites of Louis XIV accompany him on his journeys" (*The Writings of Margaret Fuller*, ed. Mason Wade [New York: Viking Press, 1941, reissued by Augustus M. Kelley, Publishers, 1973], 123). Historically, women were allowed to travel when it suited the pleasure and purposes of men. What Dawn Lander calls a wilderness taboo,

imposed on women to deny feminine wanderlust, pertained to foreign as well as wilderness travel: "The home-loving figure is repelled by all forms of wildness, including sexuality and other peoples" (Dawn Lander, "Eve among the Indians," in *The Authority of Experience: Essays in Feminist Criticism*, ed. Arlyn Diamond and Lee R. Edwards [Amherst: Univ. of Massachusetts Press, 1977], 200).

41. Veblen, *The Theory of the Leisure Class*, 81.

42. For the competitiveness of fleets across the century, see Bowen, *Century of Atlantic Travel*, 241, especially on "the glamour cast over the whole," including the smaller ships of a company, by the presence of one sensational ship in the lists.

43. Judith Adler, "Origins of Sightseeing," *Annals of Tourism Research* 16 (1989): 8.

44. See Kolodny, *The Land before Her*, 93–111.

45. Mary Thorn Carpenter, *In Cairo and Jerusalem: An Eastern Note-Book* (1894), 120–30.

46. See James Buzard, *The Beaten Track: European Tourism, Literature, and the Ways to Culture, 1800–1918* (Oxford: Clarendon Press, 1993), 149.

47. Louis Althusser defines ideology as "not the system of the real relations which govern the existence of individuals, but the imaginary relation of those individuals to the real relations in which they live" (Althusser, *Lenin and Philosophy and Other Essays*, trans. Ben Brewster [London: New Left Books, 1971], 155, quoted in Catherine Belsey, "Constructing the Subject: Deconstructing the Text," in *Feminist Criticism and Social Change: Sex, Class and Race in Literature and Culture*, ed. Judith Newton and Deborah Rosenfelt [New York: Methuen, 1985], 46). According to this understanding, women would "imagine" that they travel to study education, for example, or to immerse themselves in history and art, when in fact the "real" reason is the profit to be made from their circulation.

48. See Kolodny, *The Land before Her*, 93–111.

49. Walker, *Irreverent Pilgrims*, 24–25.

50. Mary Cadwalader Jones, *European Travel for Women: Notes and Suggestions* (New York: Macmillan, 1900), vii, 45.

51. On guidebooks, see Stowe, *Going Abroad*, 37–40.

52. See Michael Curtin, "A Question of Manners: Status and Gender in Etiquette and Courtesy," *Journal of Modern History* 57 (September 1985): 395–423.

53. Nancy Armstrong and Leonard Tennenhouse, "The Literature of Conduct, the Conduct of Literature, and the Politics of Desire: An Introduction," in *The Ideology of Conduct: Essays on Literature and the History of Sexuality*, ed. Nancy Armstrong and Leonard Tennenhouse (New York: Methuen, 1987), 5.

54. See Nancy Armstrong, "The Rise of the Domestic Woman," in *Ideology of Conduct*, 117–18.

55. See Scott, *Making the Invisible Woman Visible*, 65. Important studies of women, domesticity, and public space include Karen J. Blair, *The Clubwoman as Feminist: True Womanhood Redefined, 1868–1914* (New York: Holmes & Meier, 1980); Frances Cogan, *The All-American Girl* (Athens: Univ. of Georgia Press, 1989); Nancy F. Cott, *The Bonds of Womanhood: "Woman's Sphere" in New England, 1780–1835* (New Haven: Yale Univ. Press, 1977); Mary Kelley, *Private Woman Public Stage: Literary Domesticity in Nineteenth-Century America* (New York: Oxford Univ. Press, 1984); Linda K. Kerber, "Separate Spheres, Female Worlds, Woman's Place: The Rhetoric of Women's History," *Journal of American History* 75 (June 1988): 9–39; Glenna Matthews, *The Rise of Public Woman: Woman's Power and Woman's Place in the United States, 1630–1970* (New York: Oxford Univ. Press, 1992); Mary Ryan, *Cradle of the Middle Class: The Family in Oneida County, New York, 1790–1865* (Cambridge: Cambridge Univ. Press, 1981), 186–229; Mary P. Ryan, *Women in Public: Between Banners and Ballots, 1825–1880* (Baltimore: Johns Hopkins Univ. Press, 1990); Barbara Welter, "The Cult of True Womanhood: 1820–1860," *American Quarterly* 18 (summer 1966): 151–74. Nina Baym's analysis of the meaning of the domestic, the public, and the private between 1790 and 1860 is especially instructive (Baym, *American Women Writers*, 4–7).

56. Sklar, *Catharine Beecher*, xii.

57. See Eric J. Leed, *The Mind of the Traveler: From Gilgamesh to Global Tourism* (New York: Basic Books, 1991), 276. Leed names the 1840s and the advent of Thomas Cook, "the watchful tour guide," as the end of the genderization of mobility and journeying as a masculine or masculinizing activity (288).

58. See Elizabeth Fagg Olds, *Women of the Four Winds* (Boston: Houghton Mifflin, 1985), 5–70.

59. Veblen, *The Theory of the Leisure Class*, 181–82. Skirts also provide a certain privacy, however, serving as curtains for performing bodily functions, dressing, and so on. See Schlissel, *Women's Diaries*, 98.

60. Mary Poovey, *The Proper Lady and the Woman Writer: Ideology as Style in the Works of Mary Wollstonecraft, Mary Shelley, and Jane Austen* (Chicago: Univ. of Chicago Press, 1984), 19–25.

61. Elizabeth Bisland, "The Art of Travel," in *The Woman's Book: Dealing Practically with the Modern Conditions of Home-Life, Self-Support, Education, Opportunities, and Every-Day Problems*, 2 vols. (New York: Charles Scribner's Sons, 1894), 1:382–83. According to Mary Russell, in *The Blessings of a Good Thick Skirt: Women Travellers and Their World* (London: Collins, 1986), 181, a British traveler, Lillias Campbell Davidson, expresses virtually identical sentiments in *Hints to Lady Travellers at Home and Abroad* (1889).

62. My summary is taken from Ryan, *Women in Public*, 58–94. See, as well, Matthews, *The Rise of Public Woman*, 93–171.

63. Bisland, *The Woman's Book*, 1:382.

64. See Smith-Rosenberg, *Disorderly Conduct*, 53–76.

65. See John Tomsich, *A Genteel Endeavor: American Culture and Politics in the Gilded Age* (Stanford: Stanford Univ. Press, 1971), 16–17.

66. Olds, *Women of the Four Winds*, 14–15. Olds's study includes a bibliography of Annie Smith Peck's travel writing (299–300).

67. Brooke Kroeger, *Nellie Bly: Daredevil, Reporter, Feminist* (New York: Times Books, 1994), 161.

68. Kroeger, *Nellie Bly*, 163, 175. Nellie Bly's feat continues to be a money-maker: Simon and Schuster's list of Books for Young People includes Robert Quackenbush's *Stop the Presses, Nellie's Got a Scoop!: A Story of Nellie Bly* (New York: 1992).

69. Quoted in Madelon Golden Schilpp and Sharon M. Murphy, *Great Women of the Press* (Carbondale: Southern Illinois Univ. Press, 1983), 144.

70. Kroeger, *Nellie Bly*, 167.

71. See Ingrid Carlander, *Les Américaines* (Paris: Grasset, 1973), 11–59; Paul Eakin, *The New England Girl: Cultural Ideals in Hawthorne, Stowe, Howells, and James* (Athens: Univ. of Georgia Press, 1976); Linda K. Kerber, *Women of the Republic: Intellect and Ideology in Revolutionary America* (Chapel Hill: Univ. of North Carolina Press, 1980), 269.

72. Beecher, *A Treatise on Domestic Economy*, 12, 13.

73. See Ryan, *Women in Public*, 172, 43.

74. Baym, *American Women Writers*, 13.

75. Sklar, *Catharine Beecher*, 193–94.

76. Alexis de Tocqueville, *Democracy in America* [1835], ed. J. P. Mayer and Max Lerner, trans. George Lawrence (New York: Harper & Row, 1966), 577. Ironically, the separation of spheres to which Tocqueville ascribed the prosperity and power of the United States was to American women the arrangement that complicated the matter of citizenship and identity by removing women from the public arena.

77. Paula Baker, "The Domestication of Politics: Women and American Political Society, 1780–1920," *American Historical Review* 89 (June 1984): 620–47.

78. See Marion Marzolf, *Up from the Footnote: A History of Women Journalists* (New York: Hastings House, 1977), 17.

79. Lilian Whiting, *Kate Field: A Record* (London: Sampson Low, Marston, 1899), 69, 66–67, 276, 416. Whiting also quotes from Field a remarkable anticipation of Virginia Woolf's *A Room of One's Own*: "It seems to me that one of the greatest delights of life," Field writes, "to a thinking mind must be a study,—a room religiously your own, the open sesame of which is a charm to be broken by

none else; a sanctuary to which you retire to ponder, think, weep, write, read, *pray*, knowing that there you may indulge your feelings as the emotions and passions dictate, and no one will dare intrude—no one will scrutinize you, save the All-wise, Omnipresent God. For such a retreat have I ever sighed" (69).

80. See Sara Mills, *Discourses of Difference: An Analysis of Women's Travel Writing and Colonialism* (London: Routledge, 1991), 94–106.

81. Sara M. Evans, *Born for Liberty: A History of Women in America* (New York: Free Press, 1989), 164.

82. Sandra Gilbert and Susan Gubar, *The Madwoman in the Attic: The Woman Writer and the Nineteenth-Century Literary Imagination* (New Haven: Yale Univ. Press, 1979), 64.

83. Mary O'Brien, "Feminist Theory and Dialectical Logic," *Signs* 7 (1981): 144–57, quoted in Patricia Yaeger, *Honey-Mad Women: Emancipatory Strategies in Women's Writing* (New York: Columbia Univ. Press, 1988), 210.

84. Hamalian, *Ladies on the Loose*, x.

85. Elizabeth Bisland [Wetmore], *A Flying Trip Around the World* (1891), 27; Mrs. A. E. Newman, *European Leaflets for Young Ladies* (1872), 22; Harriet Trowbridge Allen, *Travels in Europe and the East: During the years 1858–59 and 1863–64* (1879), 4; Lucy Bronson Dudley, *Letters to Ruth* (1896), 12.

86. Ella W. Thompson, *Beaten Paths, or a Woman's Vacation* (1874), 9–10.

87. I am indebted to Gillian Brown's *Domestic Individualism: Imagining Self in Nineteenth-Century America* (Berkeley: Univ. of California Press, 1990) for the schema of domesticity, the marketplace, domestic individualism, and agoraphobia I have here applied to women's travel.

88. Georges Van Den Abbeele, "Sightseers: The Tourist as Theorist," *Diacritics* 10 (December 1980): 9; and Leed, *The Mind of the Traveler*, 292.

89. The Bishop of Africa inscribed this in Agnes McAllister's book, *A Lone Woman in Africa: Six Years on the Kroo Coast* (1896), adding that she "made a success in all departments of our mission work" and has now written a book "full of graphic delineations of what she saw, suffered, heard and did in the babble of heathen life and the ravages of war in which she took an active part as surgeon, nurse, and counselor."

90. Mrs. M. and Emma Straiton, *Two Lady Tramps Abroad, a compilation of letters descriptive of nearly a year's travel in India, Asia Minor, Egypt, the Holy Land, Turkey, Greece, Italy, Austria, Switzerland, France, England, Ireland, and Scotland* (1881), iii–v.

91. See Eakin, *New England Girl*, for the American woman as the all-purpose symbol of the culture; and Carlander, *Les Américaines*, 11–59, for the European vision of the American woman. Tocqueville, *Democracy*, 579.

92. Quoted in Ryan, *Cradle of the Middle Class,* 219. Ryan notes that Lavinia

Johnson, staying "noiselessly in her sphere," was married for thirty-one years "to a man who apparently did not live up to his responsibility in the sexual division of labor."

93. Lucy Seaman Bainbridge, *Round-the-World Letters* (1882), 14–15.

94. Quoted in Sandra Gilbert and Susan Gubar, *No Man's Land: The Place of the Woman Writer in the Twentieth Century*, 2 vols.(New Haven: Yale Univ. Press, 1988), 1:17. This same Royal Geographical Society made May French Sheldon, explorer, a Fellow in 1892.

95. Fanny Bullock Workman, *Two Summers in the Ice-Wilds of Eastern Karakoram* (New York: E. P. Dutton, 1914), 222–23. It is conceivable that Workman *uses* gender here to evade the question, but gender is nevertheless in play.

96. Bisland [Wetmore], *A Flying Trip*, 5–6.

97. Fuller, *The Writings of Margaret Fuller*, 171–72.

98. Ida Tarbell, *All in the Day's Work: An Autobiography* (1939, rpt. Boston: G. K. Hall, 1985), 114. In *Fashioning the Bourgeoisie: A History of Clothing in the Nineteenth Century*, trans. Richard Bienvenu (Princeton: Princeton Univ. Press, 1994), Philippe Perrot reports that the sensuous appeal of clothing on display in department stores created compulsive shoplifting, understood as a symptom of the female pathology of hysteria.

99. See *Elizabeth Cady Stanton*, ed. Theodore Stanton and Harriet Stanton Blatch, 2 vols. (New York: Arno Press, 1969), 1:76; Bell Gale Chevigny, *The Woman and the Myth: Margaret Fuller's Life and Writings* (Boston: Northeastern Univ. Press, 1994), 3; Joan Hedrick, *Harriet Beecher Stowe: A Life* (New York: Oxford Univ. Press, 1994), 269–70, 264. Virginia Woolf observed that Charlotte Brontë's genius would have profited enormously from travel (*A Room of One's Own* (London: Hogarth Press, 1929), 105.

100. Scott, *Making the Invisible Woman Visible*, 65.

CHAPTER TWO · LITERARY INROADS

1. Hamalian, *Ladies*, x.

2. Fussell, *Abroad*, 203.

3. Figures compiled from Smith, *American Travellers Abroad*. These numbers are of course approximate for, as Smith points out, there was "probably a large body of fugitive items . . . which did not get into trade bibliographies, and which did not come to the attention of the bibliographer." These figures raise a question of generic definition: what counts as a travel book? Deciding this question is not necessary for my purposes here, but the figures I have compiled from Smith include, as William W. Stowe observes in "Conventions and Voices in Margaret

Fuller's Travel Writing," *American Literature* 63 (June 1991): 242, n. 1, "subgenres such as the sailor's account or the diplomatic memoir." The percentage by decade of the total number of travel books (including subgenres) published by women is as follows: before 1830: 0% (0 books by women, 91 by men); 1830s: 5% (4 by women, 76 by men); 1840s: 5% (7 by women, 148 by men); 1850s: 6% (16 by women, 261 by men); 1860s: 10% (13 by women, 119 by men); 1870s: 13% (33 by women, 215 by men); 1880s: 15% (57 by women, 320 by men); 1890s: 16% (65 by women, 340 by men). After 1830, that is, and beginning with the 1850s, the percentage of women's travel books increased in each of the successive decades, rising to 13% in the 1870s, to 15% in the 1880s, and to 16% in the 1890s. Information about certain variables, however, stands to modify this picture of women's progress in publishing travel accounts. Because of the decline in the whaling and sealing industries in the second half of the century, the raw number of accounts by men may include fewer in the subgenre of sailors' accounts and relatively more, therefore, in the type that women wrote, mitigating women's relative "gains." Moreover, the phenomenon of affluent businessmen clipping coupons in New York while sending their women abroad may mean that a larger percentage of the men who traveled after the Civil War, in contrast with antebellum writers, wrote accounts. Women's "gains" measured only in percentages, that is, may distort the picture.

4. William J. Gilmore, *Reading Becomes a Necessity of Life: Material and Cultural Life in Rural New England, 1780–1835* (Knoxville: Univ. of Tennessee Press, 1989), 308, 298, 267–68. This is accounted for, Gilmore believes, by "the vast increase in knowledge of every conceivable aspect of this world, an increase ushered in by the Enlightenment" and creating a craving for novelty. Gilmore's data are taken from 396 family libraries.

5. Ronald J. Zboray, *A Fictive People: Antebellum Economic Development and the American Reading Public* (New York: Oxford Univ. Press, 1993), 176–79. Zboray finds that in the late 1840s, 19% of the books charged from the New York Society Library by men and 15% of those charged by women were books of travel.

6. Zboray, *Fictive People*, 179. Zboray explains that by the middle of the 1850s, fiction dominated the publishing market. John Tebbel, in *A History of Book Publishing in the United States*, 4 vols. (New York: Bowker, 1972), 2:675–708, prints tables from *Publishers Weekly* on the numbers of titles in various genres published annually in the United States. Books of "Description and Travel" typically rank fourth or fifth, just below history, in numbers of titles published.

7. Quoted in Tebbel, *History of Book Publishing*, 2:520. Perhaps Griswold's book sold as well as it did because it was published by the American Publishing Company, a subscription book business. According to Tebbel, it seemed impos-

sible to lose on subscription books (104). *Periodical Literature in Nineteenth-Century America*, ed. Kenneth M. Price and Susan Belasco Smith (Charlottesville: Univ. Press of Virginia, 1995), collects instructive essays on periodical literature in social and historical context.

8. *The Reader's Companion to American History*, ed. Eric Foner and John A. Garraty (Boston: Houghton Mifflin, 1991), 57, cites the following statistics: the West "increased its share of the world manufacturing output from 29 percent in 1800 to 86 percent in 1900, whereas Asia's declined from 57 to 10 percent." The lure of such a market "more than any strategic calculations, served to keep that part of the world alive in the American consciousness." According to James Buzard, revolutions in Italy and France in 1848, although they deterred continental tours, did not significantly deter travel writers (*Beaten Track,* 160).

9. Jared Sparks, "Riley's Narrative," *North American Review* 5 (1817): 390, quoted in Lawrence Buell, *Literary Transcendentalism: Style and Vision in the American Renaissance* (Ithaca: Cornell Univ. Press, 1973), 189; anon., quoted in Frank L. Mott, *A History of American Magazines*, 4 vols. (Cambridge Univ. Press, 1967), 1:422; Sedgwick, *Letters from Abroad to Kindred at Home* (1841), ix; *Harper's New Monthly Magazine* 40 (1870): 301; *Hearth and Home*, quoted in Evelyn I. Banning, *Helen Hunt Jackson* (New York: Vanguard, 1973), 86.

10. Adelaide S. Hall, *Two Women Abroad; What They Saw and How They Lived While Traveling Among The Semi-Civilized People of Morocco, the Peasants of Italy and France, as well as the Educated Classes of Spain, Greece, and Other Countries* (1897), vii.

11. Eric Savoy, "The Subverted Gaze: Hawthorne, Howells, James and the Discourse of Travel," *Canadian Review of American Studies* 21 (winter 1990): 290.

12. Harris, *The Artist in American Society*, 126.

13. Anon., *Peterson's Magazine* (August 1857): 315.

14. Buzard, *Beaten Track,* 158. Although Buzard focuses on European tourism, the attitudes he identifies also played in accounts of travel to the Middle and Far East.

15. Baym, *American Women Writers*, 3.

16. See ibid., 5; and Kerber, "Separate Spheres," 9–39.

17. *Peterson's Magazine* (December 1845): 72; *Atlantic Monthly* (August 1874): 233; quote about Jackson in Banning, *Jackson*, 93; Buzard, *Beaten Track,* 158.

18. Baker, *The Fortunate Pilgrims*, 213–24.

19. See, for example, Kerber, *Women of the Republic*, 284; and Blair, *Clubwoman*.

20. Evans, *Born for Liberty*, 72.

21. Baym, *American Women Writers*, 65–66. In *Transatlantic Manners*, 61, Christopher Mulvey quotes Harriet Martineau's sharply different view, in *Society*

in America (1831), of the situation of the woman in the United States. "While woman's intellect is confined, her morals crushed, her health ruined, her weakness encouraged and her strength punished," writes Martineau, "she is told that her lot is cast in the paradise of women: and there is no country in the world where there is so much boasting of the 'chivalrous' treatment she enjoys."

22. See Ryan, *Cradle of the Middle Class*, 218.

23. Smith-Rosenberg, *Disorderly Conduct*, 176. See also Scott, *Making the Invisible Woman Visible*, 282–83.

24. See Elaine Showalter's discussion of James's *The Bostonians* in *Sexual Anarchy: Gender and Culture at the Fin de Siècle* (New York: Penguin, 1990), 27–30. Elizabeth Ammons identifies the problem of female muteness in the fiction of the Progressive Era in *Conflicting Stories: American Women Writers at the Turn into the Twentieth Century* (New York: Oxford Univ. Press, 1991), 5. Teresa L. Ebert points out that "language acquires its meaning not from its formal system, as Saussure proposes, but from its place in the social struggle over meanings"; sign becomes an arena of social struggle ("The 'Difference' of Postmodern Feminism," *College English* 53 [December 1991]: 886).

25. Harriet Beecher Stowe, *Sunny Memories of Foreign Lands*, 2 vols. (1854), 1: iii. For the battle of the travel books, see Lockwood, *Passionate Pilgrims*, 197–207. Zboray, in *Fictive People*, xv, explains that the published accounts of European travelers "often left their onetime hosts infuriated" because the Europeans, seeking the unique American and finding a diversity of types, "chose as representative the boorish, the pretentious, the unlettered, the vulgar," none of which stood for the American from the native point of view. "Natives preferred vaguer, more celebratory models."

26. Joanne Dobson, *Dickinson and the Strategies of Reticence* (Bloomington: Indiana Univ. Press, 1989), 79.

27. Mary Louise Pratt, *Imperial Eyes: Travel Writing and Transculturation* (London: Routledge, 1992), 160.

28. My information about women in journalism is taken from Marzolf, *Up from the Footnote*, 1–31. The classic history of women in journalism is Ishbel Ross, *Ladies of the Press: The Story of Women in Journalism by an Insider* (New York: Harper's, 1936). See, as well, Sherilyn Cox Bennion, *Equal to the Occasion: Women Editors of the Nineteenth-Century West* (Reno: Univ. of Nevada Press, 1990).

29. Richard Brodhead, *Cultures of Letters: Scenes of Reading and Writing in Nineteenth-Century America* (Chicago: Univ. of Chicago Press, 1993).

30. See Buell, *Literary Transcendentalism*, 189.

31. See Shelley Fisher Fishkin, *From Fact to Fiction: Journalism and Imaginative Writing in America* (Baltimore: Johns Hopkins Univ. Press, 1985), 15, 55.

32. See Susan Coultrap-McQuin, *Doing Literary Business: American Women*

Writers in the Nineteenth Century (Chapel Hill: Univ. of North Carolina Press, 1990), 17.

33. Sarah Haight, *Letters from the Old World. By a lady of New York*, 2 vols. (1839): 1:preface.

34. See Percy Adams, ed., *Travel Literature through the Ages: An Anthology* (New York: Garland, 1988), xxiii. See, as well, Terry Caesar, "'Counting the Cats in Zanzibar': American Travel Abroad in American Travel Writing to 1914," *Prospects: An Annual of American Cultural Studies*, ed. Jack Salzman, vol. 13 (New York: Cambridge Univ. Press, 1988): 95–134.

35. Perhaps the eclectic nature of the genre explains why, in Paul Fussell's words, "Criticism has never quite known what to call books like these" (Fussell, *Abroad*, 202). Also see Buell, *Literary Transcendentalism*, 194–99.

36. William W. Stowe, "Conventions and Voices in Margaret Fuller's Travel Writing," *American Literature* 63 (June 1991): 243.

37. See Josephine Donovan, "The Silence Is Broken," *Women and Language in Literature and Society*, ed. Sally McConnell-Ginet et al. (New York: Prager, 1980), 205–18, for an extended exploration of women writers and the epistolary form. Writing about Victorian travelers to Africa, Catherine Barnes Stevenson, in *Victorian Women Travel Writers in Africa* (Boston: G. K. Hall, 1982), 9, points out that "women often cast their narratives as a series of letters home to a predominantly female audience interested in both the minutiae of everyday domestic life and the writer's psychological reactions to a new environment. The loose, accretive, epistolary form serves as an ideal vehicle for leisurely descriptions of diverse subjects."

38. Jane Marcus, "Invincible Mediocrity: The Private Selves of Public Women," in *The Private Self: Theory and Practice of Women's Autobiographical Writings*, ed. Shari Benstock (Chapel Hill: Univ. of North Carolina Press, 1988), 120. In *Pleasurable Instruction: Form and Convention in Eighteenth-Century Travel Literature* (Berkeley: Univ. of California Press, 1978), 45, 47–81, Charles L. Batten Jr. points out that in the eighteenth century, in the face of accusations of lying, and as if artless and homely narration were proof against invention, British travelers sought to underscore their fundamental veracity by denigrating their work, adopting a humble style and stressing their "inability to entertain readers with style and language." In *Discourses of Difference*, 112–16, Sara Mills associates the tradition of the travel liar as identified by Batten and the travel writing of British women with stereotypes that cast women as duplicitous.

39. Blair, *Clubwoman*, 5.

40. These features and others are insightfully analyzed in Buzard, *Beaten Track*, and Stowe, *Going Abroad*.

41. A version of my analysis of difference appears as "Women's Place in Travel

Texts," in *Prospects: An Annual of American Cultural Studies*, ed. Jack Salzman, vol. 20 (New York: Cambridge Univ. Press, 1995): 161–79.

42. David E. Johnson, " 'Writing in the Dark': The Political Fictions of American Travel Writing," *American Literary History* 7 (spring 1995): 3.

43. Roland Barthes, "The Death of the Author," trans. Geoff Bennington (1977, rpt. in *Modern Criticism and Theory: A Reader*, ed. David Lodge [New York: Longman, 1988], 170. The measure of inescapability may be the role of "travel writing" in schools. Steeped by the age of fifteen in paradigms of the world and travel, Ellen Hardin Walworth reports that her school lessons included the composition of pseudo-travel letters (*An old world, as seen through young eyes; or, travels around the world* [1877], 127).

44. Baym, *American Women Writers*, 46. Baym's study of women historians includes a chapter on women's travel writing entitled "Tourists in Time" (130–51).

45. I am indebted to Philip Glazebrook's *Journey to Kars* (1984) for this metaphor, quoted in Heather Henderson, "The Travel Writer and the Text: 'My Giant Goes with Me Wherever I Go,' " *New Orleans Review* 18 (summer 1991): 31.

46. Bayard Taylor, *A Journey to Central Africa; or, Life and Landscapes from Egypt to the Negro Kingdoms of the White Nile* (1854), 230, 502, 491–92. According to John Tebbel, in *The History of Publishing*, 2:307, Taylor's *Views Afoot* (1846), one of the publisher Putnam's earliest successes, sold 100,000 copies by 1884. Susan Warner's *Wide Wide World*, on the other hand, one of the wonders of publishing history, sold 500,000 copies in the United States alone.

47. See Annette Kolodny, "Dancing through the Minefield," in *The New Feminist Criticism: Essays on Women, Literature, and Theory*, ed. Elaine Showalter (New York: Pantheon, 1985), 154. The recurrent evocation of talismanic names is another sign of the culture's inundation in travel talk. Tourist meccas such as Venice are transformed by travelers and travel books into commonplaces and icons, which then became kernel words for other travel writers. One need write only the kernel word to call up visions. Talismanic names offer "marker involvement," in which the tourist gets "thrills from the marker instead of the sight" (Dean MacCannell, *The Tourist: A New Theory of the Leisure Class* [New York: Schocken, 1989], 115). Mrs. E. A. Forbes's words on the subject of Abbotsford, in *A Woman's first impressions of Europe. Being wayside sketches made during a short tour in the year 1863* (1865), 66, go directly to the heart of the talismanic matter: "What more is needed than the name!" she exclaims.

48. Edith Wharton, *Italian Backgrounds* (New York: Scribner's, 1905), 35.

49. Edward Said, *Orientalism* (1978, rpt. "Crisis [in Orientalism]" in *Modern Criticism and Theory: A Reader*, ed. Lodge, 295.

50. Strout, *The American Image of the Old World*, xii.

51. See John Frowe, "Tourism and the Semiotics of Nostalgia," *October* 57 (summer 1991): 125–48.

52. Roland Barthes demonstrates the operations of this phenomenon with the "Blue Guide" series, which becomes "through an operation common to all mystifications, the very opposite of what it advertises, an agent of blindness" (Barthes, "The 'Blue Guide,'" in *Mythologies*, trans. Annette Lavers [New York: Hill & Wang, 1972], 76).

53. See Buzard, *Beaten Track*, 154–216.

54. See Baym, *American Women Writers*, 131.

55. Julia Ward Howe, *From the Oak to the Olive. A plain record of a pleasant journey* (1868), 6. See my "Julia Ward Howe and the Travel Book," *New England Quarterly* 62 (June 1989): 264–79.

56. Margaret Fuller, *Summer on the Lakes* (1844; rpt. in *The Writings of Margaret Fuller*, ed. Mason Wade [New York: Viking Press, 1941]), 51.

57. Savoy, "Subverted Gaze," 288.

58. Mark Twain [Samuel Clemens], *The Innocents Abroad or The New Pilgrims' Progress* [1869], 2 vols. (New York: Harpers, 1906), 1:xxxvii, 154–55, 98, 69. Leslie Fiedler recognized that *Innocents* is a book primarily about the American tourist/consumer "rather than about the Old World itself" ("Afterword," *The Innocents Abroad* by Mark Twain [New York: Signet, 1980], 489). See, as well, Richard S. Lowry, "Framing the Authentic: The Modern Tourist and *The Innocents Abroad*," *New Orleans Review* 18 (summer 1991): 18–28.

59. [Helen Hunt Jackson], *Bits of Travel. By H. H.* (1872), 166.

60. Drawing on Mikhail Bakhtin, one might argue that any use of language is bivocal. "Our practical everyday speech," Bakhtin writes, "is full of the words of other people; we merge our voice completely with some of them, forgetting whose they are; others we take as authoritative, using them to support our own words; still others we people with aspirations of our own which are foreign or hostile to them" (*Dostoevsky's Poetics*, trans. R. W. Rotsel [Ann Arbor MI: Ardis, 1973], 161–62). Bakhtin, however, does not take gender into account.

61. Robert Scholes, *Semiotics and Interpretation* (New Haven: Yale Univ. Press, 1982), 144.

62. Linda Alcoff, "Cultural Feminism versus Post-Structuralism: The Identity Crisis in Feminist Theory," *Signs* 13 (1988): 405–36.

63. Kristeva quoted in Gilbert and Gubar, *No Man's Land*, 1:228.

64. Ross, *Ladies of the Press*, 14. On double-voiced discourse, see Elaine Showalter, "Feminist Criticism in the Wilderness," in *Writing and Sexual Difference*, ed. Elizabeth Abel (Chicago: Univ. of Chicago Press, 1982), 29–31.

65. See Nicole Tonkovich, "Traveling in the West, Writing in the Library: Margaret Fuller's *Summer on the Lakes*," *Legacy* 10 (fall 1993): 79–102.

66. For faithless readings, see Nelly Furman, "The Politics of Language: Beyond the Gender Principle?" *Making a Difference: Feminist Literary Criticism*, ed. Gayle Greene and Coppélia Kahn (London: Routledge, 1985), 59–79.

67. Washington Irving, *The Sketchbook of Geoffrey Crayon, Gent.*, (1819, rpt. in *The Literature of the United States*, ed. Walter Blair et al., 2 vols. (Chicago: Scott, Foresman, 1966), 1:589; and Fuller, *Summer*, in *Writings*, ed. Wade, 10.

68. Henry James, *Portraits of Places* (1883), 1–2.

69. Henrietta Schuck, *Scenes in China, or sketches of the country, religion, and customs of the Chinese, by the late Mrs. Henrietta Shuck, missionary in China* (1852), preface.

70. Mabel Loomis Todd, *Corona and coronet: Being a narrative of the Amherst eclipse expedition to Japan in Mr. James' schooner-yacht Coronet, to observe the sun's total obscuration, 9th August, 1896* (1898), v–vi.

71. Twain, *Innocents Abroad*, 1:91. The vehicle convention is alive and well in our time on travel videos made for television. Clive James, for example, in his "Postcard from Berlin" that aired on television in the fall of 1995, dallied for at least five of the twenty-five minutes of his "postcard" over his rented East German automobile, decrepit, unreliable, and the symbol of the political failure of the East German regime.

72. Joseph [illustrator] and Elizabeth Robins Pennell, *Two Pilgrims' Progress: From Fair Florence to the Eternal City of Rome* (1886), 23.

73. John Tomsich, *A Genteel Endeavor: American Culture and Politics in the Gilded Age* (Stanford: Stanford Univ. Press, 1971), 42. Tomsich adds that "the escape was far from complete, however, but rather more like a tourist's holiday. One flirted with the exotic, but never confronted it." See also Dulles, *Americans Abroad*, 4.

74. Mills, *Discourses of Difference*, 88–90.

75. Taylor, *A Journey to Central Africa*, 225.

76. Edith Wharton, *In Morocco* (1920, rpt. London: Century Publishing, 1984), 76, 79.

77. Baym, *American Women Writers*, 64.

78. Jackson Lears points out that by the turn of the nineteenth century, Roman Catholicism was attractive to antimodernist Americans and to aesthetes on whom medievalism and the ritual and artifacts of Catholicism exercised a certain attraction (*No Place of Grace: Antimodernism and the Transformation of American Culture, 1880–1920* [New York: Pantheon, 1981], 184–215).

79. Taylor, *Journey to Central Africa*, 333–36. Taylor is the ancestor of Indiana Jones.

80. Paine, *Tent and Harem*, 249–51.

81. Taylor, *Journey to Central Africa*, 338–39. For an account of Taylor and his place in American travel writing, see Tomsich, *Genteel Endeavor*, 27–50.

82. Claude M. Simpson and Fredson Bowers, eds., *The Centenary Edition of the Works of Nathaniel Hawthorne*, 14 vols. (Columbus: Ohio State Univ. Press, 1970), 5:48–49.

83. Twain, *Innocents Abroad*, 1:202, 243.

84. Anna P. Little, *The World as We Saw It* (1887), 223–224, 248.

85. Mrs. S. R. Urbino, *An American Woman in Europe. The Journal of Two Years & a Half Sojourn in Germany, Switzerland, France, and Italy* (1869), 19. Mrs. Urbino (Levina Buoncuore) published children's books, Italian grammars, and art handbooks from the 1860s through the turn of the century.

86. Clara Moyse Tadlock, *Bohemian Days* (1889), 380–81. Tadlock published collections of poetry entitled *Solomon Grinder's Christmas Eve and Other Poems* (1885) and *A California Idyl* (1893), *Holiday Souvenir No. 5* (1897–98).

87. Susan E. (Mrs. Lew) Wallace, *Along the Bosphorus, and other sketches* (1898), 49, 66–67.

88. See Mills, *Discourses of Difference*, 87–94.

89. Mary Wieting, *Prominent Incidents in the Life of Dr. John M. Wieting* (1889), 125, 141.

90. Emma Willard, *Journal and Letters, from France and Great Britain* (1833), 164.

91. See Leverenz, *Manhood and the American Renaissance*, 72.

92. Baker, *Fortunate Pilgrims*, 215.

93. Sklar, *Catharine Beecher*, 211.

94. Abby Morrell, *Narrative of a Voyage to the Ethiopic and South Atlantic Ocean, Indian Ocean, Chinese Sea, North and South Pacific Ocean, in the Years 1829, 1830, 1831* (1833), dedication.

95. Leverenz, *Manhood and the American Renaissance*, 72.

96. According to Katherine Frank, British women who traveled in Africa were freed by travel to perceive themselves in terms of race rather than gender. They "transcended their sexual identities" ("Voyages Out: Nineteenth-Century Women Travelers in Africa," *Gender, Ideology, and Action: Historical Perspectives on Women's Public Lives*, ed. Janet Sharistanian (New York: Greenwood Press, 1986), 71. American women textualize their self-perception quite differently. They burrow into gender until they reach the bottom of it.

97. Baym, *American Women Writers*, 215.

98. Yaeger, *Honey-Mad Women*, 83.

CHAPTER THREE · AUTOBIOGRAPHICAL OCCASIONS

1. Bénédicte Monicat, "Autobiography and Women's Travel Writings in Nineteenth-century France: Journeys through Self-Representation," *Gender, Place and Culture* 1 (1994): 64–65. I am indebted to Diana Swanson for bringing this essay to my attention.

2. Margo Culley, "What a Piece of Work Is 'Woman'! An Introduction," *American Women's Autobiography: Fea(s)ts of Memory*, ed. Margo Culley (Madison: Univ. of Wisconsin Press, 1992), 11.

3. Sidonie Smith, *A Poetics of Women's Autobiography: Marginality and the Fictions of Self-Representation* (Bloomington: Indiana Univ. Press, 1987), 58.

4. See Evans, *Born for Liberty*, 61–66.

5. On the self-made woman see Scott, *Making the Invisible Woman Visible*, 89–106.

6. Russell, *Blessings of a Good Thick Skirt*, 217.

7. Ibid., 80. A similar but more tedious and perfunctory book of travels than Abby Morrell's is *Life in Feejee, or Five Years among the Cannibals*, by a Lady [Mrs. Wallis] (1851, rpt. Ridgewood NJ: Gregg Press, 1967).

8. Morrell came home with an average of 6,500 fur-seal skins per voyage. See *Dictionary of American Biography*, vol. 13: 195.

9. Benjamin Morrell, *A Narrative of Four Voyages* (1832, rpt. Upper Saddle River NJ: Gregg Press, 1970), 350–51, 356.

10. Sara Mills finds that British women travelers in the Victorian age did not mention "'indelicate' subjects in the main; surprisingly, few of them refer to any fear of sexual harassment, one of the discursive constraints which is the strongest in the context of women and travel, especially in accounts of women travelling alone" (*Discourses of Difference*, 82). Women diarists on the Oregon Trail also avoided "indelicate" subjects such as pregnancy and contraception, and wrote euphemistically of rape. See Schlissel, *Women's Diaries*, 106–11.

11. Morrell, *A Narrative of Four Voyages*, 418. His account of the incident with the consul puts a rather different face on it. He reports that "it was finally arranged" that his wife would stay in Manilla "and not encounter the privations and dangers of the voyage. It was not without reluctance that my wife consented to this arrangement; but being very much attached to Mrs. Cannell and her pleasant little family, she at length became reconciled to a temporary separation from me,

and took up her residence in this abode of virtue, peace, and hospitality, where I knew that she would receive such protection and delicate attentions as her sex and state of health required" (387). After returning from the Fijis and leaving Manila, he refers to "the envy and perfidy of some of my own countrymen" that kept him from raising funds to outfit his ship profitably, and then he reports obliquely: "The sanctity of the tomb, combined with a delicacy for the feelings of the living, protects the memory of *one* whose name would otherwise, in this very narrative, have been stamped with irredeemable infamy. *His* perfidious machinations so far succeeded as to compel me to abandon the idea of returning to the islands of Sunday and Monday [natives he had taken on board his ship to bring to the United States] until I had first visited the United States" (469). If this passage refers to the harassment episode, its indirection may be designed to protect his wife's reputation.

12. Ibid., 418. Morrell became more than reconciled to Abby's presence. Although on one occasion she importuned him by coming on deck during a violent storm to offer him his hat, he writes that eventually his "own mental temperament [was] much improved by the influence of her society; her sweetly smiling vivacity and exuberance of spirits operated on my own feelings like a charm— I was insensibly awakened from my despondency, hope was rekindled in my bosom, and, as far as respected myself, I could contemplate my recent misfortunes [an attack by Feejee islanders] without a sigh of regret. The safety of the Antarctic [his ship] was identified with that of one who was dearer to me than life. What stronger security could exist for the care and vigilance of her commander!" His next remarks join the culture's discourse about wives accompanying husbands at sea. He writes: "Were I a merchant and a ship-owner, so far from opposing the wishes of an affectionate wife who would accompany her husband on a long and hazardous voyage, I would recommend such a measure to every ship-master in my employ, and consider it of more value to my interest than the policy of ensurance" (378).

13. Carl N. Degler, *At Odds: Women and the Family in America from the Revolution to the Present* (New York: Oxford Univ. Press, 1980), 31–35.

14. Russell, *Blessings of a Good Thick Skirt*, 162.

15. Cott, *Bonds of Womanhood*, 8.

16. See Russell, *Blessings of a Good Thick Skirt*, 162. For women travelers on the Oregon Trail, see Schlissel, *Women's Diaries*, 82.

17. See Evans, *Born for Liberty*, 57.

18. Karen R. Lawrence, *Penelope Voyages: Women and Travel in the British Literary Tradition* (Ithaca: Cornell Univ. Press, 1994), 20.

19. Mary Kelley quoting Catharine Sedgwick's autobiography, *Life and Letters*

of Catharine Maria Sedgwick (1872), in "Legacy Profile: Catharine Maria Sedgwick," *Legacy* 6 (fall 1989): 46.

20. See Scott, *Making the Invisible Woman Visible*, 102, 238.

21. Morrell, *Narrative of Four Voyages*, 468.

22. Georges Gusdorf, "Conditions and Limits of Autobiography," trans. James Olney, *Autobiography: Essays Theoretical and Critical*, ed. James Olney (Princeton: Princeton Univ. Press, 1980), 29.

23. Eleanor Smith Bowen, *Return to Laughter: An Anthropological Novel* (1954, rpt. Garden City: Doubleday Anchor, 1964), xiv.

24. A version of this analysis of the Hawthornes has appeared in my "Difference of Signatures: Sophia and Nathaniel Hawthorne," coauthored with Ranjini Philip in *Commonwealth and American Women's Discourse: Essays in Criticism*, ed. A. L. McLeod (New Delhi: Sterling, 1995), 365–75.

25. James R. Mellow, *Nathaniel Hawthorne in His Times* (Boston: Houghton Mifflin, 1980), 131. The *Cuba Journal* is available through University Microfilms, Ann Arbor, Michigan. See also "A Sophia Hawthorne Journal, 1843–1844," ed. John J. McDonald, *Nathaniel Hawthorne Journal* 4 (1974): 1–30.

26. Randall Stewart, *Nathaniel Hawthorne: A Biography* (New Haven: Yale Univ. Press, 1947), 62.

27. Ibid., 189.

28. Mellow, *Nathaniel Hawthorne*, 529.

29. Sophia Hawthorne, *Notes in England and Italy* (1870), preface. Reprinted in 1874 and 1875.

30. For a provocative analysis of Sophia's reaction to portraits, see T. Walter Herbert, *Dearest Beloved: The Hawthornes and the Making of the Middle-Class Family* (Berkeley: Univ. of California Press, 1993), 218–22.

31. Ibid., 121.

32. Ibid., 49.

33. Raymona E. Hull, *Nathaniel Hawthorne: The English Experience, 1853–1864* (Pittsburgh: Univ. of Pittsburgh Press, 1980), 228–29.

34. Nathaniel Hawthorne, *The English Notebooks*, ed. Randall Stewart (New York: Russell & Russell, 1941), xiv.

35. Anon., *Harper's New Monthly Magazine* 40 (January 1870): 301.

36. Cott, *Bonds of Womanhood*, 78.

37. Hawthorne, *English Notebooks*, 473.

38. Ibid., 154.

39. Stewart, *Nathaniel Hawthorne*, 240.

40. *Passages from the American Notebooks*, by Nathaniel Hawthorne, ed. Sophia Hawthorne (1876), xix, xviii, xii.

41. The precarious financial circumstances of the Hawthornes necessitated frugality. In their early married life their situation was sometimes desperate, but Sophia loyally concealed this "lest anyone dare accuse her husband of failing to provide properly for his wife and child." In the late 1840s, Sophia painted lamp shades and fire screens for needed income, and their expenses in England consumed their entire income. According to the Hawthorne household account book, Sophia served as the family accountant and did well as a household manager at a time when the Hawthornes were impecunious. See Louise Hall Tharp, *The Peabody Sisters of Salem* (Boston: Little, Brown, 1951), 176, 189; and Hull, *Nathaniel Hawthorne*, 35.

42. Herbert, *Dearest Beloved*, 37.

43. Lockwood, *Passionate Pilgrims*, 327.

44. Quoted in Hull, *Nathaniel Hawthorne*, 181–82. Hawthorne concludes his remarks with this: "I doubt whether she would find sufficient inspiration in writing directly for the public."

45. Patricia Dunlavy Valenti, "Sophia Peabody Hawthorne: A Study of Artistic Influence," *Studies in the American Renaissance*, ed. Joel Myerson (Charlottesville: Univ. Press of Virginia, 1990), 7.

46. Tharp, *Peabody Sisters*, 46–50.

47. Quoted in ibid., 55.

48. Ibid., 107.

49. Ibid., 130–31, 153.

50. Quoted in Julian Hawthorne, *Nathaniel Hawthorne and His Wife*, 2 vols. (1884), 1:353.

51. Rose Hawthorne Lathrop, *Memories of Hawthorne* (1897), 70.

52. Ibid., 72–73; Tharp, *Peabody Sisters*, 181.

53. Mellow, *Nathaniel Hawthorne*, 482.

54. Herbert, *Dearest Beloved*, 217.

55. Tharp, *Peabody Sisters*, 6.

56. Valenti, "Sophia Peabody Hawthorne," 2.

57. Hawthorne, *Nathaniel Hawthorne and His Wife*, 1:211.

58. Quoted in Hull, *Nathaniel Hawthorne*, 182.

59. Lathrop, *Memories of Hawthorne*, 422–23.

60. Quoted in ibid., 88–89. On Rose, see Patricia Dunlavy Valenti, "Memories of Hawthorne: Rose Hawthorne Lathrop's Auto/Biography," *Auto/Biography Studies* 8 (spring 1993): 1–15.

61. Hull, *Nathaniel Hawthorne*, 228–29. Sophia edited Nathaniel's *Passages from the American Notebooks* (1863), *Passages from the English Notebooks* (1870), and *Passages from the French and Italian Notebooks* (1871). While Hawthorne's travel books were very successful, Sophia's *Notes* was diminished. One reviewer,

cited earlier (note 35), found himself attracted to Sophia's "delightfully gossipy" style, despite the "absolutely innumerable books of European travel. . . . Of course the chief value of such a book is as a memento to those [Nathaniel Hawthorne?] who have travelled the same ground in person."

62. Valenti, "Sophia Peabody Hawthorne," 20–21, lists Sophia's works and their locations. Valenti also makes the case that although Sophia Peabody learned from her male mentors, it was her separation from them during her Cuban so-journ that "provided her with the respite necessary to coalesce her artistic strength" (16). Valenti construes this as preparation to become a "mentor to a great artist [Hawthorne]," but one might also construe this as Sophia's preparation for her own artistic pursuits.

63. Martha J. Coston, *A Signal Success: The Work and Travels of Mrs. Martha J. Coston: An Autobiography* (1886), 142.

64. See Nina Baym, *Woman's Fiction: A Guide to Novels by and about Women in America, 1820–1870* (Ithaca: Cornell Univ. Press, 1978), 22–50.

65. Howells, *Suburban Sketches* (1893), 96. Howells says that the female sex "is born tired" and that "our climate and customs have drained" women's health. David Schuyler asserts that to think of the nineteenth-century genteel woman as idle is to project the twentieth century back onto the nineteenth ("Inventing a Feminine Past," *New England Quarterly* 51 [September 1978]: 299).

66. Smith, *Poetics*, 52.

67. Georg Misch, *A History of Autobiography in Antiquity*, trans. E. W. Dickes (Cambridge: Harvard Univ. Press, 1951), 12.

68. Tompkins, *Sensational Designs*, xi–xix.

CHAPTER FOUR · POLITICAL OCCASIONS

1. Madeleine Vinton Dahlgren, *South Sea Sketches: A Narrative* (1881), 144. Dahlgren was not alone in ruing the sewing machine. Catharine Beecher and Harriet Beecher Stowe claimed that "the sewing-machine, hailed as a blessing, has proved a curse to the poor; for it takes away profits from needlewomen, while employers testify that women who use this machine for steady work, in two years or less become hopelessly diseased and can rear no children. Thus it is that the controlling political majority of New-England is passing from the educated to the children of ignorant foreigners" (*The American Woman's Home: or, Principles of Domestic Science* [1869], 467).

2. Gail Hamilton, *Woman's Wrongs: A Counter-Irritant* (Boston: Ticknor & Fields, 1868), 97; quoted in Hedrick, *Stowe*, 359.

3. Hedrick, *Stowe*, 361.

4. See Henry Adams, *Henry Adams and His Friends: A Collection of His Unpublished Letters*, comp. Harold Dean Carter (Boston: Houghton Mifflin, 1947), 263, quoted in Stowe, *Going Abroad*, 207.

5. Richard Bridgman, *Traveling in Mark Twain* (Berkeley: Univ. of California Press, 1987), 1.

6. Margaret Fuller, *These Sad But Glorious Days: Dispatches From Europe, 1846–1850*, ed. Larry J. Reynolds and Susan Belasco Smith (New Haven: Yale Univ. Press, 1991), 161. Karen R. Lawrence finds that "travel *writing* has provided discursive space for women, who sometimes left home in order to write home, discovering new aesthetic as well as social possibilities" (*Penelope Voyages*, 18).

7. Ishbel Ross, *Sons of Adam*, 134. Ross names many women, such as Mary A. Bickerdyke, Mary Livermore, Mrs. A. H. Hoge of Chicago, and Louisa Lee Schuyler, who were part of "the first great quickening in the outlook of American women" following the Civil War (137).

8. S. D. Fry, "Newspaper Woman," *Journalist* 10 (19 November 1892), col. 3; quoted by Elizabeth V. Burt in "From Literary Ladies to Journalists: Networking in Nineteenth-Century Woman's Press Clubs," paper delivered 1 June 1996 at the Conference on 19th-Century American Women Writers in the 21st Century, Trinity College, Hartford, Connecticut.

9. I take this definition of ideology from Amy Kaplan, *The Social Construction of American Realism* (Chicago: Univ. of Chicago Press, 1988), 6.

10. Fuller was paid $10 per dispatch. See Stowe, "Conventions and Voices," 243. For Fuller's relationship to literary genres, see Sandra M. Gustafson, "Choosing a Medium: Margaret Fuller and the Forms of Sentiment," *American Quarterly* 47 (March 1995): 34–65. See Bell Gale Chevigny's account of Fuller's travels in *The Woman and the Myth: Margaret Fuller's Life and Writings* (Boston: Northeastern Univ. Press, 1994), 294–303; Larry J. Reynolds's analysis in *European Revolutions and the American Literary Renaissance* (New Haven: Yale Univ. Press, 1988), 55–78; and Joan von Mehren, *Minerva and the Muse: A Life of Margaret Fuller* (Amherst: Univ. of Massachusetts Press, 1994), 230–332. Biographical information and quotations are taken from Fuller's letters in *These Sad But Glorious Days*, 1–35.

11. Reynolds, *European Revolutions*, 63.

12. Nineteenth-century travel writers berated the railroad until the turn of the century, when Edith Wharton took it up and marked the beginning of its touristic decline with this compelling first line: "The motor-car has restored the romance of travel" (*A Motor-Flight Through France* [New York: Scribner's, 1908, rpt. DeKalb: Northern Illinois Univ. Press, 1991], 1).

13. Margaret V. Allen, "The Political and Social Criticism of Margaret Fuller,"

South Atlantic Quarterly 72 (autumn 1973): 565–66; Baym, *American Women Writers*, 124. For Fuller's rhetoric of citizenship, see P. Joy Rouse, "Margaret Fuller: A Rhetoric of Citizenship in Nineteenth-Century America," in *Oratorical Culture in Nineteenth-Century America: Transformations in the Theory and Practice of Rhetoric*, ed. Gregory Clark and S. Michael Halloran (Carbondale: Southern Illinois Univ. Press, 1993), 110–36.

14. Entreaties to return home came from Ralph Waldo Emerson and from Fuller's family. See Chevigny, *Woman and Myth*, 375.

15. A. William Salomone analyses America's pre-Cavourian use of Italy as a mirror in which to catch America's reflection of itself as it sought its identity, followed by a recoil when the events of the period of the Risorgimento intervened in this Arcadian vision, in "The Nineteenth-Century Discovery of Italy: An Essay in American Cultural History. Prolegomena to a Historiographical Problem," *American Historical Review* 73 (June 1968): 1372–91.

16. Chevigny, *Woman and Myth*, 2, 222.

17. Mary Hannah Krout, *Hawaii and a Revolution: The Personal Experiences of a Correspondent in the Sandwich Islands during the Crisis of 1893 and Subsequently* (1898), 33–34. In addition, Krout was on the staff of the Denver *Times* from 1900 to 1901 and traveled in Australia in 1906, giving a series of lectures. Her other publications include *A Looker On in London* (1899); *Alice's Visit to the Hawaiian Islands* (1900) and *Two Girls in China* (1903), children's stories drawn from her travels and including citations of authorities and sources; *The Memoirs of Hon. Bernice Pauahi Bishop* (1908); and *Platters and Pipkins* (1910), an advice book "Dedicated to all housekeepers: the many who are still striving and the few who have been perfected through suffering."

18. *Platters and Pipkins* (Chicago: A. C. McClurg, 1910), Krout's book of advice for homemakers, marshals similes that, in their extravagance, reveal the tension circulating around the debate over woman's sphere. "The woman who looks well to the ways of her household is a conservator of the greatest forces that shape the destinies of the race, and in what is required of her there is nothing inconsequential or of little account," Krout writes. "She influences and nurtures in their incipiency the economic measures that better the nations and which make all wholesome life possible. A home under fine supervision is like a fertile land through which flow a myriad crystal streams; over which are spread rich fields of ripening grain; in which are rooted the fruitful trees of the orchard, the giants of the forest that lend their strength to civilization, to the building of bridges along the thoroughfares of the world, of ships that carry the traffic of the high seas, of roofs that shelter the life of the race.

It behooves the home-maker, then, to honor her place with efficiency, and to meet its demands with willingness and fortitude in which there shall be neither regret nor repining, for that which is mistakenly called a wider sphere. There is, in all the varied affairs of this world, none wider and none so sacred" (208–9).

19. Nina Baym, "Rewriting the Scribbling Women," *Legacy* 2 (fall 1985): 8.

20. Biographical information is taken from Lilian Whiting, *Kate Field: A Record* (1899) unless otherwise indicated. For Kate Field among her peers in journalism, see Ross, *Sons of Adam*, 125–33.

21. Kate Field, *Hap-Hazard* (1873), 21–22.

22. Smith-Rosenberg, *Disorderly Conduct*, 109.

23. Gerda Lerner distinguishes history from History in *The Creation of Patriarchy* (New York: Oxford Univ. Press, 1986), 3–14.

24. Stowe, *Sunny Memories*, 1:lx–lxi.

25. Field was once barred because of her sex from speaking at the Lowell (Massachusetts) Institute on the subject of Mormonism. She responded to the prohibition with three questions about the policy of Lowell Institute Fund: Did the donor of the fund specify the sex of the lecturer? Would a man be allowed to lecture on the Mormon Treason before the institute? Could she delegate a man to deliver her lecture? See Whiting, *Kate Field*, 439.

26. Field refused to side publicly with woman suffrage until 1891, at which late date she was welcomed into the sisterhood by Lucy Stone and Elizabeth Cady Stanton. Kate Field's community of women friends included Julia Ward Howe, Helen Hunt Jackson, Charlotte Cushman, Adelaide Phillips, and Louise Chandler Moulton, all hard at work as she was.

27. For accounts of British women travelers in the Victorian era, see Dea Birkett, *Spinsters Abroad: Victorian Lady Explorers* (Oxford: Blackwell, 1989); Dorothy Middleton, *Victorian Lady Travellers* (New York: E. P. Dutton, 1965); Russell, *The Blessings of a Good Thick Skirt*; Mills, *Discourses of Difference*; and Stevenson, *Victorian Women Travel Writers in Africa*.

28. According to Carl N. Degler, in *At Odds*, 152, less than 13% of women in Massachusetts in 1830 remained unmarried before reaching the age of fifty, while by 1870 the proportion reached almost 18%; and by the federal census, "the highest proportion of women who never married for any period between 1835 and the present [1980] were those born between 1860 and 1880." For discussion of the double standard, male sexual license, and women as guardians of their own sexual integrity, see Smith-Rosenberg, *Disorderly Conduct*, 109–28. For the extent to which women's travel activities, including modes of transportation, were monitored for their gender propriety, see Ellen Gruber Garvey, "Reframing the Bicycle: Advertising-Supported Magazines and Scorching Women," *American Quarterly* 47 (March 1995): 66–101.

29. Matthews, *The Rise of Public Woman*, 100–171.

30. Jones, *European Travel*, vii. The desire of the "lady" for inconspicuousness was so thoroughgoing that Jones recommends women travelers *not* affix their names to their luggage; a name tag is of no use and "only serves to make her conspicuous, which is always disagreeable to a lady, besides offering an opportunity to adventurers" (35).

31. Jones, *European Travel*, 15.

32. Mary E. Hitchcock, *Two Women in the Klondike: The Story of a Journey to the Gold-Fields of Alaska* (1899), vii.

33. Carpenter, *In Cairo and Jerusalem*, 177–78.

34. Quoted in Kroeger, *Nellie Bly*, 163.

35. Elizabeth Cochrane Seaman, *Nellie Bly's Book: Around the World in 72 Days* (1890), 5.

36. Lilian Leland, *Traveling Alone: A Woman's Journey around the World* (1890), vii.

37. See Lockwood, *Passionate Pilgrims*, 327. Lockwood writes, "There is a continual, carping, querulous tone in so many commentaries by American women in the later decades of the century that one comes to the conclusion that they must have been very wearing as traveling companions."

CHAPTER FIVE · CULTURAL OCCASIONS

1. Elizabeth Robins Pennell, "The Italy of Virgil and Horace," *Harper's Magazine* 104 (May 1902): 867–68, 874.

2. Brodhead, *Cultures of Letters*; Levine, *Highlow/Lowbrow*. Jackson Lears also discusses professionalization and the effort to shore up authority at the turn of the century in *No Place of Grace*, 186–88.

3. Levine, *Highbrow/Lowbrow*, 149, 21–23.

4. See Lawrence Buell, *New England Literary Culture: From Revolution through Renaissance* (Cambridge: Cambridge Univ. Press, 1986), 371–74.

5. See Brodhead, *Cultures*, 85, 161.

6. For the making of canonical writers, see, for example, Richard Brodhead, *The School of Hawthorne* (New York: Oxford Univ. Press, 1986); Tompkins, *Sensational Designs*; Russell J. Reising, *The Unusable Past: Theory and the Study of American Literature* (London: Methuen, 1986); Coultrap-McQuin, *Doing Literary Business*; and *Redefining American Literary History*, ed. A. LaVonna Brown Ruoff and Jerry W. Ward, Jr. (New York: Modern Language Association of America, 1990). The list of leading writers is taken from Tebbel, *A History of Book Publishing*, 2:527.

7. See Nelson Lichtenstein, "Authorial Professionalism and the Literary Marketplace 1885–1900," *American Studies* 19 (spring 1978): 35–53; and Buell, *New England*, 58.

8. See Brodhead, *Cultures*, 124–35.

9. According to Frank Mott, "The new woman found the more scientific, more realistic, more newspaperish magazine fitted to her needs." These paid writers better fees than such magazines as *Harper's* and *Scribner's*. See *A History of American Magazines*, 5 vols. (Cambridge: Harvard Univ. Press, 1957), 4:223, 722; and Donald Sheehan, *This Was Publishing: A Chronicle of the BOOK TRADE in the Gilded Age* (Bloomington: Indiana Univ. Press, 1952), 44.

10. See Brodhead, *Cultures*, 155.

11. See Cheryl Torsney, *Constance Fenimore Woolson: The Grief of Artistry* (Athens: Univ. of Georgia Press, 1989), 7–10.

12. See Torsney, *Woolson*, 32.

13. Wharton, *A Backward Glance*, 112, 144.

14. Stowe, *Sunny Memories*, 1:23.

15. Hedrick, *Stowe*, 266. Hedrick provides an account of the journey that produced *Sunny Memories* and of two other journeys abroad on two other occasions, in 1856 and 1859 (233–52).

16. On contemporary politics, see my "Assuming a Public Voice: The Travel Writing of Margaret Fuller and Harriet Beecher Stowe," *Femmes de conscience: Aspects du féminisme américain (1848–1875)*, ed. Susan Goodman and Daniel Royot (Paris: Presses de la Sorbonne Nouvelle, 1994), 137–48.

17. Hedrick, *Stowe*, 265–70. I am indebted to Hedrick's astute analysis of the voice of *Sunny Memories*.

18. Calvin was, however, supportive of Harriet's career. He wrote to Harriet: "You must be a *literary woman*. It is so written in the book of fate. Make all your calculations accordingly . . . your husband will lift up his head at the gate [at the name of Harriet Beecher Stowe], and your children will rise up and call you blessed" (quoted in Hedrick, *Stowe*, 138).

19. Harriet used Charles's journal not simply as a reminder of their itinerary but as a source of passages for *Sunny Memories* "in lieu of chapters she worked up herself" (Hedrick, *Stowe*, 292). The journal of Charles Beecher has been published as *Harriet Beecher Stowe in Europe: The Journal of Charles Beecher*, ed. Joseph S. Van Why and Earl French (Hartford CT: Stowe-Day Foundation, 1986).

20. Information on parlor literature is taken from Hedrick, *Stowe*, 76–88, to whom I am indebted for my analysis.

21. Willard, *Journal and Letters*, 15.

22. Quoted in Hedrick, *Stowe*, 78.

23. Ibid., 80.

24. Catherine Gilbertson, *Harriet Beecher Stowe* (New York: D. Appleton-Century, 1937), 189.

25. Baym, *Woman's Fiction*, 48, 47.

26. Woolson may have known that John Bruce Ford was the name of a subscription publisher who worked for Appleton until the fall of 1867, when he started his own subscription business, J. B. Ford & Company. Subscription publishers sought highly marketable materials and sent out traveling salesmen to woo subscribers. William Dean Howells equated subscription publications with trash (Tebbel, *A History of Book Publishing*, 2:520, 522, 527).

27. In Constance Fenimore Woolson, *Dorothy and Other Italian Stories* (1896), 268.

28. Torsney, *Woolson*, 7–10.

29. Quoted in Leon Edel, *Henry James: The Middle Years* (New York: Lippincott, 1962), 90, 92.

30. Torsney, *Woolson*, 29. Also, Woolson was "acutely conscious of her situation as a woman writer." As the great-niece of James Fenimore Cooper and a friend of Henry James, who included her in his 1888 *Partial Portraits*, "she could hardly be anything else" (Joan Myers Weimer, "Women Artists as Exiles in the Fiction of Constance Fenimore Woolson," *Legacy* 3 [1986]: 3. See, as well, Sharon Dean, *Constance Fenimore Woolson* [Knoxville: Univ. of Tennessee Press, 1995]).

31. Torsney, *Woolson*, 31.

32. James, of course, wrote international novels across his career, from *Roderick Hudson* (1876) to *The Golden Bowl* (1904). Howells's accounts of travel are *Venetian Life* (1866) and *Italian Journeys* (1877). His novels that travelize fictions are *Their Wedding Journey* (1872), *A Chance Acquaintance* (1873), and *A Foregone Conclusion* (1875). He drew on his travels for characters in *The Lady of the Aroostook* (1879) and *A Fearful Responsibility* (1881). In addition to numerous travelized fictions set in the United States, Marietta Holley's fictions of foreign travel are *Samantha in Europe by Josiah Allen's Wife* (1896) and *Around the World with Josiah Allen's Wife* (1905). In addition to travelized short fictions, Wharton travelized many novels, among them *The Valley of Decision* (1902), *Madame de Treymes* (1907), *The Reef* (1912), *The Custom of the Country* (1913), *Hudson River Bracketed* (1929) and *The Gods Arrive* (1932). She was working on a travelized fiction, *The Buccaneers* (published posthumously in 1938), at the time of her death.

33. G. R. Carpenter, "Mrs. Wharton's *Italian Backgrounds*," *Bookman* 21 (August 1905): 610, (rpt. in *Edith Wharton: The Contemporary Reviews*, ed. James W. Tuttleton, Kristin O. Lauer, Margaret P. Murray [Cambridge: Cambridge Univ. Press, 1992], 100).

34. See Torsney, *Woolson*, 25–29.

35. Biographical information is taken from Rayburn S. Moore, *Constance Fenimore Woolson* (New York: Twayne, 1963), and *Women Artists, Women Exiles: "Miss Grief" and Other Stories*, ed. Joan Myers Weimer (New Brunswick: Rutgers Univ. Press, 1988), ix–xliii.

36. Quoted in Moore, *Woolson*, 31–32. Her image of her nomadic self was shaped by gender norms. She wrote to a friend, "It is a curious fate that has made the most domestic woman in the world . . . a wanderer for nearly twenty years." Unlike Edith Wharton, she never put down permanent roots in Europe or elsewhere, and yet she continued to define herself as domestic and to define domesticity in opposition to "wanderer." She loved "the romance and color" of Europe, and wrote: "What do you say to my trying Algiers next winter? Wouldn't that be a bold move!" It is unlikely that a man "trying" Algiers would conceive of it as "a bold move."

37. Moore, *Woolson*, 30–31.

38. Constance Fenimore Woolson, *Mentone, Cairo, and Corfu* (1896), 189–90. The essays constituting the collection originally appeared in *Harper's New Monthly Magazine*: "At Mentone," 55–56 (January–February 1884): 189–216, 367–91; "Cairo in 1890," 83 (October–November 1891): 651–74, 828–55; "Corfu and the Ionian Sea," 85 (August 1892): 351–70. She also published accounts of her travels in the United States. Bibliographical information is compiled from John Dwight Kern, *Constance Fenimore Woolson: Literary Pioneer* (Philadelphia: Univ. of Pennsylvania Press, 1934), 180–94. See Mott, *A History of American Magazines*, 4, for the status and interests of American periodicals between 1885 and 1905.

39. Paine, *Tent and Harem*, 228–29.

40. See Van Wyck Brooks, *The Dream of Arcadia: American Writers and Artists in Italy, 1760–1915* (New York: Dutton, 1958), 196. Brooks devotes a full chapter to Woolson (189–96).

41. Her other travel accounts are *The Cruise of the Vanadis* (Amiens, France: Sterne, 1992), discovered in 1991; *Fighting France: From Dunkerque to Belfort* (New York: Scribner's, 1915) and *In Morocco* (New York: Scribner's, 1920). Sarah Bird Wright counts *The Decoration of Houses, Italian Villas and Their Gardens*, and *French Ways and Their Meaning* as works of travel (see *Edith Wharton Abroad: Selected Travel Writings, 1888–1920*, ed. Sarah Bird Wright (New York: St. Martin's Press, 1995). The Wharton papers at the Beinecke Library at Yale University include two travel fragments: an undated, four-page typescript named *A Motor-Flight through Spain*, and *Italy Again* (Yale Collection of American Literature, Box 19, Folder 604).

42. "Italian Backgrounds," *Nation* (22 June 1905): 508; Carpenter, "Mrs. Wharton's *Italian Backgrounds*," *Bookman* (21 August 1905): 609–10; "Italian Back-

grounds and Views," *New York Times Saturday Review* (9 September 1905): 588; "*A Motor-Flight Through France*," *Spectator* 101 (5 December 1908): 947; "*A Motor-Flight Through France*," *Review of Reviews* 38 (December 1908): 760. Reprinted in *Edith Wharton: The Contemporary Reviews*, 97, 103, 100, 101, 165, 166.

43. Wright, *Edith Wharton Abroad*, 9.

44. Wharton, *A Backward Glance*, 140–41.

45. Kaplan, *Social Construction*, 65–87.

46. Elizabeth Ammons, *Edith Wharton's Argument with America* (Athens: Univ. of Georgia Press, 1980), 19–20.

47. See Wharton, *A Backward Glance*, 64–76, and Shari Benstock, *No Gifts from Chance: A Biography of Edith Wharton* (New York: Scribner's, 1994), 172–73, on Wharton's reading while she completed articles for the *Atlantic Monthly* that were gathered in *A Motor-Flight Through France*. Carol Singley's *Edith Wharton: Matters of Mind and Spirit* (Cambridge: Cambridge Univ. Press, 1995) thoroughly explores the relationship between Wharton's intellectuality and her work.

48. For Wharton, Beecher, and architecture, see Judith Fryer, *Felicitous Space: The Imaginative Structures of Edith Wharton and Willa Cather* (Chapel Hill: Univ. of North Carolina Press, 1986), 5–74.

49. Benstock, *No Gifts from Chance*, 81, 136.

50. Millicent Bell, *Edith Wharton and Henry James: The Story of Their Friendship* (London: Peter Owen, 1965), 45. When the difficulties of traveling by car are taken into account, the intensity of Wharton's love of the road becomes even more evident. In her time, when "motoring was making a great deal more headway in Europe than in America" and there were no garages or filling stations, a motorist had to be prepared with all sorts of paraphernalia, from spark plugs to extra bolts and nuts (see Dulles, *Americans Abroad*, 144–45, paraphrasing an article entitled "Taking an Automobile Abroad" that Dulles attributes to *Outing*, 1906.) Virginia Scharff finds that "whether they took the wheel themselves, or rode as passengers, motoring women asserted not only their intention to conquer distance, but also their right to control a costly piece of property they might not even own outright. Little wonder that observers of the time saw something incongruous, something fundamentally disruptive, in the spectacle of women on wheels" (*Taking the Wheel: Women and the Coming of the Motor Age* [New York: Free Press, 1991], 22). Wharton had drivers, but she was delighted to be liberated from rail travel (a sentiment she shared with Margaret Fuller, who called trains "that convenient but most unprofitable and stupid way of travelling").

51. Percy Lubbock, *Portrait of Edith Wharton* (New York: Appleton, 1947), 123.

52. Letters from Edith Wharton to Bernard Berenson in the Berenson Archive, Villa I Tatti, Harvard University Center for Italian Renaissance Studies, Florence, Italy. Reprinted by permission of the author and the Watkins/Loomis Agency.

53. Yale Collection of American Literature, Ms. 42, Box 19, Folder 604. Beinecke Library.

54. Edith Wharton, "Seven Books of Some Importance," *Bookman* 13 (August 1901): 563 (a review of E. and E. W. Blashfield's *Italian Cities*).

55. The first article that became part of *Italian Backgrounds* appeared in *Atlantic Monthly* in June of 1900, followed later by others in *Scribner's Magazine* in January, March, and August of 1902 and February of 1903. *Italian Backgrounds* saw one edition and printing by Scribner's in 1905; a second printing by Macmillan, London, in 1905, and three later printings from the first edition: Scribner's in 1907 and 1927, and a facsimile reprinting by Ecco Press in 1989.

56. See my "Edith Wharton and Travel Writing as Self-Discovery," *American Literature* 59 (May 1987): 257–67; my introduction to *A Motor-Flight Through France* (1991), xvii–xlix; and my "Edith Wharton and the Dog-Eared Travel Book," in *Wretched Exotic: Essays on Edith Wharton in Europe*, ed. Katherine Joslin and Alan Price (New York: Peter Lang, 1993), 147–64.

57. See Benstock, *No Gifts from Chance*, 81. Bicycling was such a craze that publishers worried over the demise of reading and, consequently, the demise of the publishing business. See Sheehan, *This Was Publishing*, 18.

58. A staunch admirer of the travel volumes of writers such as Walter Pater and Arthur Symonds, Vernon Lee and Paul Bourget, Wharton devotes two pages of her autobiography to travel books and claims that when Bernard Berenson's first volumes on Italian painting were published, she felt "almost guilty for having read Pater and even Symonds with such zest, and ashamed of having added my own facile vibrations to the chorus" (Wharton, *Backward Glance*, 141).

59. Wharton, *A Motor-Flight Through France*, 166–67. *Motor-Flight* was serialized in the *Atlantic Monthly* in December 1906, January and February 1907, and January, February, and March 1908. Scribner's reprinted it in 1908, 1909, and 1927. (See Stephen Garrison, *Edith Wharton: A Descriptive Bibliography* [Pittsburgh: Univ. of Pittsburgh Press, 1990].) The Scribner's volume includes part 3, "A Flight to the Northeast," absent from the *Atlantic Monthly* articles. The *Atlantic Monthly* assigns a title, "A Second Motor-Flight Through France," to the portion of the text that stands as part 2 of the otherwise untitled Scribner's volume.

60. Fussell, *Abroad*, 204.

61. Kaplan, *Social Construction*, 73.

62. On Wharton's use of the picturesque, see Brigitte Bailey, "Aesthetics and Ideology in *Italian Backgrounds*," in *Wretched Exotic*, 181–200.

63. For Wharton's love of scholarly standards and architectural design, and her dislike of "sentimental undergrowth," see her *Backward Glance*, 140–41. I am indebted to Sarah Bird Wright's "Garden Plans and 'Dabby Sketches': Edith

Wharton and the Illustrated Travel Book," paper delivered at the meeting of the American Literature Association in Baltimore, May 1995, for drawing my attention to Edith Wharton's concern with illustrations for her texts.

64. Wharton, *Backward Glance*, 378.

65. Ibid., 209.

66. Robert Scholes, *Structuralism in Literature: An Introduction* (New Haven: Yale Univ. Press, 1974), 130.

67. Yaeger, *Honey-Mad Women*.

CODA

1. Benstock, *No Gifts from Chance*, 311.

2. For full biographical information on Wharton's war efforts see R. W. B. Lewis, *Edith Wharton: A Biography* (New York: Harper & Row, 1975), 363–403; Benstock, *No Gifts from Chance*, 301–49; and Alan Price, *The End of Innocence: Edith Wharton and the First World War* (New York: St. Martin's, 1996).

3. In "Narrative Practices and Construction of Identity: Edith Wharton" (*Commonwealth and American Women's Discourse: Essays in Criticism*, 278–91), Radhika Mohanram argues that because Wharton was "other" in America because she was an artist, and "other" in Europe because she was a colonial, she constructed in her letters and her autobiography, as well as in her fiction, a spiral of identities. She was always the *sujet-en-procès*.

4. Wharton, *Backward Glance*, 352.

5. The articles that became *Fighting France* appeared as "In Argonne," *Scribner's Magazine* 57 (June 1915): 651–60; "In Lorraine and the Vosges," *Scribner's Magazine* 58 (October 1915): 430–42; and "In the North," *Scribner's Magazine* 58 (November 1915): 600–610. Wharton calls *Fighting France* a "little book" and "scribbles" in *A Backward Glance*, 339, 352–53.

6. Wright, *Edith Wharton Abroad*, 36.

7. Wharton, *A Motor-Flight Through France*, 160.

8. For Wharton's own account of this, see *A Backward Glance*, 345–57.

9. For a full discussion of the characteristics and evocations of *Motor-Flight*, see my "Edith Wharton and Travel Writing as Self-Discovery," 257–67.

10. See MacCannell, *The Tourist*, x.

Index